Analysis & Study Guide: Dr Jekyll & Mr Hyde

Francis Gilbert

ABOUT THE AUTHOR

Francis Gilbert is a writer who has been a secondary school
teacher for over twenty years in various state schools. He has
published numerous books, including *I'm A Teacher, Get Me Out
Of Here* and *The Last Day of Term* as well as a series of study
guides on classic texts such William Blake's *Songs of Innocence
and Experience, Frankenstein, Wuthering Heights* and *Jane Eyre*
-- all published on Kindle. For more: www.francisgilbert.co.uk

DEDICATION

To all my GCSE classes, especially the ones who have studied
Stevenson's mysterious novel with me.

ACKNOWLEDGMENTS

Thanks, as ever, to Erica Wagner for helping me with my writing &
all the teachers who have supported me over the years.

Contents

PART ONE: INTRODUCTION TO THE NOVEL

1 Contexts

Understanding Contexts

In order to fully appreciate a text, you need to understand the context, or background, in which it was written – known as its contexts of writing – and the contexts in which you read the book, or the contexts of reading. This is potentially a huge area to explore because 'contexts' essentially mean the 'worlds' from which the book has arisen and the worlds it creates in the reader's mind. For the best books, these are many and various. The most obvious starting point is the writer's own life: it is worth thinking about how and why the events in a writer's life might have influenced his or her fiction. However, you do have to be careful not to assume too much. For example, you must remember that Dr Jekyll, while he might have been based upon some real people that Robert Louis Stevenson knew in his life, is a character in his own right in the novel – a vital cog in the narrative wheel, a literary construct and not a real person.

It is particularly fruitful to explore other contexts of writing. We can look at the broader world from which Stevenson arose (Victorian society and the values that it promoted), and consider carefully how, in his writing, he both adopted and rejected the morals of his time. Other contexts might be the influence of the literary world that Stevenson inhabited (what other authors were writing at the time), how religion shaped his views, and so on.

Just as important as the contexts of *writing* are the contexts of *reading*: how we read the novel today. Most of us before we read *The Strange Case of Dr Jekyll and Mr Hyde* will actually know the outcome of the story and many of the major incidents; this will affect the way we read it profoundly, particularly if we have seen one of the many filmed versions. Your own personal context is very important too. If you have particular views about human nature, you may find the novel even more interesting. If, for example, you feel that human beings may have two sides to their nature, a good and evil side, then you may feel more engaged with the novel. In order for you to fully consider the contexts of reading rather than my telling you what to think, I have posed open-ended questions that get you thinking about your own views.

Contexts of Writing: Stevenson's Life

You can watch a YouTube video about Stevenson's life here: http://www.youtube.com/watch?v=yRxC5ETN8Zc

Stevenson was born in 1850: the middle of the nineteenth century. He is a figure who straddles both the Victorian and the modern age: his writing appears Victorian on the surface, in its language, settings and characters, but dig deeper and you find a modern interest in the darker sides of the human mind.

Growing up in Edinburgh, the son of an engineer and a religious mother, he suffered numerous illnesses as a child which were tended to by his fundamentalist Christian nurse, Alison Cunningham or 'Cummy'. Both his nurse and his parents instilled in him a strong sense of good and evil, talking to him at length about the consequences of sin, which was to perish eternally in the flames of Hell on Judgment Day. Cummy's talk of Hell gave the young Stevenson nightmares that were to plague him for the rest of his life. Most significantly, Stevenson saw humans as essentially "dualistic" creatures, split personalities who were both good and evil in equal measure.

This dualism was reflected in the world that Stevenson inhabited. Edinburgh had both an 'Old' and 'New Town'. Being from a rich family, Stevenson lived in the pleasant, wide streets of the New Town, but was aware of the filthy, disgusting over-crowded conditions of the Old Town. As he grew older, he came to realise that the New Town derived its wealth in part from the labourers who lived in the Old Town: Stevenson worked out that the two worlds were reliant upon each other.

Moreover, Edinburgh also had a dark past, which Stevenson was fascinated by. There were stories of William 'Deacon' Brodie who appeared to be an upright craftsman by day, but was a criminal at night until he was hanged in 1788. As a teenager, Stevenson worked upon a script based on Brodie's life. Stevenson also knew about Burke and Hare, who in the 1820s, would murder people in order to supply Edinburgh Medical College with bodies to experiment upon. The respectable Dr. Knox was their main customer.

Stevenson himself led something of a double life. While a student studying engineering at Edinburgh University, he would spend a great deal of time in the dives of the Old Town, drinking and probably sleeping with prostitutes. He left Edinburgh in 1873, and travelled abroad. This was the real beginning of his literary career. After suffering from a physical collapse, he travelled widely and frequently in France: the warmer climate suited him better than the cold of Scotland. In France, he made many trips to the Forest of Fontainebleau, staying at Barbizon, Grez-sur-Loing and Nemours, visiting art galleries and joining artists' communities there. He also made the journeys described most famously in his travel book, *Travels with a Donkey in the Cévennes*. Although his parents thought he was wasting his time, he was developing a powerful voice as a writer.

While in Grez, France, he met Fanny Osbourne: she was married with two children but this did not stop him from falling in love with her. A year later, he met her again and spent much of his time with her and her children. Fanny returned to American and began divorce proceedings in San Francisco. Desperate to see her again, against the wishes of his friends and parents, Stevenson embarked upon the long journey to join her, sailing to New York, and then taking the train to California.

After many adventures, including a total breakdown of his health, he arrived in San Francisco, where he married Fanny. Later the couple returned to Scotland, where he wrote in collaboration with W.E. Henley, *Deacon Brodie*, his first play. In 1882, he moved to France, publishing *Treasure Island* in 1883. However with his health getting worse, he returned to England and settled in Bournemouth, which remained his home until 1887. Thus began the most productive and successful period of his writing career. Despite being gravely ill, he wrote and published, *A Child's Garden of Verses*, *Dr Jekyll and Mr Hyde* and *Kidnapped* during this time. The death of his father in 1887, Thomas Stevenson, prompted Stevenson to look again for a warm climate to live in. He visited the South Seas. He chartered a yacht and spent three years sailing around the eastern and central Pacific, visiting important island groups and stopping off for extended stays in Hawaii, getting to know the local royalty and railing against the stupidity and arrogance of the missionaries. In 1890, he settled with his family on one of the Samoan islands, becoming known as Tusitala, or "story-writer" in Samoan. Once again, he came into conflict with the Europeans on the island, feeling that the colonists were running the island in a corrupt and incompetent fashion. After suffering from depression, he resumed writing, but died suddenly of a cerebral hemorrhage in 1894, at the age of 44.

His writing of *Dr Jekyll and Mr Hyde* is now, like the writing of *Frankenstein*, the stuff of legend. He wrote it in 1885 while living in Bournemouth, publishing it in 1886. Mrs Stevenson recounted:

> In the small hours of one morning, I was awakened by cries of horror from Louis. Thinking he had a nightmare, I woke him. He said angrily, 'Why did you wake me? I was dreaming a fine bogey tale.' I had awakened him at the first transformation scene. He had had in his mind an idea of a double life story, but it was not the same as the dream. He asked me, as usual, to make no criticisms until the first draft was done...In this tale I felt and still feel he was hampered by his dream. The powder – which I thought might be changed – he couldn't eliminate because he saw it so plainly in the dream. In the original story he had Jekyll bad all through, and working for the Hyde change only for a disguise. I didn't like the opening, which was confused – again the dream – and proposed that Hyde should run over the child showing that he was an evil force without humanity. After quite a long interval his bell rang for me, and ...I went upstairs. As I entered the door Louis pointed with a long dramatic finger (you know) to a pile of ashes on the hearth of the fireplace saying that I was right and there was the tale. I nearly fainted away with misery and horror when I saw all was gone. He was already hard at work at the new version which was finished in a few days more.

There is some debate as to exactly how the story was written, with some critics agreeing that Mrs Stevenson played a pivotal role in shaping the story, but others disagreeing. No one will know for sure. But whatever the exact history of the writing of the story, the drafting process was intensive but furiously quick. Lloyd Osbourne, Stevenson's stepson, said: "I don't believe that there was ever such a literary feat before as the writing of *Dr Jekyll*. I remember the first reading as if it were yesterday. Louis came downstairs in a fever; read nearly half the book aloud; and then, while we were still gasping, he was away again, and busy writing. I doubt if the first draft took so long as three days". Having listened to his wife's criticisms and thought about the story further Stevenson re-wrote the story again in three to six days. He then re-wrote the story again over the space of four to six weeks. In truth, although written quickly, the story was the product of a life-time interest in dreams, the Gothic genre, and the fundamental duality of man. The story was more or less an immediate bestseller, with forty thousand copies being sold in six months. By 1901, it was estimated to have sold over 250,000 copies -- a huge number for a book of that time. Critics of the day generally received the story favourably. One reviewer was quick to perceive that Stevenson's narrative was truly original in one respect. When talking about Edward Hyde, the critic said:

> with its unlikeness to its master, with its hideous caprices, and appalling vitality, and terrible power of growth and increase, is, to our thinking, a notion as novel as it is terrific. We would welcome a spectre, a ghoul, or even a vampire gladly, rather than meet Mr Edward Hyde.

Questions

Why was Stevenson's religious upbringing influential in shaping the themes of *Dr Jekyll and Mr Hyde*?

How did growing up in Edinburgh influence the writing of *Dr Jekyll*?

In what ways was Stevenson's behaviour in his life similar to that of Dr Jekyll? In what ways was it different?

How did Stevenson make his living from writing?

How did *Dr Jekyll and Mr Hyde* come to be written? Who was influential in the re-drafting of the manuscript?

How successful was the novel? Why was it successful do you think?

POSSIBLE ANSWERS in brief & bold

Why was Stevenson's religious upbringing influential in shaping the themes of *Dr Jekyll and Mr Hyde*? **Although Stevenson became an atheist later on in life, he was profoundly affected by the tales he heard about sinners being punished for their sins in hell, and the ways in which religion made people feel shame about sex and desire. *Dr Jekyll* is full of religious references to the Devil and to behaviour which religion deemed sinful. Jekyll pretends to be religious and pious but desperately wants to be** sinful. Stevenson's religious upbringing – including his nanny's "hellfire" stories – affected him deeply.

How did growing up in Edinburgh influence the writing of *Dr Jekyll*? **Although *Dr Jekyll* is set in London, many critics think Stevenson is describing the Edinburgh of his childhood where there was an "Old Town", which was run-down and poverty-stricken like the place where Hyde lives, and a "New Town" which was posh and rich, like Jekyll's house. This "dualism" – having two sides – was the central theme of the book: how a city and people themselves have a good and an evil side.**

In what ways was Stevenson's behaviour in his life similar to that of Dr Jekyll? In what ways was it different? **Stevenson probably led a "secret" life as a student: he probably visited prostitutes, and took drugs such as alcohol. He also took the painkiller opium to help him with his illnesses: this drug-taking is similar to Jekyll's drug-taking. However, Stevenson did not feel the desire to appear respectable in the way that Jekyll does: he led a Bohemian life that was very different from most middle-class people of his day.**

How did Stevenson make his living from writing? **He wrote many different types of texts: he found success as a children's writer but was also a poet, critic, essayist and adult novelist, as we see with *Dr Jekyll*.**

How did *Dr Jekyll and Mr Hyde* come to be written? Who was influential in the re-drafting of the manuscript? **The novel was the result of a nightmare Stevenson had where he dreamt about a man having a double which haunted him. His wife made him re-write the novel because she felt that it didn't have a clear moral or point.**

How successful was the novel? Why was it successful do you think? **The novel was tremendously successful, by far the most successful book Stevenson wrote, and sold a quarter of a million copies in Stevenson's life-time, a huge number for a novel of its day. It explored the nightmares of the Victorian middle-class in the form of a thrilling, "sensational" story: it showed how supposedly respectable people were, in fact, evil.**

Selected Reading on Stevenson's Life

One of the best places to start learning about Stevenson is the Robert Louis Stevenson website:
http://www.robert-louis-stevenson.org/
The Wikipedia entry on Stevenson is useful:
http://en.wikipedia.org/wiki/Robert_Louis_Stevenson

Clare Harman: *Robert Louis Stevenson – A Biography* (Harper Perennial; 2006) A landmark book on Stevenson, brilliantly researched.

G.K. Chesterton: *Robert Louis Stevenson* (House of Stratus; 2001)

Chesterton's biography written in the early 20th century is a concise classic.

Contexts of Reading

We read the story of *Jekyll and Hyde* very differently now. For us, the story is less about a battle between good and evil and more about one man's battles with his repressed nature. Above all, it seems to us now that the novel is about 'repression'. It is clear from the text that Dr Henry Jekyll is a deeply repressed man: a man who wishes to appear very respectable to the outside world and yet deep down harbours many secret desires that he is not able to pursue openly. Thus the transformation into Hyde becomes a wonderful 'disguise'.

While we are a more open society now, many powerful people are still "Jekyll and Hyde" characters. It is clear that important people in the media, politics and education have to put on a respectable facade in order to further their careers, and yet harbour secret desires that they would not want anyone to know about. The most spectacular case of this is the story of Bill Clinton's presidency, which was ruined by what has come to be known as the 'Monica Lewinsky' scandal. Clinton had an affair with a young intern in the White House and attempted to cover it up: the 'cover up' nearly led to him being impeached for lying to the American people about the truth of the affair. Obviously, people like Clinton would benefit greatly if they had had a potion like Henry Jekyll's!

Many critics have also begun to view the narrative as an allegory about addiction. One of the central issues of the notion is Jekyll's addiction to taking the potion and to being "transformed" into another person. Towards the end of the novel, it is clear that Jekyll can't wean himself off the drug. As a result, like a junkie, his whole physical and mental condition deteriorates. The last section of the book could be viewed as a horrific description of the nightmare of addiction: his ransacking the town for the drug, his violent mood swings, his wish to hide away from everyone. In such a way, we could say that the novel has become more relevant than ever because it tackles issues which are problems in our society.

Questions

Why is the novel about repression?

Why has the novel become so influential in popular and literary culture?

What issues does the novel raise that are still in our minds today?

POSSIBLE ANSWERS in brief & bold

Why is the novel about repression? **Dr Jekyll buries and hides his secret desires and wishes, and this repression leads to him developing a "Hyde" character who is a way of finding an outlet for these desires.**

Why has the novel become so influential in popular and literary culture? **Stevenson revealed something which is prevalent in modern culture: he showed that people in power, who are respectable, often have secret, inner lives which can come to dominate them at the expense of their careers, e.g. President Clinton.**

What issues does the novel raise that are still in our minds today? **Apart from its focus upon repression, the novel explores the consequences of drug addiction and possibly madness.**

2 Structure

How Stevenson shapes his narrative around certain themes

> You can watch a YouTube video I made about the plot of the book, entitled 'Learn the Plot of Dr Jekyll in Five Minutes' here:
> http://www.youtube.com/watch?v=zV3QxszjtPE

The novel has a complex structure because it has several different narrators. This is largely because Stevenson wishes to make the story a mystery story with the central issue being: who is Edward Hyde and what is his connection to Henry Jekyll? In order to construct a mystery story, Stevenson could not have Jekyll narrating until the very end of the book when the mystery has been solved. In this sense, the novel is a proto-type detective novel. The lawyer Utterson plays the role of the detective, narrating more or less continuously, the first three sections of the book. The fourth section is Lanyon's narrative, which at the end reveals that Jekyll is Hyde, and then the final section is Jekyll's narrative, which tells us, with the mystery solved, how he became Hyde.

As has been already noted, the novel is structured around the theme of repression. Most of the novel's most striking images are connected in one form or another around the idea of repression. The locked doors and curtained windows of Jekyll's house are images of a man locking away the truth that lurks inside; the image of Jekyll turning into Hyde could possibly be a metaphor of what happens when the unconscious mind is revealed; the murder of Carew is possibly a symbol of the repressed mind striking out at the conscious one. The narrative is about the unpeeling of the layers that hide the repressed desires inside Jekyll. We could break down the novel into the following structure:

Opening (Section 1: Story Of The Door, Search for Mr Hyde, Dr Jekyll was quite at ease)
This is Utterson's narrative, in which he tells us about his cousin witnessing a brutal assault upon an eight-year-old
- Suspecting that Jekyll is involved with this terrible character, Utterson spies upon Hyde and meets him. He believes that Jekyll is being blackmailed by Hyde.
- We meet the slick, superficial Dr. Lanyon and hear about Jekyll's strange experiments.

Complications (Section 2: The Carew Murder Case)
- London is shocked by the murder of Danvers Carew, a respectable MP. Hyde is suspected. His flat is raided but he is not found.
- When Utterson visits Jekyll, he finds him sick and depressed. He suspects that Jekyll has forged a letter to protect Hyde.

Crisis (Section 3: Remarkable Incident Of Dr Lanyon)
- Hyde has vanished. Jekyll joins society, socialising widely. For two months, Jekyll is once again respectable man, but then returns to seclusion.
- The pompous Lanyon is also much changed, apparently mortally ill and wanting nothing to do with Jekyll.
- Lanyon dies. He has written a letter which is not to be opened until Jekyll dies or disappears.

- Jekyll continues to decline. A strange man is spotted in his house. At the request of Jekyll's servant, Poole, Utterson breaks into Jekyll's laboratory and finds Hyde lying dead, dwarfed by Jekyll's larger clothes.

Climax (Section 4: Dr Lanyon's narrative)
- Utterson reads Lanyon's account in which he learns that Lanyon was asked to find some powders for Jekyll.
- Hyde arrives at Lanyon's house, mixes a potion and becomes Jekyll before Lanyon's eyes.

Resolution (Section 5: Henry Jekyll's Statement Of The Case)
- Jekyll tells his story, talking about his essential dual nature, his search for a potion which enable him to become someone else, his transformation into Hyde
- He explains how Hyde begins to take over. He can no longer control his transformations. Jekyll has become utterly corrupted.

Questions
What themes does Stevenson explore in the novel?
How and why does he structure the novel around these themes?

POSSIBLE ANSWERS in brief & bold

What themes does Stevenson explore in the novel? **Stevenson explores the theme of repression in the novel and the ways in which people repress their inner-most desires and hide their secret wishes.**
How and why does he structure the novel around these themes?
The novel is structured around the themes of repression and dualism because it slowly reveals Jekyll's inner life and desires as the mystery is unraveled. Hyde is Jekyll's inner-most repressed desires and this is why he is so destructive.

3 Genre

The blending of science fiction, the gothic and the detective genres

The most influential genre upon this work is the Gothic. Stevenson's descriptions of the smoggy London streets, his vivid imagery when describing the horrible Mr Hyde, the mysterious narrative with its kernel of horror at the heart of it are all elements which you might find in a Gothic story. The Gothic emerged as a very popular form of entertainment in the 18th century with writers like Horace Walpole and Mrs Radcliffe writing novels about nasty aristocrats living in haunted castles and attempting to seduce innocent damsels in distress. The novels were extremely successful because they combined haunted settings with racy narratives that were about beautiful girls being pursued by unscrupulous men.

The Gothic influenced Mary Shelley when she wrote the first science fiction novel, *Frankenstein*, in 1818. The impact of Mary Shelley's novel *Frankenstein* cannot be underestimated in terms of its influence upon Stevenson's novella, *Dr Jekyll and Mr Hyde*. In many ways, Shelley set the template which all other science fiction narratives have imitated since: an obsessive scientist who pays the consequences for his meddling with the structure of the human body and brain. Stevenson's fiction contains a similar 'Promethean' figure to Mary Shelley's Victor Frankenstein. Henry Jekyll is like the Greek hero Prometheus who brought fire to mankind – he offers man the chance to become another person entirely with his potion. Like Victor Frankenstein, he creates a 'new being' in the form of Hyde.

Another Gothic story which influenced Stevenson is Edgar Allen Poe's story about a man who has a double called 'William Wilson'. There are also strong correlations to James Hogg's *Private Memoirs and Confessions of a Justified Sinner*. Stevenson's narrative has many similarities with Hogg's in that it has overlapping third and first person narratives, and contains a man who is motivated to murder by a strange, ghost-like demonic alter ego.

However, Stevenson's novel takes the Gothic one stage further than all of these novels by being more 'concentrated' and, in some ways, more simple. Stevenson intensifies the horror in his novel by concentrating upon the character of Hyde and not introducing lots of peripheral characters. The novel is more psychological than any other previous efforts in that it makes it clear that it is Jekyll's psychology which creates Hyde: that Hyde is a manifestation of Jekyll's character. More than other writers, Stevenson takes the time to establish a memorable setting, evoking the foggy London streets, the locked doors, the mysterious laboratories in intense detail. He is a much more technically accomplished writer than Mary Shelley: he does not need to pile event upon horrific event to create the horror in the book. He is able to build suspense by evoking character and setting.

Most significantly, Stevenson creates many of the trademark features of the science fiction and detective genres here. His descriptions of the making of the potion and the transformation of Jekyll into Hyde are masterful set-pieces which have been imitated so much since that it is difficult now to appreciate their power when they were first written. Likewise, Utterson's uncovering of the mystery has now become the template for most detective stories: his spying on his suspects, his investigations into the relevant documents, his interviews with various characters from different social settings are all the stock-in-trade of the detective story now.

Thus we can see that the novel is a brilliantly successful blend of genres: the Gothic, the science fiction narrative, and the detective story.

Key ways in which Dr Jekyll conforms to the Gothic genre:

Its focus upon a horrible **villain**;

Description of **horrific incidents**: the death of Carew and Hyde;

The **atmosphere** is ghostly and spooky with lots of darkness and fog;

There are **innocent victims**: a girl of eight, Danvers Carew, and possibly Henry Jekyll – who is both guilty and innocent?

Ways in which it doesn't conform:

The **structure** of the story: the narrative operates like a detective novel in that we have one character, Utterson, searching for the solution to the mystery;

The **urban setting**: most Gothic novels are set in castles or the remote countryside. Stevenson invented an entirely new genre, the "urban gothic", which was later imitated by Sir Arthur Conan-Doyle in his Sherlock Holmes stories and many films such as *Seven*;

The **psychology** of the characters: all the characters in the novel are psychologically convincing, they are not stereotypical heroes and villains;

The lack of any **hero**: the closest the story gets to a hero is Utterson, who fails to save his friend but does, like a detective, uncover the mystery;

The **solution** to the mystery. There had been many Gothic stories with doppelgangers (doubles) in which the hero was hunted by a double or alter ego, someone who looks very like him but behaves in an evil fashion. But no story until this one had the "double" – in this case Mr Hyde – being the same as the main protagonist, Dr Jekyll.

Questions
In what ways does the story operate like a detective novel?
In what ways does it contain elements of the Gothic novel?
In what ways is the novel different from many Gothic novels?

POSSIBLE ANSWERS in brief & bold

In what ways does the story operate like a detective novel? **Mr Utterson is like a detective in the novel, slowly unearthing and discovering the truth about Dr Jekyll and Mr Hyde, finding clues about Hyde's violence and misdemeanours, and interviewing people, reading documents and breaking down doors to discover the truth about Jekyll.**
In what ways does it contain elements of the Gothic novel? **The foggy atmosphere, the monstrous Hyde, the violence and the extreme emotions expressed are all Gothic in atmosphere.**
In what ways is the novel different from many Gothic novels? **The lack of any hero and the solution to the mystery are not typically Gothic in that when we discover Hyde is Jekyll the whole novel becomes psychological.**

4 Critical Perspectives

Is this novel about the unconscious?

Dreams played a central role in the writing of the story and form an important part of the narrative. His wife's view of the dream being a distraction from writing the story was not an opinion shared by Stevenson himself, who, in an interview, said:

> At night I dreamed the story, not precisely as it is written, for of course there are always stupidities in dreams, but practically it came to me as a gift...Even when fast asleep I know that it is I who am inventing, and when I cry out it is with gratification to know that the story is so good...For instance, all I dreamed about Dr Jekyll was that one man was being pressed into a cabinet, when he swallowed a drug and changed into another being...

Here we can see how it was Stevenson's 'unconscious' mind – the part of the mind that is expressed in dreams – which helped shape the narrative.

Stevenson was writing at a time when many philosophers and scientists were beginning to examine the role of dreams and the unconscious in influencing human behaviour. Stevenson wrote the book at a time when people's interest in the 'unconscious' – which is supposed to influence our actions without us knowing it – was growing. In 1885, the French neurologist Charcot had given a public display of hypnotism in Paris. The great French scientist used hypnosis to induce a state of hysteria in patients and studied the results, and was single-handedly responsible for changing the medical community's perception of hypnosis: previously they'd thought of it as 'mesmerism', effectively no better than supernatural hokum. But Charcot showed how there were powerful 'unconscious forces' at work in shaping what people do, particularly in hysterics and neurotics.

Perhaps even more relevant to an understanding of *Jekyll and Hyde* is an appreciation of the work of Krafft-Ebing and Freud. While it is unlikely that Stevenson had heard of either, there is no doubt that the ideas that they explored and theorised about interested Stevenson. It's clear that there was a 'zeitgeist' at this time: a coming together of ideas, art and science. Many of the top writers, thinkers and scientists were fascinated by the realm of the 'unconscious'. Krafft-Ebing's *Psychopathia Sexualis* was published in 1886. For the first time, Krafft-Ebing's work charted the different sorts of sexual desire, male and female, homosexual and heterosexual. While many of his views now would be regarded as offensive, at the time they were very progressive. Fundamentally, he began to uncover the role of sexuality in society, showing that these hidden desires are often battling with the conventional moral standards of the day. Thus, like Stevenson, he suggests that man is a 'dualistic' creature, appearing respectable and pleasant, but deep down suffering from frustrated, repressed desires. Sigmund Freud took these ideas a step further and proposed that sexual desire was the main motivation in life.

In his book, *The Interpretation of Dreams* (1899), Freud explored this notion in some depth. He called dreams the "royal road to the unconscious". This meant that dreams can tell us about the language of the unconscious. In particular, they can tell us about the desires we "repress" in our life. In such a way, Freud would interpret certain objects in dreams as being sexual symbols: apertures of any sort could be metaphors for the vagina, while protruding objects could represent the erect penis, being what Freud calls a 'phallic symbol'. Freud argued that the human mind was divided into three main components: the 'Super-Ego', which is the part of the mind which "controls" you and makes you behave, the "Id" which is the part that expresses pure desire, such as sexual desire, while the 'Ego' tries to mediate or deal with the differing demands of the Id and the Super-Ego.

While many of his ideas were clearly not known by Stevenson, there is no doubt that Hyde is an intensely sexual creature, playing out his sexual fantasies in the smoggy streets of London: he is in many ways a literary embodiment of Freud's 'Id'. It could be argued indeed that Hyde is a metaphor for the 'unconscious' of man: he is the ape-like creature that we would all rather hide from civilised society. While our unconscious might want to punch people who annoy us, our civilised side prevents us from doing so. While we might want to have sex much more frequently than we do, our desire to appear respectable and not "randy" stops us from propositioning every person we fancy. It is clear that Hyde suffers from no such inhibitions. Thus, there is a powerful argument that the novel is very disturbing still because Hyde represents the unconscious in all of us.

Questions

What might be a "Freudian" reading of the novel?

Why could you argue that the novel is actually about the "unconscious"?

POSSIBLE ANSWERS in brief & bold

What might be a "Freudian" reading of the novel? **One could see Hyde as an expression of Freud's the "Id": he is pure desire unchecked by the Ego or the Super-Ego, desire let off the leash, able to do exactly what it wants. Meanwhile, Dr Jekyll has a "Super-Ego", a controlling, moralizing part of his mind, but it grows weaker as Hyde, the "Id" becomes stronger. In the middle, the real Jekyll, the "Ego" becomes hopelessly lost trying to deal with the competing demands of the Id and the Super-Ego.**

Why could you argue that the novel is actually about the "unconscious"? **Hyde might be an expression of the unconscious desires of mankind: what men really want to do if they weren't "hemmed in" by modern society's rules and regulations.**

Selected Reading

Norton Critical Editions: *The Strange Case of Dr Jekyll and Mr Hyde* (Norton: 2003) This is by far and away the best "academic" edition of the book, packed with great critical essays as well as comprehensive notes: it is aimed at undergraduates studying the book at university.

David Daiches: *Robert Louis Stevenson and His World* (Pictorial Biography: 1973) Although this is an old book, it remains the best for evoking the world that Stevenson lived in and has an excellent section of Jekyll and Hyde.

5 Use of language

A writer's first and only tool is language. Writers create settings, characters, and stories out of language. This is no mean feat: unlike film-makers they don't have moving images, sound, and music to create atmosphere, believable people and engaging narratives. Stevenson's audience would have been highly educated but the vast majority of people in his day were not literate: they could not read and write – and obviously could not read his books. They were expected to be servants, factory-workers and assistants in shops. However, there was a growing group of people called the middle class who had been well-educated and were highly literate. In the days before cinema, television, the internet, one of the main forms of entertainment for wealthy, educated people was reading stories in magazines and novels. Many well-off families would read to each other in the evenings and avidly bought the latest fashionable book. As a result, some writers could make a living by selling their fiction to this eager audience.

Until *Jekyll and Hyde*, Stevenson had struggled to make money, but this novel was to change everything. It was sensationally popular. In terms of style, it was written like many novels of the day: in a highly literary, ornate style in places, but in a more simple style in others. We may find this difficult to understand but educated readers took delight in reading complex sentences and sophisticated vocabulary: it was a "badge of honour" to know difficult words. However, the writing couldn't be too difficult as to be unreadable. Stevenson strikes a balance in *Jekyll and Hyde*: some parts – particularly when Jekyll explains his psychology – are very complicated, but others are fairly simple to understand, particularly the dialogue.

In some of the most dramatic parts of the novel, Stevenson thinks and writes like a playwright. Hyde does not speak very much but when he does the effect is electrifying and suspenseful. Let's look at this interaction between Hyde and Utterson in Chapter 2, *The Search for Mr Hyde*:

> "Yes," returned Mr. Hyde, "It is as well we have met; and apropos, you should have my address." And he gave a number of a street in Soho.

"Good God!" thought Mr. Utterson, "can he, too, have been thinking of the will?" But he kept his feelings to himself and only grunted in acknowledgment of the address.

"And now," said the other, "how did you know me?"

"By description," was the reply.

"Whose description?"

"We have common friends," said Mr. Utterson.

"Common friends," echoed Mr. Hyde, a little hoarsely. "Who are they?"

"Jekyll, for instance," said the lawyer.

"He never told you," cried Mr. Hyde, with a flush of anger. "I did not think you would have lied."

Notice in the dialogue how Stevenson generates a powerful "subtext": what matters is what is not said. We see this very vividly in Hyde's first comment about how it is good that he has met Utterson because Utterson needs to know where he lives. Utterson realises that this is because Hyde is aware that he is in the will and Utterson, being Jekyll's lawyer, will need to contact him if Jekyll dies or disappears and give him all of Jekyll's money. Thus we can see that a simple comment is laced with menace and double meaning. The dialogue then becomes even more sinister when Hyde turns the tables and begins questioning Utterson by asking him how he knows him. It is only when we know the solution to the mystery that we realise how Hyde knows that Utterson is lying about Jekyll having given a description of Hyde.

Much of the tension in the dialogue is created by the way Utterson, the "detective" figure in the story, seeks to find out information by talking to the main characters involved. In Chapter 3, 'Dr Jekyll was quite at ease', Utterson is convinced that Jekyll is being blackmailed by Hyde. He says:

> "Jekyll," said Utterson, "you know me: I am a man to be trusted. Make a clean breast of this in confidence and I make no doubt I can get you out of it."

The dialogue creates tension because Utterson does not "speak plainly" – he does not ask outright "Jekyll, are you being blackmailed?" – instead he urges his friend to "make a clean breast of this in confidence". In other words, he tells Jekyll that whatever it is that Jekyll is being blackmailed for can be confessed to him, and he will "get you out of it". The dialogue is emotional and secretive in atmosphere: this is a world where people do not share secrets easily and where the wrong words can ruin a man's reputation. Utterson is one of the few people in this world who can be trusted to keep a secret. And yet, Jekyll does not tell his friend what his secret is other than to reassure him that he is not being blackmailed.

Stevenson is wonderful at evoking a Gothic atmosphere in his descriptions of London; this is what is known as "urban Gothic" (see my chapter on this). If we examine the description of Soho in *The Carew Murder Case* we can see this:

> The dismal quarter of Soho seen under these changing glimpses, with its muddy ways, and slatternly passengers, and its lamps, which had never been extinguished or had been kindled afresh to combat this mournful reinvasion of darkness, seemed, in the lawyer's eyes, like a district of some city in a nightmare.

The use of adjectives like "dismal", "muddy", "slatternly" evoke a miserable, depressing and sinister atmosphere, while the visual image of the flickering, feeble lamps in this dark morning suggest a world where evil predominates. Meanwhile, the simile "like a district of some city in a nightmare" emphasizes a key idea in the novel: nightmares can become real; our worst dreams can become true.

Stevenson excels in various "set pieces": key scenes of action which are central to the plot of the story. These set-pieces are, in my view, the description of Poole's breaking into the laboratory in 'The Last Night' and Lanyon's description of Hyde's transformation into Jekyll. This latter description has set the template for many "transformation" scenes in literature and the movies:

> He put the glass to his lips and drank at one gulp. A cry followed; he reeled, staggered, clutched at the table and held on, staring with injected eyes, gasping with open mouth; and as I looked there came, I thought, a change—he seemed to swell—his face became suddenly black and the features seemed to melt and alter—and the next moment, I had sprung to my feet and leaped back against the wall, my arms raised to shield me from that prodigy, my mind submerged in terror.
>
> "O God!" I screamed, and "O God!" again and again; for there before my eyes—pale and shaken, and half fainting, and groping before him with his hands, like a man restored from death—there stood Henry Jekyll!

Here Stevenson uses powerful dynamic verbs "reeled, staggered, clutched...gasping" to describe the physical contortions and agony that Hyde undergoes as he changes back into Jekyll. Meanwhile, other dynamic verbs vividly convey the actual transformation: "swell...melt...alter". The effect of these verbs is to make the reader see a bewildering and disturbing transformation, while the use of descriptive noun phrases "injected eyes" and "opened mouth" brilliantly give a powerful visual image of someone appearing like they are being tortured. The use of colour "black" adds a very ambivalent edge to the description: does Jekyll literally go "black" as in "black skinned" or does he look like he's black because he's bruised? To then follow this description with the adjectives "pale and shaken" creates a strong contrast: Hyde had been having spasms but now is half-dead. Syntactically, Stevenson leaves the fatal name, Henry Jekyll, to the last words in the sentence to underline the shock Lanyon feels at seeing his former friend before him. Lanyon's responses only serve to suggest his shock and horror. He "sprung" to his feet, and "leapt back against the wall," raising his arms to hide the vision. The verbs here suggest violent, shocked movements. Thus the reader has two pictures in his head: he sees the transformation of Henry Jekyll but he also sees the terrified response of Lanyon. The short exclamation "Oh God!" also tells us of Lanyon's panic-stricken fear.

While this novel makes masterful use of language, it is interestingly in part about how some things – particularly horrifying things – cannot be described in language. There are a number of instances in the novel of people trying to describe Hyde but failing because words cannot capture the feelings people have when they see him. In 'Story of the Door', Enfield says:

> "No, sir; I can make no hand of it; I can't describe him. And it's not want of memory; for I declare I can see him this moment."

Stevenson's novel reaches beyond the words that are used to evoke the situation. He seems to be saying that language is not adequate to describe the feelings of horror that some people and situations create. This only adds to the chilling, dream-like atmosphere of the book.

TASKS

This is a good series of exercises to help you analyse the language of the book. Look at these different word classes (nouns, verbs, adjectives etc.) used in the story, and think about the connotations of the words: what do the words make you think, feel and see within the context of the novel? Look up the meanings of words you don't know.

NOUNS

Names: "Dr Henry Jekyll, Mr Edward Hyde, Mr. John Gabriel Utterson, Dr Hastie Lanyon." What do the sounds and connotations of these names suggest about the characters?

> POSSILBE ANSWER: The phrase "Dr" embodies "male respectability", power and prestige. Jekyll and Lanyon are both doctors and appear to be very respectable as a result. The irony is that Jekyll is the absolute opposite of "respectability" when he becomes "Mr Edward Hyde". For me, the word "Jekyll" has sinister overtones in that it sounds like "jackal" – a deadly wolfish animal. The word "Lanyon" has connotations of laziness and smugness for me, much like the character. Meanwhile the surname of "Hyde" is very important because it is, of course, a different spelling of "hide"; this is the surname Jekyll has given himself in his "alter ego" state. The lawyer in the novel, Utterson has the first name of "Gabriel" which suggests the Angel Gabriel, who was very good and I think it's no coincidence that Utterson is fundamentally a good man. His surname contains the word "utter" which means to "speak" or say something; Utterson often dares to say the unsayable and will listen to the unsayable when asks Jekyll to confess to him if he has something that he is being blackmailed for.

CONCRETE NOUNS

Describing the city: "thoroughfares, streets, lamps, fog, mist, labyrinths, and darkness." Why are these nouns used to describe the city?

> POSSIBLE ANSWER: Stevenson peppers his text with these concretes nouns to evoke both a "real" city of streets and thoroughfares but also suggest its nightmarish qualities: its "labyrinths" and "darkness". Both these concrete nouns are symbolic as well: the "labyrinth" is symbolic of the confusion that the reader and many of the characters feel because they are trapped in the maze of Jekyll's deceit. Similarly, the "darkness" of the city is symbolic of Jekyll's evil and deceit as well; he is swamped by the darkness of Hyde in much the same way the city is swamped by the foggy darkness of corruption and social injustice.

The house: "hallway, laboratory, cabinet, cheval-glass, phial." Why are these nouns emphasized in the descriptions of the house and laboratory?

> POSSIBLE ANSWER: Stevenson takes time to evoke Jekyll's house and laboratory by using concrete nouns that evoke both a respectable house and a working laboratory. Concrete nouns like "hallway" and "cabinet" suggest the luxury and spaciousness of Jekyll's house: this is such a big house that Hyde can go un-noticed while he lives for days at a time in the laboratory. Meanwhile, an old-fashioned noun phrase like "cheval-glass" suggests the vanity of Jekyll: this is a big mirror which is used to adjust clothing all over the body.

Nouns connected with the drugs/potions: "ebullition, salt, drugs, mixture."

> POSSIBLE ANSWER: The noun "ebullition" means "fizzing liquid": it is slightly archaic but it connotes the mysterious nature of Jekyll's potion; however it has scientific connotations and makes the drinking of the drug sound much less like something that might happen in a fairy-tale. If Stevenson had used "potion" consistently instead of this word, there would have been suggestions of Jekyll being rather like the wicked stepmother in *Snow White* who transforms herself from a beautiful woman into an old pedlar. The word "salt" and "drugs" both conjure a more scientific atmosphere as well.

RELIGIOUS LEXIS

"Devil, fiend, Satan, Juggernaut": Why are these religious nouns associated with Hyde?

> POSSIBLE ANSWER: Many critics have commented upon (Gray, 2004) the religious nature of the tale and how much Stevenson was influenced by the strict Christianity of his country, Scotland. Hyde is consistently linked with the "Devil": he is called by this emotive noun a number of times. He is the antithesis (opposite) of Jesus Christ. These religious nouns create a fevered, "Satanic" atmosphere and greatly increase the horror.

ABSTRACT NOUNS

"Duality, evil, horror, terror, good, goodness, dreams, nightmares, geniality." What role do these abstract nouns play in the novel?

> POSSIBLE ANSWER: These abstract nouns create the intellectual qualities of the book. The abstract noun "duality" is absolutely vital because it evokes the central theme of the novel, what Mighall (Mighall, 2003) calls the "double-consciousness" of Jekyll: he is a man of "two minds" and approaches to life, one which is wholly good and nice (Jekyll) and one which is wholly evil and anti-social (Hyde).

VERBS

What are the connotations of the following verbs and why are they important in the novel? Verbs connected with Mr Hyde: "sneering, stumping, trampling, murdering, striking, running, swearing, twitching."

> POSSIBLE ANSWER: The dynamic verbs associated with Hyde are very important in suggesting the violence of the character. He is even violent in the way he walks, being described as "stumping". He "tramples" on the girl at the beginning of the story and "strikes" Sir Danvers Carew to death: these dynamic verbs convey the power and evil of the man. Verbs like "whispering" describe the way he speaks: again this suggests his menace. He is not someone who needs to shout to be heard; people are transfixed by him and will listen even when he whispers.

Verbs connected with Jekyll: "sighing, crying, and pleading."

> POSSIBLE ANSWER: In stark contrast to Hyde, Jekyll often has rather "pathetic" verbs attached to him, particularly at the end of the book. He "sighs", "cries" and "pleads"; these verbs evoke how lost he is, how confused his situation is, and how desperate this once powerful and respectable man has become.

Verbs connected with Utterson: "seeking, dreaming, asking, and inquiring."

> POSSIBLE ANSWER: Utterson is always "seeking" the answer to the solution of the mystery of Hyde, but never

quite discovers it. The verbs connected with him suggest his curiosity and his inquiring nature: he is both fascinated and concerned by what has happened to his friend.

ADJECTIVES

What are the connotations of the following adjectives and why are they important in the novel? Adjectives connected with the city: "misty, foggy, dark, and black."

> POSSIBLE ANSWER: As has been said when talking about the concrete nouns connected with the city, much lexis suggests the mysterious and evil-nature of the city. These adjectives are both descriptive and symbolic: the "foggy" atmosphere not only tells us what the city looks like but also evokes the confusion people feel in this malign, nightmarish place.

Adjectives connected with Hyde: "displeasing, down-right detestable, deformed, sordid, evil, mis-shapen, small, energetic, ape-like, and troglodytic."

> POSSIBLE ANSWER: This is possibly the most interesting lexis to examine in the novel; each adjective connected with Hyde could be analysed at great length. The most important ones are connected with Hyde's physical appearance: he is "deformed" and "mis-shapen" and yet the irony is that there is never anything specific which categorically proves he is like this. In other words, while the adjectives are technically inaccurate in their physical description of him, these words evoke the "feeling" or "atmosphere" Hyde creates in the people that meet him. Hyde is someone who cannot be described: he has to be "felt" to be understood. This is a real paradox: he is a made-up character who "lives beyond the page"; he is the demon that lives within all of us. He is our worst aspects; the deformity of our souls. He is also the "primitive" side of our natures; he is described as "ape-like" and "troglodytic". In other words, he seems to convey what we were once like when we first evolved as humans: he is our violent, unfettered ancestor who would club anyone he didn't like to death without any feelings of guilt.

ADVERBS

What are the connotations of the following adverbs and why are they important in the novel? Adverbs connected with people talking: "hoarsely, peevishly, and complainingly."

POSSIBLE ANSWER: These adverbs suggest the nightmarish qualities of Hyde: he is "hoarse". There is something "painful" to hear in his voice. Many people in the novel are irritated or anxious; they behave "peevishly" and "complainingly".

DIFFERENT LITERARY STYLES

Look at the way Stevenson uses different literary forms in the novel. At times, the book uses "third-person" narration – people are described in the "third person", i.e. "he/she/it/they". When does this happen and what is the effect of this?

At other times, Stevenson makes use of first person narration, using letters, first-hand testimonies, wills and confessions to show what is happening. When does this happen and why do you think he switches "person" like this?

POSSIBLE ANSWER: Stevenson brings real variety to the novel by using so many different styles: the reader is never bored by being subjected to one style for long. He also provides the novel with what we might call "veracity" or the "ring of truth" by using forms which are largely "non-fictional", that is they are used to convey truths and facts. For example, Jekyll's notes to the chemist convey very vividly his desperation for drugs, while the first hand testimonies of Lanyon and Enfield turn what are actually rather unbelievable events into ones that are believable because they are written in a non-fictional form.

6 Characterisations

It is important to realise that the characters in the novel are not "real people" but invented creations. The author has invented them to engage our interest in their stories, to make us feel certain emotions towards them, to use them as a way to explore certain issues. A good literary critic must think about the techniques an author uses to make a character interesting, and the thoughts, feelings and images a character provokes in the reader's mind.

Dr Jekyll

Dr Jekyll is a complex character. He is a rich man who lives what appears to be a very "respectable" life as a scientist, except that this appearance of respectability hides a darker side. In his confession, he talks about having a "dual" nature from an early age: he indulges in things that are not respectable in the society he lives in. We never really learn what these things are but we can guess: he probably likes having sex with people who were not deemed as suitable partners during that time.

Stevenson's first description of him is informative:

> Dr. Jekyll was no exception; and as he now sat on the opposite side of the fire—a large, well-made, smooth-faced man of fifty, with something of a stylish cast perhaps, but every mark of capacity and kindness—you could see by his looks that he cherished for Mr. Utterson a sincere and warm affection.

It's important to note that Jekyll is a kind man who does "good works": he helps out the poor, various charities and religious causes. He is the embodiment of Victorian respectability and seems to take pleasure in helping people and being a good friend. Except, of course, this is, to a degree, a "sham", a "façade": he appears this way, but in reality he is not. Stevenson uses him as a way of exploring the hypocrisy of Victorian England: this is a world where appearances mean everything and, as a result, many rich people are being blackmailed because they are not as "squeaky clean" as they pretend to be. Jekyll believes that becoming Hyde is wonderful because it allows him to be the person he could never be if he was Jekyll: he can be violent, anti-social, and can go to places of "sin" and "vice" that might mean Jekyll's disgrace if he were seen in them. In his confession, this passage is perhaps the most revealing of Jekyll:

> Not that I dreamed of resuscitating Hyde; the bare idea of that would startle **me** to frenzy: no, it was in my own person that I was once more tempted to trifle with my conscience; and it was as an ordinary secret sinner that I at last fell before the assaults of temptation.

After deciding to stop being Hyde, Jekyll finds he can't stop himself in indulging in Hyde's pleasures as himself and, as a consequence, becomes an "ordinary secret sinner" who "fell before the assaults of temptation". The language here is important: Jekyll sees "temptation" or desire as an "assault"; it is like being attacked. This shows how terrified Jekyll is of his secret desires. What are they though? We never really learn in the novel, but in various filmed versions of the book we see him acting like a paedophile, a sex maniac and a psycho-path. Part of the book's power may be that we never learn what he has been doing, thus leaving us to imagine his depravity.

Jekyll is "vindictive" and settles old scores in the novel. This is particularly the case with Lanyon. Just before Hyde turns back into Jekyll in front of Lanyon, Jekyll speaking as Hyde says:

> And now, you who have so long been bound to the most narrow and material views, you who have denied the virtue of transcendental medicine, you who have derided your superiors —behold!

Here we see Jekyll "tell off" Lanyon for holding "narrow and material views", in other words for being blinkered and unimaginative. He calls himself a "superior" to Lanyon and makes it very clear that Lanyon was wrong to "deride" or mock him. This is a clear example of Jekyll settling an old score: although he pretended to be relaxed about Lanyon criticising his scientific methods earlier on in the novel, we learn here, through the voice of Hyde, that he definitely is not.

It important to note that Hyde is Jekyll; this seems like an obvious point but it is easy to forget. Jekyll is portrayed in a psychologically convincing fashion: he is a fully-fleshed out character who reveals a striking array of different emotions and personas. The portrayal is psychological because we see that when Jekyll represses his inner-most desires he causes serious problems for himself: Hyde has been created out of his repressed desires. This is most clearly seen with the murder of Carew in Jekyll's confession: he tells us that before the murder he had been deliberately trying to avoid taking the potion and that when he did, the potion had a doubly strong effect; his repressed anger came out in a terrifying fashion.

Questions
Why and how is Jekyll a complex character?
Why is Stevenson's characterisation of Jekyll a "psychological" portrayal?

POSSIBLE ANSWERS in brief & bold

Why and how is Jekyll a complex character? **Jekyll is complex because we learn by the end of the story that there are many sides to him. There is the "good", the side that helps charities and the poor and is a loyal friend; there is the "respectable", the part of him that wants to be seen as "decent" and "upstanding"; and then there is the side that enjoys inflicting pain upon people, the sadistic side; and there is also the "undignified" side, the side that does things that no respectable person would condone.**
Why is Stevenson's characterisation of Jekyll a "psychological" portrayal? **The portrait is psychological because Stevenson really tries to work out WHY Jekyll behaves in this way: we see in Jekyll's 'Full Statement' an explanation of Jekyll's decline; we learn how Jekyll felt he had Hyde under control to begin with, but then Hyde becomes "monstrous" as Jekyll takes more and more of the drug. This is a very psychological portrait of Jekyll because we see how he doesn't suddenly turn into an evil monster: it happened by degrees.**

Mr Hyde

Utterson's first meeting with Hyde is revealing. Stevenson writes:

> Mr. Hyde was pale and dwarfish, he gave an impression of deformity without any nameable malformation, he had a

> displeasing smile, he had borne himself to the lawyer with a sort of murderous mixture of timidity and boldness, and he spoke with a husky, whispering and somewhat broken voice; all these were points against him, but not all of these together could explain the hitherto unknown disgust, loathing and fear with which Mr. Utterson regarded him.

Hyde is, in many ways, the opposite of Jekyll. Where Jekyll is tall and kind-looking, Hyde is "dwarfish" and has a "displeasing smile" that has a "murderous mixture of timidity and boldness". He clearly smiles in a perverted or unpleasant fashion, and is both cowardly and bold. Many film versions of the book do not capture this aspect of Hyde, making him appear quite a brave but psychopathic character: he isn't brave at all. When he is confronted with what he has done to the little girl, he backs down and pays the family compensation because he is frightened of what they might do to him. When he suddenly appears in Regent's Park at the end of the novel, he is terrified of being caught and hung.

On the other hand, he is not afraid of getting away with what he can; he is not worried about what people think of him. He does not observe the normal rules of politeness: he hits people he doesn't like, and appears to dislike people for irrational reasons – we see this particularly with Sir Danvers Carew. He is probably highly sexual. We are told that he is "troglodytic"; this means that he is like a cave man. In Stevenson's time, this was probably code for being highly sexual (Mighall, 2003 & Luckhurst, 2006): it was thought by the Victorians that our ancestors behaved like apes and had no sexual inhibitions.

His true character comes out towards the end of the novel when we learn of his emotions towards Jekyll:

> The hatred of Hyde for Jekyll was of a different order. His terror of the gallows drove him continually to commit temporary suicide, and return to his subordinate station of a part instead of a person; but he loathed **the** necessity, he loathed the despondency into which Jekyll was now fallen, and he resented the dislike with which he was himself regarded. Hence the ape-like tricks that he would play me, scrawling in my own hand blasphemies on the pages of my books, burning the letters and destroying the portrait of my father; and indeed, had it not been for his fear of death, he would long ago have ruined himself in order to involve me in the ruin. But his love of me is wonderful; I go further: I, who sicken and freeze at the mere thought of him, when I recall the abjection and passion of this attachment,

and when I know how he fears my power to cut him off by
suicide, I find it in my heart to pity him.

We learn here that Hyde temporarily "commits suicide" – in other
words he drinks the potion that makes him Jekyll – only because
he wants to avoid being hung, not because he wants to be Jekyll
again. He hates Jekyll's "despondency" or depression suggesting
that Hyde is a high-spirited, bizarrely joyful person: he is
described as being in a "transport of glee" as he murders Carew.
Although it has to be said there is a problem here because Jekyll
uses the pronoun "I" to describe Hyde's feelings while he is killing
Carew, thereby implying that Jekyll felt this way too. He is also a
joker who loves to swear and desecrate things: he writes
"blasphemies" in the pages of Jekyll's books, he burns the portrait
of Jekyll's father. There is almost something pathetic about Hyde
for all his horrible selfishness: he is like an unruly child.

It is important to note that Hyde, according to Jekyll's 'Full
Statement' is not immediately evil. We learn when first appeared
what Hyde does is "undignified" but his pleasures become
"monstrous" as he gains in power. In other words, Hyde seems to
gain strength by being allowed to exist, and progressively becomes
more and more violent. When Jekyll gives up taking the drug for
two months after being shocked to find that he has woken up as
Hyde, Hyde comes back even stronger and more uncontrolled
after Jekyll takes the potion again, and murders Carew as a result.
In fact he becomes so strong that he appears without Jekyll taking
the potion: once Jekyll has decided to stop being Hyde altogether,
Hyde springs back to life in Regent's Park without Jekyll ingesting
the drug. From then onwards, Jekyll has to swallow stronger and
stronger doses of the drug to stop being Hyde. This suggests that
Hyde rather than being a fully-rounded character is an "aspect" or
element of Jekyll: a Freudian critic might argue that he is the "Id"
or the inner-desires of Jekyll which becomes stronger the longer
he is allowed to exist. A religious interpretation might be that
Hyde is the "Devil", the inner "evil" of mankind, who thrives when
God is ignored or deliberately disobeyed. Some other critics, called
"cultural theorists", have examined the culture that allows
someone like Hyde to thrive and have argued that Hyde is a
product of the society that he lives in (see Katherine Linehan in
Literary Criticism chapter); he is allowed to get away with his
crimes because someone with money and anonymity can. It is only
when he angers the upper-classes with the murder of Carew that
he is actually stopped.

Questions

What does Hyde look like? Why do people say that he seems "deformed"?
Why is he compared to being an "ape" or a cave man at times?
What does Hyde symbolise?

POSSIBLE ANSWERS in brief & bold

What does Hyde look like and how does he act? **Hyde is small and muscular, and appears in some way "deformed". He is described as "stumping", that is, moving by violently putting his feet on the ground. When he speaks he seems to "whisper" in a "hoarse" fashion.**
Why do people say that he seems "deformed"? **Although he does not explicitly look ugly, everyone who meets him feels there is something abnormal about him. Just his presence makes people feel "icy". It could be that he arouses a primitive feeling of fear in people, in the same way wild animals or snakes make people feel afraid.**
Why is he compared to being an "ape" or a cave man at times? **Stevenson, like many writers of the time, was very affected by the science of evolution developed by Charles Darwin. Hyde seems at times to be a "throwback" to when humans were "ape-like": it almost as if Jekyll has accessed our evolutionary past when he takes the potion** (Mighall, 2003).
What does Hyde symbolise? **Hyde symbolises different things to different critics. For people interpreting the book as a Christian "allegory" (a long symbolic religious story) he represents the Devil, and all the temptations of the Devil and evil. There is a great deal of religious imagery in the book which suggests this interpretation has validity: Hyde is compared to the devil and he himself, when he is taking the potion before Lanyon, referencing the name of Satan.**

Mr Utterson

One could argue that Utterson is the "protagonist" – the main character -- of the novel in that he plays the detective figure searching out for the clues as to what is happening to Jekyll. In the first chapter Stevenson describes him in this way:

But he had an approved tolerance for others; sometimes
wondering, almost with envy, at the high pressure of spirits
involved in their misdeeds; and in any extremity inclined to
help rather than to reprove. "I incline to Cain's heresy," he
used to say quaintly: "I let my brother go to the devil in his
own way." In this character, it was frequently his fortune to
be the last reputable acquaintance and the last good
influence in the lives of downgoing men. And to such as
these, so long as they came about his chamber, he never
marked a shade of change in his demeanour.

Utterson is a boring man who does not seem to have the desires,
dreams or contradictions of Jekyll. He does not judge people
however -- but helps them. He lets people do what they want
without interfering. This is what makes him an excellent character
to investigate the case of Jekyll because he is not easily shocked:
he helps "downgoing" men, that is, people who are losing their
reputations for respectability. In the novel, we see him being very
persistent: he tracks down Hyde after much waiting around for
him at his door. We see him being caring: he tries continually to
help Jekyll. He is also non-judgemental, offering to listen to Jekyll
if he has anything to confess. He is also decisive: he makes the
decision to knock down the door to Jekyll's room in order to see
where Jekyll is. Ultimately, it is his desire to find out the truth
about Jekyll which leads to Jekyll's destruction.

In literary terms, Utterson serves as a good counter-point to the
extremes of Jekyll and Hyde and provides the narrative with a
good "anchor" in that his realistic, ordinary approach to life
contrasts greatly with Jekyll and Hyde's fantastical experiments
and misdemeanours.

Questions
Why could you argue that Utterson is the main protagonist in the novel?
How and why does he behave like a detective?

Answers in brief and bold
Why could you argue that Utterson is the main protagonist in the novel?
**For the first half of the novel, before Jekyll gives his 'Full
Statement', Utterson is the main character in that the reader
follows his journey as he gradually uncovers the truth about
Jekyll. Some critics have argued that he ultimately destroys
Jekyll in his quest for the truth because Jekyll/Hyde takes the
poison that kills himself after Utterson says he will knock
down the door.**

How and why does he behave like a detective? **Utterson operates like a detective because he is continually looking for clues as to what is going on with Hyde: he takes some time to search for Hyde, he thinks about the problem of Jekyll's will, he questions Poole, Lanyon and Jekyll himself about what is happening with Jekyll, he finds clues such as the broken walking stick, and he confronts Jekyll/Hyde by breaking down the door to his laboratory. All of these things make him like your "classic detective", except of course there were very few detective novels before this one was written. Some people have argued that Stevenson invented the form of the detective novel with this book.**

Dr Lanyon

This is an early description of Lanyon:

> Dr. Lanyon sat alone over his wine. This was a hearty, healthy, dapper, red-faced gentleman, with a shock of hair prematurely white, and a boisterous and decided manner.

In many ways, Lanyon is very similar to Jekyll in that he is a respectable, wealthy scientist who has a happy life. However, he has disassociated himself with Jekyll because of Jekyll's scientific experiments which Lanyon believes are "unscientific balderdash". Lanyon is a "smug" and patronising man who believes he knows best. He learns a terrible lesson when he sees Jekyll turn into Hyde. After this time, all his certainties about life are shattered and he becomes a broken man:

> He had his death-warrant written legibly upon his face. The rosy man had grown pale; his flesh had fallen away; he was visibly balder and older; and yet it was not so much these tokens of a swift physical decay that arrested the lawyer's notice, as a look in the eye and quality of manner that seemed to testify to some deep-seated terror of the mind.

Lanyon seems to represent the self-satisfied certainties of Victorian England: he appears to be someone who thinks he knows it all and then learns to his cost that he does not. There is a suggestion too that he too may have tried the potion or may be tempted to use it: the "terror of the mind" is his horror that he is just like Jekyll and harbours secret, terrifying desires.

Lanyon serves an important role in the novel in that he witnesses Hyde's transformation into Jekyll; Stevenson deliberately engineers the narrative so that it is a scientist who witnesses this transformation because a scientist is a more trustworthy observer than someone who already believes in "supernatural" transformations.

Questions

How does Stevenson present Dr Lanyon?
Why is it Lanyon who observes Hyde's transformation into Hyde?

POSSIBLE ANSWERS in brief & bold

How does Stevenson present Dr Lanyon? **Stevenson presents Lanyon as a self-satisfied scientist who is a "materialist", i.e. he doesn't believe in mystical transformations or magic. He has a very happy and successful life in Cavendish Square, one of the wealthiest areas of London. His confidence in his scientific views is shattered when he witnesses Hyde's transformation into Jekyll. Stevenson uses a mixture of description, dialogue and first-hand testimony to make Lanyon a plausible and interesting character. Initially, we hear about Lanyon's beliefs that Jekyll's scientific methods are "balderdash", thus setting him up in what seems to be a minor conflict of opinion with Jekyll. However, we learn later that Jekyll has been greatly angered by Lanyon's dismissal of his science and that he achieves a kind of revenge upon him when he shows how Hyde can change into Jekyll. Lanyon's shock and horror at having his logical, scientific beliefs shattered ultimately kill him.**

Why is it Lanyon who observes Hyde's transformation into Hyde?
Stevenson gives the narrative more "credibility" or makes it more believable by having Lanyon observe Hyde's transformation because Lanyon is a skeptical, rational scientist who is a "truthful" observer. If a mystical person had seen the change, then we might have doubted his word because he would merely be endorsing what he already believes. However, Lanyon has to deny all his previous beliefs in order to say that the transformation really happened.

Poole

Poole is Jekyll's elderly butler who shows surprising strength in knocking down Jekyll's stout door. He is the embodiment of the Victorian servant: he is loyal and obedient even when his master's demands are outrageous. Like Lanyon he has all his certainties about life shattered: he comes to believe that his master's supposed friend, Hyde, has murdered him. He cannot act though without the support of his social superiors. This is why he asks Utterson to visit in the chapter 'The Last Night': although he would like to break down the door to Jekyll's room he knows he doesn't have the authority, but Utterson his social superior does.

Poole serves an important literary function in the novel in that he is used to heighten the sense of mystery and suspense. We see this in 'Search for Mr Hyde' when he tells Utterson that the servants have to obey Hyde and that Hyde is a familiar figure in the household. Most strikingly, he generates a huge amount of suspense in 'The Last Night' by the way he suddenly appears and says that there has been "foul play" to Utterson: the fact that he, of all people, is so upset shows how terrible the situation is. Thus we can see how Stevenson uses his character to convey a sense of horror at Jekyll's predicament: if Poole can be upset then we all should be. The way Poole calls Hyde "it" is particularly chilling: Poole dehumanises Hyde in a way that no one else has been willing to do. He seems to realise that Hyde is not the same as the human race. Other people like Lanyon, Utterson and Enfield are more easily fooled by the social codes of the day and view Hyde as a gentleman, if a bad one. Poole though knows that Hyde is different. His theory that his master has been "made away with" turns out to be the closest guess of all. In such a way, we could argue that despite the fact that Poole speaks in "slang", he is actually one of the more intelligent characters.

His character also illustrates how Hyde has managed not only to destroy and abuse people, but his actions have threatened the social order of the society. Utterson notes with horror that it is not good that all the servants are not doing their jobs anymore; furthermore, we see Poole, who should be preserving his master's household, destroying his master's door with an axe.

Questions
What function does Poole serve in the narrative?

What evidence is there that Poole is actually quite perceptive and intelligent?

POSSIBLE ANSWERS in brief & bold

What function does Poole serve in the narrative? **Poole is important in the narrative because he helps heighten the suspense considerably. At first, the introduction of Poole helps heighten the mystery about the connection between Hyde and Jekyll because he tells Utterson that Jekyll has given orders for the servants to obey Hyde. In 'The Last Night' Poole creates a great deal of the suspense by appearing so worried about Jekyll, and theorising that he has been "made away with". By calling Hyde "it", he creates a sense of horror regarding Hyde, suggesting Hyde's inhuman qualities.**
What evidence is there that Poole is actually quite perceptive and intelligent? **Of all the characters in the novel, it is Poole who gets closest to the truth when he suggests that Jekyll has been "made away with" or murdered by Hyde. This is something that Utterson doesn't believe; preferring to think Jekyll is ill and needs drugs. Poole also subtly engineers the breaking down of Jekyll's door by revealing the truth about the situation to Utterson in stages, and not all at once. This suggests he knows Utterson well and realises that he can't tell Utterson the full extent of knowledge until Utterson has witnessed Jekyll's house himself.**

7 Themes

Good versus evil

This might seem to be an obvious theme because one could argue that Jekyll represents "good" and Hyde represents "evil". However, a close reading of the novel shows that this theme is more complicated than that. In his full statement of the case, Jekyll confesses:

> I was no more myself when I laid **(put)** aside restraint **(self-control)** and plunged **(dived into)** in shame, than

when I laboured **(worked)**, in the eye of day, at the furtherance **(development)** of knowledge or the relief of sorrow and suffering.

When Jekyll "plunges" into "shame" we must assume that he is behaving in an "evil" fashion, while when he works for the "relief of suffering", he is doing "good". In other words, Jekyll is both "evil" and "good"; the two elements sit side by side within him. It is not a question of "good versus evil" but more the case that good needs evil to exist and vice versa. This is a radical thought and one that questions certain religious ideas which state that God is wholly good. By this account, this could not be the case because goodness only exists because its opposite exists. Thus we can say that there appears to be a fight within Jekyll between his good and evil side, but, as we have seen, it is more complicated than saying they are opposing forces. The novel is full of Christian imagery which references things which many Christian people regard as "sinful" or evil. There are many things to note that Jekyll does that are, in his eyes, sinful; he calls them "undignified pleasures", "irregularities", and a "gaiety of disposition" for which he feels a sense of "shame". Some critics believe that Stevenson's religious upbringing is important here in that he was taught to feel a sense of "shame" at the pleasures of the body: eating, drinking, sensuality, and sex. The strict Scottish Calvinism which Stevenson's family adhered to believed that the body or the flesh was essentially evil and needed to be constantly punished in order to be "good".

Question
In what way does the novel explore the theme of good and evil?
Please re-read the above section to find the answer.

The duality of man

This is Stevenson's main theme: the "two-sided" aspect of man. He shows that co-existing within all human beings are both the good and the bad:

> It was on the moral side, and in my own person, that I learned to recognise the thorough and primitive duality of man; I saw that, of the two natures that contended in the field of my consciousness, even if I could rightly be said to be either, it was only because I was radically both; and from an early date, even before the course of my scientific discoveries had begun to suggest the most naked possibility of such a miracle, I had learned to dwell with pleasure, as a beloved daydream, on the thought of the separation of these elements.

Henry Jekyll's great idea is that he can "separate" the two sides of man: the animal and the divine, the good and the bad, the ugly and the beautiful. However, his idea is revealed to be naïve because the author shows that the two elements are inter-dependent – as has already been discussed in the section "Good versus evil". This duality is "primitive" because all that is good about man is spoilt by the bad side. Therefore Jekyll proposes separating the bad side off entirely. This was a problem that preoccupied many Victorians who agreed with Darwin's theory of evolution but were horrified that there might be something "ape-like" about their beings, their personalities, their bodies. So Jekyll's quest is very much the secret quest of many people of the time: a quest to "get rid of" the "animal" and "primitive" side, to expunge the "ape" in the "man". His narrative reveals that this can't be done because the "ape" or "Hyde side" takes over.

Question

In what way does the novel explore the theme of the duality of man?
Please re-read the above section to find the answer.

Appearance versus reality

A key theme in this book is the lengths men will go to appear respectable: to hide their inner-most desires. We learn from Utterson that he is well aware that many men are black-mailed for the "indiscretions of their youth". This is a society where "appearance is all" (Luckhurst, 2006): if it was learnt that you were actually homosexual or had no money then you would be ruined.

Some critics think that Utterson suspects that Jekyll is being blackmailed by Hyde because he is homosexual. Homosexuality was a crime in England until 1968 and men were jailed for it, most famously an acquaintance of Stevenson's, the writer Oscar Wilde, was jailed a few years after the publication of this book for homosexuality. His entire career was ruined. This book is radical in that it suggests that within all men lurk secret desires: in other words, many so-called respectable people lead "phoney" lives, pretending to be people they are not.

Question
In what ways does the novel explore the theme of appearance versus reality?
Please re-read the above section to find the answer.

The limits of science

This theme is clearly exemplified in the characterisation of Lanyon who is a self-satisfied scientist who has all his beliefs shattered when he sees Hyde transform into Jekyll. Stevenson seems to be suggesting that modern, rational science simply isn't adequate to explain the world. Let's look at this quote in order to explore this issue:

> "We had," was the reply. "But it is more than ten years since Henry Jekyll became too fanciful for me. He began to go wrong, wrong in mind; and though of course I continue to take an interest in him for old sake's sake, as they say, I see and I have seen devilish little of the man. Such unscientific balderdash," added the doctor, flushing suddenly purple, "would have estranged Damon and Pythias."

Here we see Dr Lanyon become annoyed at the thought of Dr Jekyll's science: he feels that Jekyll has been conducting experiments which are "unscientific balderdash", in other words are worthless rubbish. He says that their disagreement would have made even the best of friends, Damon and Pythias, fall out. We, the reader, however find it difficult to see why this would be the case: certainly Utterson doesn't regard their disagreement as important and sees it as an irrelevance. However, in the context of the novel, it turns out that their disagreement is vital because we learn that Jekyll has actually shown that Lanyon's "narrow" and "material" views of the world are wrong, and that transformation into another creature is possible. Thus we can see that the novel is, in a way, showing that science is limited in its ability to explain the mysteries of life and the human character, which are far more complex than science would have us believe.

Question
In what way does the novel explore the theme of the limits of science?
Please re-read the above section to find the answer.

The "nightmarish" city

One could argue that the city is a personality in the novel in its own right. At certain critical points in the novel, Stevenson takes great care to describe the atmosphere and physical environment of London. Some critics have argued that he is actually describing his hometown of Edinburgh in Scotland rather than London because Stevenson's London has a split personality in much the same way that Edinburgh had -- and Jekyll does too. Edinburgh was divided into the "Old" and "New Town": the "Old Town" was extremely run-down and very much like where Hyde lives, while the "New Town" had houses similar to Jekyll's: grand, large, well-proportioned. Of course, Jekyll's house has Hyde's living quarters at the back so we can see how the two sides of the city – the respectable and the disgraceful – are inter-connected. It's worth examining his descriptions of the city in detail. Here's an account in 'The Carew Murder' of Utterson and the police visiting Hyde's flat:

As the cab drew up before the address indicated, the fog lifted a little and showed him a dingy street, a gin palace, a low French eating house, a shop for the retail of penny numbers and twopenny salads, many ragged children huddled in the doorways, and many women of many different nationalities passing out, key in hand, to have a morning glass; and the next moment the fog settled down again upon that part, as brown as umber, and cut him off from his blackguardly surroundings. This was the home of Henry Jekyll's favourite;

The description would have provoked the fears of middle-class Victorians because it evokes child poverty, prostitution and immigration. Stevenson describes children who are "ragged", in other words dressed in rags, and who appear to have no parents or proper guardians: they are possibly orphans who have been abandoned. He talks about a number of shops and restaurants all of which are unpleasant: there is a "gin palace" which is place to buy very cheap and strong alcohol, a "low French eating house" which is a nasty, inexpensive restaurant, and a shop where you can get very cheap takeaway food "twopenny salads" and stories of sensational crimes, "penny numbers". He talks about women who have their own "keys" to their houses; this would have been a signal that they were prostitutes or "corrupted" women to Victorian readers because normally only husbands were allowed to carry front door keys (Luckhurst, 2006). The surroundings are described as "blackguardly"; they are perceived as wicked, morally corrupt, and evil. This is the world that Hyde thrives in because he can "hide" within it.

Question

In what way does the novel explore the theme of the city being like a nightmare?

Please re-read the above section to find the answer.

Desire

A dominating theme of the novel is the nature of Henry Jekyll's desires. He has a number of desires which are contradictory: he wants to appear respectable but also to indulge in violent and possibly sexual behaviour; he wants to have good friends and yet he doesn't want to share his "secret" life with them. This passage from his "Testament" is instructive:

> And indeed the worst of my faults was a certain impatient gaiety of disposition, such as has made the happiness of many, but such as I found it hard to reconcile with my imperious desire to carry my head high, and wear a more than commonly grave countenance before the public.

More than any other passage this tells us what he is really like: he has a "gaiety" of disposition. In Stevenson's time, "gaiety" was slang for men who liked to sleep with many women, while disposition meant "character" (Luckhurst, 2006). But this desire to live the life of a "playboy" was not really permitted for someone who wanted to wear a "grave countenance" – or respectable face – in public. In other words, his desires are utterly contradictory. This is, at root, his major problem.

Question
In what way does the novel explore the theme of desire?
Please re-read the above section to find the answer.

Repression

Shortly after Stevenson wrote his novella, the psycho-analyst Sigmund Freud developed a theory for human nature which suggested that our characters are composed of three key elements: the "Id", which represents our true desires whatever they may be, the "Ego" which is the part of the mind that seeks to satisfy the "Id", and the "Superego" which the part of our mind which obeys the rules of society rather than our own desires. The critic William Gray (p. 54, Gray, 2004) points out that Henry Jekyll's predicament lends itself to a "Freudian" analysis in that it's clear that Jekyll's "Superego" which is, at bottom, the problem, because it crushes his true desires, and represses (or tries to ignore them) to such an extent that the "Id" forces itself upon when he takes a drug which takes away his inhibitions. Stevenson makes it clear that when Jekyll really represses his true desires, when they eventually surface they are much stronger than they would have been if he had allowed them to naturally express themselves. This is very obviously seen in Jekyll's description of the murder of Sir Danvers Carew:

> My devil had been long caged, he came out roaring. I was conscious, even when I took the draught, of a more unbridled, a more furious propensity to ill.

Jekyll had "caged" or imprisoned his "devil" – his innermost desires – and, as a result of this repression, it comes out "roaring" like a terrible monster. It is fascinating to note Jekyll's use of pronouns here. Sometimes, he describes Hyde in the third person as "he" but here he uses the first person "I" which makes it very clear that it is Jekyll who is essentially committing these crimes – not Hyde. This is obviously because Jekyll is Hyde: but this fact is easy to forget unless you read the text very carefully. Jekyll's desires are "unbridled" and he has a "furious propensity to ill": his desires have totally taken over him; there is no "Superego" to stop him doing what he really wants to do. However, it is clear that his violence has been generated by the repression that his Superego has imposed upon him: because he has repressed his desires, when they are expressed they all the more violent. Thus we can see Stevenson exploring a theory of repression here which anticipates the theories of Sigmund Freud.

Question
In what way does the novel explore the theme of repression?
Please re-read the above section to find the answer.

Dreams and nightmares

Linked to the theory of repression is Stevenson's exploration of dream-like states. The book itself was the outcome of a nightmare so it is possibly not surprising that the whole of the novel has the quality of a nightmare. Many of the most famous images in the book are dream-like in nature: the violence of Hyde trampling on the girl and murdering Carew; the discovery of the suicidal Hyde's small, twitching body in Jekyll's clothes; and the way Hyde magically transforms into Jekyll in such a violent and surprising fashion. One of the scariest images in the book is a description of Utterson's dream:

as he lay and tossed in the gross darkness of the night and the curtained room, Mr. Enfield's tale went by before his mind in a scroll of lighted pictures. He would be aware of the great field of lamps of a nocturnal city; then of the figure of a man walking swiftly; then of a child running from the doctor's; and then these met, and that human Juggernaut trod the child down and passed on regardless of her screams. Or else he would see a room in a rich house, where his friend lay asleep, dreaming and smiling at his dreams; and then the door of that room would be opened, the curtains of the bed plucked apart, the sleeper recalled, and lo! there would stand by his side a figure to whom power was given, and even at that dead hour, he must rise and do its bidding. The figure in these two phases haunted the lawyer all night

The image of this "faceless figure" is possibly even more unpleasant than the actual appearance of Hyde: this is a truly nightmarish image of inhuman brutality. It's a dream-like image which haunts the reader: there is something particularly disturbing about faceless figures that chase after children for no apparent reason other than to commit violence. The idea of such a figure hovering over our beds is also extremely unpleasant: we're at our most vulnerable when we're asleep.

Question
In what way does the novel explore the theme of dreams and nightmares?
Please re-read the above section to find the answer.

Friendship

Friendship doesn't appear to be an immediately obvious theme in the book, but it is an important one. After all, it is Utterson's friendship for Dr Jekyll that compels him to investigate his case at some considerable danger to himself; this is particularly the case when he breaks down the door to Jekyll's cabinet in 'The Last Night'; there is no telling what Hyde might have done at this point . It is important to note that Utterson is the opposite of a "fair weather" friend: he tells Jekyll that he can confess his sins to him without fear that he will judge him or disown him. And yet, Jekyll consistently rejects the chance to have a "deeper" friendship with

Utterson because it is clear that he enjoys his secret life too much. Jekyll's true friendship is with Edward Hyde, the dark side of his character. Although this friendship is very troubled and ultimately destroys both of them, it is a very deep friendship; each man knows the truth about each other. Lanyon is presented by Stevenson as a man who is ruined by his friendship with Jekyll: after he carries out Jekyll's instructions to fetch the drugs for him in 'Dr Lanyon's Narrative', Lanyon decides to look at Hyde take the drug, despite Hyde's warning. What he sees ultimately results in his death, even though he disowns Jekyll as a friend. Jekyll has broken the bonds of friendship with Lanyon because he has revealed himself as he really is: degraded, corrupted, evil. Lanyon cannot endure having a friend of this type.

This prompts the thought as to what would have happened if it had been Utterson that Hyde had transformed into Jekyll before. One suspects that Utterson would not have been destroyed by the revelation in the way Lanyon is because Utterson is a less pretension, pompous man, who already has a pretty jaundiced view of human nature. Thus we can see Stevenson reveals to us the different variety of friends one encounters in life: the judgemental friends like Lanyon who reject people if they are not who they believe them to be; the more forgiving friends like Utterson; and finally, the friend we make with ourselves in our own minds such as Jekyll makes with Hyde. If we see ourselves as, at root, as a bad person we clearly form destructive relationships with ourselves, and set ourselves on the road to ruin.

Question
In what way does the novel explore the theme of friendship?
Please re-read the above section to find the answer.

Secrecy & blackmail

Enfield, a friend of Utterson's, points out where Hyde lives and says this to Utterson:

> "Black Mail House is what I call the place with the door, in consequence. Though even that, you know, is far from explaining all," he added, and with the words fell into a vein of musing

Clearly Enfield is well aware of the concept of blackmail. As a respectable man about town who probably enjoyed "capers" – as he calls them – in his youth, Enfield may well be worried that he may be blackmailed at some point. In Victorian Britain, it was very important to appear "respectable" and "morally upright" if you were going to succeed in society; if it was known that you had slept with the "wrong person", or were homosexual, or a bankrupt, then it was very likely that you would be sacked from your job, rejected by your friends, and generally cast out from wealthy society. As a result, people could make considerable amounts of money by blackmailing respectable, rich people and threatening to expose their secrets if they did not pay up. There were very few people that a "gentleman" with a secret could trust. One such person is Utterson. This becomes clear when Utterson speaks to Jekyll alone in the chapter 'Dr Jekyll was quite at ease':

> "Jekyll," said Utterson, "you know me: I am a man to be trusted. Make a clean breast of this in confidence; and I make no doubt I can get you out of it."

Utterson makes an offer to Jekyll by saying that he can speak to him "in confidence", i.e. in secret. Utterson is possibly worried that Jekyll is being blackmailed because he had a homosexual relationship with Hyde, or because Hyde, looking much younger than Jekyll, is Jekyll's illegitimate son (Mighall, 2003). Jekyll reassures Utterson that his case is not as bad this and that he can get rid of Hyde at any time he wants. The wonderful thing about Hyde from Jekyll's perspective is that, while he has to remain a secret, there is no threat that he will be blackmailed for doing what he wants to do. Hyde has been created because Jekyll lives in a world where it is very easy to be blackmailed: he can't go out openly and sleep with prostitutes or do things like gamble without worrying that someone might see him and he'll get blackmailed as a result. In a world where people can do what they want, there would be no need for Hyde.

Question
In what way does the novel explore the themes of secrecy and blackmail?
Please re-read the above section to find the answer.

8 Imagery, symbols and motifs

One of the most striking aspects of the novel is its use of repeated images. For the purposes of definition we could say that imagery refers to all the poetic devices a writer uses, while a symbol is an image which represents a particular concept or idea, and a "motif" is a repeated image or symbol which is threaded throughout the novel.

The door

The first chapter of the book is called 'Story of the Door' and describes Hyde's scruffy, derelict door in detail. The door here symbolizes the gateway to more evil world; it is the access point for violence and unpleasantness. Its very aspect emphasizes the evil of its inhabitant because it is a door which suggests its owner doesn't care about how he appears to the world:

> The door, which was equipped with neither bell nor knocker, was blistered and distained. Tramps slouched into the recess and struck matches on the panels; children kept shop upon the steps; the schoolboy had tried his knife on the mouldings

In a sense it is true that Hyde doesn't care about appearances: he has made no attempt to mend the door because it is "blistered" and "disdained". This description works on a symbolic level because the door could symbolize Hyde's character, personality or soul: like the door there is something "blistered" about his being, he is mentally diseased. He certainly is "distained", which here carries a double meaning because it can mean "discoloured" or "disliked by people". Hyde doesn't care what people think of him, but Jekyll does. In stark contrast, Jekyll's door is well-kept and large. Here we see Utterson knocking on it:

> One house, however, second from the corner, was still occupied entire; and at the door of this, which wore a great

air of wealth and comfort, though it was now plunged in
darkness except for the fanlight, Mr. Utterson stopped and
knocked. A well-dressed, elderly servant opened the door.

The description of Jekyll's door is symbolic too because it suggests
how Jekyll wants to appear to the world: with a "great air of wealth
and comfort". However, we realize that the fact that it is "plunged
in darkness" is significant too because Jekyll himself, we learn
later, is plunged in the darkness of Hyde. Here then is a door
which presents the public face of Jekyll to the world is there for
everyone to see, while Hyde's door is hidden away in an alley
where respectable people rarely go. Later on in the novel, doors
become even more significant because it is the door which
generates the mystery regarding the whereabouts of Jekyll. Poole
is very upset when he says to Utterson in 'The Last Night':

> Do you think I do not know where his head comes to in the
> cabinet door, where I saw him every morning of my life?

Poole had seen "something" through the door and was able to
judge the person's height by measuring it against the door; thus
we see the door assisting him with the realisation that it is not
Jekyll. The door here, as before, becomes another clue that
something is terribly wrong. Poole also points out that the
servants have had to deal with a "closed door" and not Jekyll for a
week. The door is a symbol of Jekyll's secrecy and his desperation.
Poole says to Utterson:

> We've had nothing else this week back; nothing but papers,
> and a closed door, and the very meals left there to be
> smuggled in when nobody was looking.

The opening of the door allows Jekyll/Hyde to eat and to survive,
while the fact that it is shut upon his servants and friends
symbolises Jekyll's "social death"; his inability to communicate
properly with people and the world. Ultimately, the door to
Jekyll's laboratory stands between Utterson and the truth of what
has happened to Jekyll. The knocking down of this door is one of
the great set-pieces of the novel, and again like the descriptions
analysed above is symbolically significant; finally Jekyll's secret is
being destroyed with the destruction of the door.

> "Ah, that's not Jekyll's voice—it's Hyde's!" cried Utterson. "Down with the door, Poole!"
>
> Poole swung the axe over his shoulder; the blow shook the building, and the red baize door leaped against the lock and hinges. A dismal screech, as of mere animal terror, rang from the cabinet. Up went the axe again, and again the panels crashed and the frame bounded; four times the blow fell; but the wood was tough and the fittings were of excellent workmanship; and it was not until the fifth, that the lock burst and the wreck of the door fell inwards on the carpet.

The door here is of "excellent workmanship" and its wood is "tough"; this could symbolize the power of Jekyll's disguise, the power of Hyde himself, because this strong, heavy door has stopped the world learning the truth about his terrible experiment.

Essay question
Discuss the symbolism of doors in this novel.

Possible essay plan
Introduction:
Discuss why doors can be viewed as a symbol in poetry and novels: they are often "openings" to other worlds, metaphors for change
Main body:
Discuss what Hyde's door symbolizes: his evil, his neglect and contempt for the world, his secrecy, his escape from blame
Discuss what Jekyll's door symbolizes: his respectability, his public face to the world
Discuss the symbolism of the "knocking down" of Jekyll's cabinet door, and how the door symbolizes Jekyll's destruction
Conclusion:
Sum up your findings; discuss how doors symbolize a few different ideas and themes in the novel

Fog and darkness

Stevenson uses descriptions of fog and darkness to great effect in the novel. Dickens had described the fog in London very famously at the beginning of *Bleak House* in order to evoke a decayed, anxious atmosphere. Stevenson uses fog in London to create an atmosphere of horror and claustrophobia. In 'Search for Mr Hyde' Utterson is described in this fashion:

> In the morning before office hours, at noon when business was plenty, and time scarce, at night under the face of the fogged city moon, by all lights and at all hours of solitude or concourse, the lawyer was to be found on his chosen post.

Here the fog isn't as bad as it becomes later on in the novel. Utterson is represented as a man who is determined to find the truth in the fog, braving it at all hours of the day. The fog here is used not so much as a symbol but to create the atmosphere of Utterson's lonely vigil. Later on though, the fog becomes more sinister. Just before the murder of Carew, the fog is described in this fashion:

> Although a fog rolled over the city in the small hours, the early part of the night was cloudless, and the lane, which the maid's window overlooked, was brilliantly lit by the full moon.

We have here a mixed picture of London: it is a beautiful, cloudless night, lit by the full moon. The atmosphere makes the maid think of romance and her loved one, but the fog gives the night a sinister tinge as does the full moon on reflection because this is, of course, when madness is at its height. The word "lunacy" comes from the Latin word for moon "luna": people believed that the full moon could cause madness. This is certainly what we see happening with Hyde who kills Carew for no good reason at all.

During the morning after the murder though, the atmosphere has changed completely. In one of the most horrifying descriptions in the novel, Stevenson writes:

> It was by this time about nine in the morning, and the first fog of the season. A great chocolate-coloured pall lowered over heaven, but the wind was continually charging and routing these embattled vapours; so that as the cab crawled from street to street, Mr. Utterson beheld a marvellous number of degrees and hues of twilight; for here it would be dark like the back-end of evening; and there would be a glow of a rich, lurid brown, like the light of some strange conflagration; and here, for a moment, the fog would be quite broken up, and a haggard shaft of daylight would glance in between the swirling wreaths.

Of all the descriptions in the novel, this description best reveals a literary device known as the "pathetic fallacy": this is when the weather reflects or mirrors the mood of a character or the story. This is certainly the case here: the wind is surging violently around the city, reflecting the violence of Hyde, while the daylight is described as "haggard", tired and ugly and defeated, which certainly reflects Utterson's mood, and is symbolic of his desperation to find a solution to the Jekyll/Hyde problem. But it is interesting to note that the darkness is "man-made" because the "chocolate-coloured pall" has almost certainly been created by the factories and chimneys in the city. The fact that this made-man smog is compared to a "pall" is important: a "pall" is the cloth put over a coffin during a funeral, thus suggesting that the city itself is a dead body with the pall thrown over it. Even though it is morning, it feels like the onset of night, or the "back-end of evening", with the streets revealing lots of different twilit colours. While this is a nightmarish vision of the city, it is a rather marvellous one: this is more like the city of a nightmare or bad dream than a real one. In such a way, we could speculate that the fog and darkness symbolises a few different things here: it symbolises Utterson's confusion and bewilderment, it symbolises the destructiveness of the modern city, it symbolises Hyde's evil intent, but it also symbolises the ghastly, dream-like wonder of Hyde.

Essay

Explore what the fog and darkness symbolise in this novel.

Possible plan

Introduction:
Discuss the ways in which fog and darkness can symbolise confusion and evil in various works of literature. Discuss the context of Stevenson's novel, and the fact that London and most cities were covered in industrial smogs, which were artificial fogs and created darkness during the day-time

Main body:
Discuss the way in which Stevenson uses fog and darkness early on in the novel to create a Gothic atmosphere, and that this fog lightly suggests mystery

Discuss how after the murder of Carew, the descriptions of darkness and fog in the morning are richly symbolic and work on many different levels.
Analyse this passage in detail

Conclusion:

Sum up your points, showing that Stevenson uses fog as a motif to suggest the confusion of Utterson and the mystery and horror of Hyde as well as the "modern city".

The bogeyman

The novel was described by Stevenson as a "bogeyman" tale. In Hyde, Stevenson created the most horrifying "bogeyman" of all, the bogeyman that is within all of us: what we are like in our worst moments, a representation of our most despicable desires and hatreds. The idea of the novel began with Stevenson having a dream which was very similar to the one that he writes for Utterson in 'Search for Mr Hyde':

> The figure in these two phases haunted the lawyer all night; and if at any time he dozed over, it was but to see it glide more stealthily through sleeping houses, or move the more swiftly and still the more swiftly, even to dizziness, through wider labyrinths of lamplighted city, and at every street corner crush a child and leave her screaming. And still the figure had no face by which he might know it; even in his dreams, it had no face, or one that baffled **(confused)** and melted before his eyes;

The dream is truly nightmarish because it visualises two of our most common fears: that an adult would want to kill a child, and that a figure might be stalking over us while we are sleeping, which Utterson sees happening to Jekyll in his dream. To make matters even worse, the figure has no "face" and when he does catch sight of it, it "melts" before his eyes. The bogeyman then is both human and not-human: he is shadowy and evil, he seems to have super-human powers to be here, there and everywhere, and he catches people at their most vulnerable, either by picking on children or while we are asleep. This bogeyman is more than a ghost: he is a symbol of our deepest fears. Stevenson's skill as a novelist is to reveal that the bogeyman though is not a monster that exists outside us, but actually is part and parcel of who we are. Hyde behaves like a psychotic as we see in the murder of Carew, but he is not an "alien" from outer space, but more of a throw-back to our evolutionary ancestors, the apes:

And next moment, with ape-like fury, he was trampling his victim under foot and hailing down a storm of blows, under which the bones were audibly **(could be heard)** shattered and the body jumped upon the roadway.

The description of Hyde as "ape-like" is important, and is imagery that is sustained throughout the novel: Hyde is merely who we used to be, an "ape". He also is visibly child-like in this description: he stamps on Carew in the same way that a child might stamp on a toy, revelling in the sound of the toy shattering. This sense that Hyde symbolises our inner-most natures is heightened and explored in Jekyll's "Full Statement of the Case" when he recounts how he woke up one morning as Hyde:

But the hand which I now saw, clearly enough, in the yellow light of a mid-London morning, lying half shut on the bedclothes, was lean, corded, knuckly, of a dusky pallor (colour) and thickly shaded with a swart growth of hair. It was the hand of Edward Hyde.

Here Stevenson develops the "ape-like" imagery by describing Hyde's hand more or less as an "ape's" hand, one which is hairy, muscly, "corded" and dark. This is a murderer's hand, this is the bogeyman's hand, and it is actually Jekyll's, the supposedly respectable doctor who helps charitable causes.

Essay
Analyse the role that the "bogeyman" plays in this novel.

Possible plan
Introduction:
Discuss how Stevenson intended the novel to be a "bogeyman" tale, discuss why they were and are popular stories to write
Main body:
Discuss Utterson's dream, analysing the role of the bogeyman in it.
Discuss the representation of Hyde as being "ape-like", a psychotic, and child-like
Discuss why Stevenson made Jekyll and Hyde be the same person, and the implications of that
Conclusion:
Sum up your points, pointing out how the bogeyman is symbolic of our deepest fears that the bogeyman lurks within us

Expressions

Stevenson pays particular attention to how people look and make faces in this novel. His description of their expressions is a running "motif", a repeated pattern of images which are used to convey the personality and hidden natures of the characters. In this regard, he was probably influenced by some prominent criminologists of the day, such as Cesar Lombroso, who believed that you could work out whether someone was a criminal by the way they looked. This is certainly the case with both Hyde and Jekyll. Let's look at one of the first descriptions of Hyde, in 'Story of the Door'. Enfield describes Hyde in this way:

> there was the man in the middle, with a kind of black sneering coolness—frightened too, I could see that—but carrying it off, sir, really like Satan

The "black sneering coolness" is a suggestive description. The "black" is a manifestation of Hyde's evil, the darkness of his soul, the "sneering" reveals Hyde's contempt and dismissal of other people and their troubles, while the "coolness" suggests the way in which Hyde has no feelings of empathy. Hyde's looks are in marked contrast to Jekyll's, which are described here when Utterson brings up the matter of Hyde:

> The large handsome face of Dr. Jekyll grew pale to the very lips, and there came a blackness about his eyes. "I do not care to hear more," said he. "This is a matter I thought we had agreed to drop."

Jekyll is not ugly or deformed like Hyde, but has a "large handsome face": this suggests someone who is successful, wealthy, and high up on the evolutionary scale, a successful manifestation of the species. However, we see intimations of Hyde in the description of him when the name of Hyde is mentioned because a "blackness" comes about his eyes. This is the same blackness we saw when Hyde was challenged about trampling upon the little girl. Thus we can see that Stevenson is possibly challenging the thinkers of his day, such as Lombroso, who believed you could tell whether someone was a criminal by their physical features: Jekyll doesn't look like a criminal at all. However, at times, his expressions reveal his inner-most blackness; it is not his immediate looks that give him away, but his behaviour. Later on in the novel, after the murder of Carew, Jekyll's looks are described again in 'Incident at the Window'. Jekyll is sits talking to Enfield and Utterson from his window when this happens:

> "That is just what I was about to venture to propose," returned the doctor with a smile. But the words were hardly uttered, before the smile was struck out of his face and succeeded by an expression of such abject terror and despair, as froze the very blood of the two gentlemen below.

Jekyll's expression of "abject terror and despair" deeply affects Enfield and Utterson who are looking at him, freezing their blood. We realise later on that Jekyll is aware that he is about to turn into Hyde again and that he has no choice over the matter. The expression on his face reveals how powerless he is, and how he has become a victim of his own experiment. Stevenson uses the description of the expression to heighten both mystery and horror at this moment in the novel, as he has done before when he described Jekyll's "blackness about the eyes" because we never quite know why, at this point, Jekyll is looking this way.

In 'Remarkable Incident of Dr Lanyon', we learn about the change that has happened to Lanyon's looks:

> He had his death-warrant written legibly upon his face. The rosy man had grown pale; his flesh had fallen away; he was visibly balder and older; and yet it was not so much these tokens of a swift physical decay that arrested the lawyer's notice, as a look in the eye and quality of manner that seemed to testify to some deep-seated terror of the mind.

This description works because of the contrasts it makes between how Lanyon used to appear and how he appears now that he has learned the truth about Jekyll. His "rosy" or healthy complexion has become "pale", his "flesh had fallen away", his hair has fallen out and he looks older. However, as with Jekyll, it is not so much how he looks which is the most important thing but the way his eyes reveal a "deep-seated terror of the mind". This terror is in contrast to the blackness about Jekyll's eyes: Lanyon has seen Jekyll/Hyde's blackness and it has terrified him. He is in a worse state than Jekyll in the 'Incident of the Window'. Stevenson uses this description to heighten the mystery of the novel because at this point we don't know exactly what Lanyon knows. There is a real sense of pathos as well because it is terrible to see such a successful, happy man brought down so low. Thus, we, the reader, who had very little for the pompous Lanyon at the beginning of the novel, now do.

It is worth looking at the description which Jekyll gives when he first sees Hyde because his reaction to Hyde is quite different to other people:

> Again, in the course of my life, which had been, after all, nine tenths a life of effort, virtue and control, it had been much less exercised and much less exhausted. And hence, as I think, it came about that Edward Hyde was so much smaller, slighter and younger than Henry Jekyll. Even as good shone upon the countenance of the one, evil was written broadly and plainly on the face of the other. Evil besides (which I must still believe to be the lethal side of man) had left on that body an imprint of deformity and decay. And yet when I looked upon that ugly idol in the glass, I was conscious of no repugnance, rather of a leap of welcome. This, too, was I. It seemed natural and human. In my eyes it bore a livelier image of the spirit, it seemed more express and single, than the imperfect and divided countenance I had been hitherto accustomed to call mine. And in so far I was doubtless right. I have observed that when I wore the semblance of Edward Hyde, none could come near to me at first without a visible misgiving of the flesh. This, as I take it, was because all human beings, as we meet them, are commingled out of good and evil: and Edward Hyde, alone in the ranks of mankind, was pure evil.

It is fascinating to see that when Jekyll sees Hyde he feels not "repugnance" but a "leap of welcome". He realises that Hyde is "I". Jekyll knows that Hyde is ugly but thinks that Hyde reveals a "livelier image of the spirit", the face seems more "express" – i.e. quicker – and "single" – i.e. purposeful – than his face which was "imperfect" and "divided". In Jekyll's view his face conveys "dividedness"; it shows complexity while Hyde's face is "single" or simple in its purpose. There is no moral confusion about Hyde, he just feels that he can do what he wants, and this is what his ugly face reveals: the fact that he is "pure evil". So Hyde's face is an expression of Jekyll's inner evil. This, Jekyll explains, is why people have a "visible misgiving of the flesh" when they see Hyde.

Essay

Discuss the role that people's facial expressions play in the novel.

Possible plan

Introduction:

Discuss the context of the time and now and the reasons why people think they can see someone's inner character in a person's face and expressions.

Main body:

Discuss the descriptions of Hyde's expressions and facial characteristics, and why people feel uneasy around him. Discuss the symbolism of the blackness of his expression.

Discuss the descriptions of Jekyll's face and expressions.

Discuss Lanyon's change in appearance and how this creates sympathy for his character.

Conclusion:

Sum up your thoughts on the role that the descriptions of physical expressions play in the novel, showing that they are a running motif in the novel.

PART TWO: THE NOVEL WITH STUDY GUIDE NOTES

EXPLANATION & RATIONALE

What follows is the full text of *The Strange Case of Doctor Jekyll and Mr Hyde* by Robert Louis Stevenson interspersed with my notes, explanation, analysis and questions. I have decided not to footnote this edition so that the book can be read quickly without interrupting your reading. I have loosely based the questions on Bloom's taxonomy, with comprehension questions first, checking understanding of the text; then analytical questions; followed by evaluative and creative response questions – the "higher order skills" according to Bloom.

Simple explanations are basic accounts of the plot of the story.

Analysis sections are more academic discussions of the section that has just been read.

Thematic questions start the chapters to help the reader think about key themes and ideas which are part of the chapter.

Comprehension questions and fill-in-the-blanks passages are there to help check understanding.

Analytical questions require more than understanding: you will need to think about HOW a writer achieves a certain effect, like creating a feeling of suspense or horror.

Evaluative questions ask the reader to evaluate the story, thinking about how effective it is.

Creative response tasks invite the reader to respond creatively to the novel by writing their own fiction/diary entries/letters etc. They are there to get the reader to empathise with the characters and situations.

Discussion points are more open-ended questions which are there to help the reader respond in a personal and original way to the novel, many of the questions asked are analytical in nature, but should be, if possible, discussed with someone else who has read the book.

1 Story of the Door

YouTube reading:
http://www.youtube.com/watch?v=BMhePVqxdS8
Thematic questions
Who do you trust? Why do you trust them?
Are boring, quiet people like Utterson more trustworthy than exciting
people?
What do "run-down" places tell us about the people who live there?
What are the most shocking things you have heard about?

Mr. Utterson the lawyer was a man of a rugged **(rough)** countenance **(face)** that was never lighted by a smile; cold, scanty **(small)** and embarrassed in discourse **(talk)**; backward in sentiment **(feeling)**; lean **(thin)**, long, dusty **(old fashioned)**, dreary **(boring)** and yet somehow lovable. At friendly meetings, and when the wine was to his taste, something eminently **(very)** human beaconed **(shone)** from his eye; something indeed which never found its way into his talk, but which spoke not only in these silent symbols of the after-dinner face, but more often and loudly in the acts **(deeds)** of his life. He was austere **(strict)** with himself; drank gin when he was alone, to mortify **(stop)** a taste for vintages **(expensive wines)**; and though he enjoyed the theatre, had not crossed the doors of one for twenty years. But he had an approved **(admired)** tolerance **(willing to put up with bad behaviour etc.)** for others; sometimes wondering, almost with envy, at the high pressure of spirits involved in their misdeeds; and in any extremity inclined to help rather than to reprove. "I incline to Cain's heresy," **(ignoring other people's faults. Cain is the Bible's first murderer, killing his brother Abel in Genesis 4:9. Utterson may be mis-remembering the Bible since it is Cain who goes to the devil, not Abel. However some early Christian sects believed that Cain was a good man who was superior to Abel)** he used to say quaintly: "I let my brother go to the devil in his own way." **(I don't try and stop people behaving badly)** In this character, it was frequently his fortune to be the last reputable **(respectable)** acquaintance **(friend/person you know)** and the last good influence in the lives of downgoing men **(men who are losing their reputation)**. And to such as these, so long as they came about his chambers **(rooms)**, he never marked a shade of change in his demeanour.

Simple explanation: Utterson is a lawyer for respectable people; he is quite a boring person but helps men when they are in trouble without judging them.

Analysis: Stevenson begins the novel with a description of Utterson, describing him as an unappealing, down-to-earth, "dreary" individual who is both loyal and intelligent. It's important in the context of what is to come that Utterson is very ordinary, but clever. Utterson becomes the detective figure in the novel, searching for the terrible truth about his friend Dr. Jekyll. If he had been a more interesting individual, the narrative could have become too focused upon his personality as opposed to his reactions to events. Because he is so very ordinary, the reader values his responses more: he is you or I investigating the matter, an everyman figure. The story could never have worked if a character like Sherlock Holmes had investigated because the detective himself would have over-burdened the narrative, and made everything too fantastical. Above all, Stevenson, for all the fantasy elements in his narrative, wants to tell the truth about mankind.

Discussion Point

What sort of person is Mr Utterson? Why do you think Stevenson begins the novel with this description of such a dull man? Why does Stevenson begin the novel by describing the character of Utterson?

No doubt the feat was easy to Mr. Utterson; for he was underdemonstrative **(not showing feelings)** at the best, and even his friendship seemed to be founded in a similar catholicity **(generosity/openness to a wide variety of views)** of good-nature. It is the mark of a modest **(humble/not showing off)** man to accept his friendly circle ready-made from the hands of opportunity; and that was the lawyer's way. His friends were those of his own blood or those whom he had known the longest; his affections **(feelings)**, like ivy, were the growth of time, they implied no aptness in the object. Hence, no doubt the bond that united him to Mr. Richard Enfield, his distant kinsman **(cousin/family member)**, the well-known man about town **(a man who is very fashionable, possibly with many lovers)**.

Simple explanation: Enfield is a distant cousin of Utterson's and they enjoy going on walks together.

Analysis: There is an irony about the description of Utterson's attachment to Enfield here: Utterson is undiscriminating (doesn't care who he is friends with) in his friendship, his "affections" grow like "ivy over time". As we have seen Utterson tends to befriend men on their way "down" in society. Perhaps Enfield, who has been out all night, is one of these people. Enfield is possibly like Jekyll because he is someone who may like the "high life" – what pleasures he enjoys, we never find out. Re-reading the novel, we realise that Enfield is a potential Jekyll/Hyde figure himself: his moral disgust at Hyde is possibly because he too secretly might relish committing such a deed. Enfield marks the beginning of Utterson's delving into the mystery of his friend Dr. Jekyll; Stevenson's skill as a writer is to make the reader realise at the end of the novel that Enfield is a potential Hyde himself. Thus the beginning of the novel is enriched by the end.

Discussion Point

Why does Stevenson have Enfield and not Utterson describe the assault?

It was a nut to crack for many, what these two could see in each other, or what subject they could find in common. It was reported by those who encountered them in their Sunday walks, that they said nothing, looked singularly **(very)** dull and would hail **(greet)** with obvious relief the appearance of a friend. For all that, the two men put the greatest store by these excursions **(walks/trips)**, counted them the chief jewel of each week, and not only set aside occasions of pleasure, but even resisted the calls of business, that they might enjoy them uninterrupted.

It chanced on one of these rambles **(walks)** that their way led them down a by-street in a busy quarter of London. The street was small and what is called quiet, but it drove a thriving **(successful)** trade on the weekdays. The inhabitants **(people that live in a place)** were all doing well, it seemed and all emulously **(copying in order to compete)** hoping to do better still, and laying out the surplus **(additions)** of their grains **(clothes/accoutrements)** in coquetry **(flirtatious behaviour)**; so that the shop fronts stood along that thoroughfare with an air of invitation, like rows of smiling saleswomen.

Simple explanation: Enfield and Utterson walk down a street one Sunday which usually has lots of shops open on it.

Analysis: There is a suggestion here that the shops are like prostitutes who are "emulously" showing off their clothes and goods in a flirtatious manner. The style is possibly deliberately obscure because Stevenson was aware that he would not be allowed to talk directly about prostitutes in a popular piece of fiction for fear of being censored.

Discussion Point

This novel is clearly about Hyde's sexual behaviour but never mentions it directly. Why do you think this is?

Even on Sunday, when it veiled its more florid **(flowery)** charms and lay comparatively empty of passage, the street shone out in contrast to its dingy **(miserable, dull)** neighbourhood, like a fire in a forest; and with its freshly painted shutters, well-polished brasses, and general cleanliness and gaiety of note, instantly caught and pleased the eye of the passenger.

Two doors from one corner, on the left hand going east the line was broken by the entry of a court; and just at that point a certain sinister block of building thrust forward its gable **(the triangular upper part of a wall at the end of a ridged roof)** on the street. It was two storeys high; showed no window, nothing but a door on the lower storey and a blind forehead of discoloured wall on the upper; and bore in every feature, the marks of prolonged and sordid **(dirty)** negligence **(neglect/ failure to take proper care over something)**. The door, which was equipped with neither bell nor knocker, was blistered and distained **(stained/discoloured)**. Tramps slouched into the recess and struck matches on the panels; children kept shop upon the steps; the schoolboy had tried his knife on the mouldings **(a shaped strip of wood or other material fitted as a decorative architectural feature, especially in a cornice)**; and for close on a generation, no one had appeared to drive away these random visitors or to repair their ravages **(damages)**.

Mr. Enfield and the lawyer were on the other side of the by-street; but when they came abreast of the entry, the former lifted up his cane and pointed.

"Did you ever remark that door?" he asked; and when his companion had replied in the affirmative **(saying yes)**. "It is connected in my mind," added he, "with a very odd story."

Simple explanation: There is a door which is very run-down where tramps stay and children play. Enfield has a story to tell about the door.

Analysis: Throughout the novel, the pages are soaked with imagery which is established here: the idea that behind the respectable facade of the street, with its clean, respectable houses, there is this place of "prolonged and sordid negligence". Thus the very city itself becomes a metaphor for the disease of mankind: our "prolonged and sordid negligence" of our inner desires and dreams. Moreover, the door is part of this metaphor: it is the gateway to the dark parts of the human soul, a threshold through which we step to find our true desires. Thus, Stevenson cleverly manages to make much of his novel metaphorical: the city itself is a metaphor for the divided human soul. Furthermore, the ordinary, everyday objects of the city become full of sinister resonances: doors, pavements, windows, shops, even parks are merely facades, "cover-ups", disguising the inherent Hyde-like ugliness of mankind.

Discussion Point
Why does Stevenson take such care to describe the city in this novel?

"Indeed?" said Mr. Utterson, with a slight change of voice, "and what was that?"

"Well, it was this way," returned Mr. Enfield: "I was coming home from some place at the end of the world, about three o'clock of a black winter morning, and my way lay through a part of town where there was literally nothing to be seen but lamps. Street after street and all the folks asleep—street after street, all lighted up as if for a procession and all as empty as a church—till at last I got into that state of mind when a man listens and listens and begins to long for the sight of a policeman. All at once, I saw two figures: one a little man who was stumping along eastward at a good walk, and the other a girl of maybe eight or ten who was running as hard as she was able down a cross street. Well, sir, the two ran into one another naturally enough at the corner; and then came the horrible part of the thing; for the man trampled calmly over the child's body and left her screaming on the ground. It sounds nothing to hear, but it was hellish to see. It wasn't like a man; it was like some damned Juggernaut.

Simple explanation: Enfield saw a small, short man trample on a girl, aged 8-10 years, at 3am in the morning.
Analysis: Some commentators from Stevenson's time, including the famous poet, Gerald Manley Hopkins, thought that Hyde was doing something worse than trampling on the girl. Stevenson probably felt he wasn't allowed to write what

he wanted to write about Hyde: there are hints throughout the book that Hyde is a rapist, or certainly someone with perverted sexual tastes (Luckhurst, p. 184). Notice how Enfield's description of Hyde – who we don't know the identity of yet – is full of wonder, almost admiration. The adverb "calmly" suggests that Hyde has no scruples about crushing the child. When Enfield says that it "sounds like nothing to hear" he means that he can't quite convey in words how "hellish" it was to see. His description of Hyde as "some damned Juggernaut" suggests that his horror of the deed is tinged with admiration. Obviously, in Stevenson's time, the word "Juggernaut" did not mean a lorry, it actually meant a massive, immoveable force which crushes everything in its way, the origin of the word coming from the Indian: Jagannath is an avatar of Vishnu, a crude idol of Krishna, in Hinduism. Some critics have suggested that Enfield's description is actually a veiled account of a brutal rape. This is possibly the case. Certainly though, on re-reading, we made aware that there is a sense of wonder from Enfield that Hyde should be so brazen, so open, so unstoppable in his actions.

Discussion Point

How does Stevenson create a sense of horror at this point?

I gave a few halloa, took to my heels, collared **(grabbed)** my gentleman, and brought him back to where there was already quite a group about the screaming child. He was perfectly cool and made no resistance, but gave me one look, so ugly that it brought out the sweat on me like running. The people who had turned out were the girl's own family; and pretty soon, the doctor, for whom she had been sent put in his appearance. Well, the child was not much the worse, more frightened, according to the Sawbones **(Victorian slang for a doctor, who would "saw" up bones)** and there you might have supposed would be an end to it. But there was one curious circumstance. I had taken a loathing **(hatred)** to my gentleman at first sight. So had the child's family, which was only natural. But the doctor's case was what struck me. He was the usual cut and dry apothecary **(chemist/doctor)**, of no particular age and colour, with a strong Edinburgh accent and about as emotional as a bagpipe. Well, sir, he was like the rest of us; every time he looked at my prisoner, I saw that Sawbones turn sick and white with desire to kill him. I knew what was in his mind, just as he knew what was in mine; and killing being out of the question, we did the next best. We told the man we could and would make such a scandal out of this as should make his name stink from one end of London to the other. If he had any friends or any credit, we undertook that he should lose them. And all the time, as we were pitching **(shouting)** it in red hot **(very angry)**, we were keeping the women off him as best we could for they were as wild as harpies **(devil-like women)**. I never saw a circle of such hateful faces; and there was the man in the middle, with a kind of black sneering coolness—frightened too, I could see that—but carrying it off, sir, really like Satan **(the Devil)**. `If you choose to make capital out of this accident,' said he, `I am naturally helpless. No gentleman but wishes to avoid a scene,' says he. `Name your figure.' Well, we screwed him **(forced)** up to a hundred pounds for the child's family; he would have clearly liked to stick out; but there was something about the lot of us that meant mischief **(trouble)**, and at last he struck. The next thing was to get the money; and where do you think he carried us but to that place with the door?—whipped out a key, went in, and presently **(after a while)** came back with the matter of ten pounds in gold and a cheque for the balance on Coutts's **(a bank for wealthy and respectable people)**, drawn payable to bearer and signed with a name that I can't mention, though it's one of the points of my story, but it was a name at least very well-known and often printed. The figure was stiff **(high/expensive)**; but the signature was good for more than that if it was only genuine. I took the liberty of pointing out to my gentleman that the whole business looked apocryphal **(hidden/made-up)**, and that a man does not, in real life, walk into a cellar door at four in the morning and come out with another man's cheque for close upon a hundred pounds. But he was quite easy and sneering. `Set your mind at rest,' says he, `I will stay with you till the banks open and cash the cheque myself.' So we all set off, the doctor, and the child's father, and our friend and myself, and passed the rest of the night in my chambers; and next day, when we had breakfasted, went in a body to the bank. I gave in the cheque myself, and said I had every reason to believe it was a forgery. Not a bit of it. The cheque was genuine."

> **Simple explanation:** a crowd gathers around Hyde, including a doctor, and the parents of the hurt child, and demand that he pays for the hurt he has caused. He goes into the door and comes out with a cheque for £100 paid for by a different man, a respectable man. No one believes that the cheque is genuine. Hyde goes to the bank with the parents and they find out the cheque is "good".

Analysis: The mystery of the man deepens. His offer to pay for his misdeeds is initially regarded with skepticism, but, after waiting with him until the banks open, Enfield finds that the cheque is genuine. In other words, the brute is not a common criminal. Notice also how our notions of justice have changed: now Hyde would have been jailed for a brutal assault, then paying the father of the child was enough recompense. At the heart of the novel, there is a huge contradiction: Hyde behaves like a thug, but has all the resources of a 'gentleman'. In other words, he does not behave like his "class" of person should.

Discussion Point

How and why does Stevenson deepen the mystery here?

"Tut-tut," said Mr. Utterson.

"I see you feel as I do," said Mr. Enfield. "Yes, it's a bad story. For my man was a fellow that nobody could have to do with, a really damnable **(hateful)** man; and the person that drew the cheque is the very pink of the proprieties **(good behaviour)**, celebrated too, and (what makes it worse) one of your fellows who do what they call good. Black mail I suppose; an honest man paying through the nose for some of the capers **(bad behaviour, high jinks, jokey behaviour)** of his youth.

Analysis: Some critics have argued that the blackmail being referred to is homosexuality, which was illegal in the UK until 1968. The clue is that Hyde is a young male who is getting money from an older man: this could lead one to think that Hyde had an affair with Jekyll and is now blackmailing him, threatening to make it public about their affair. If this was true, this could result in Jekyll being jailed: the writer Oscar Wilde was jailed a few years later for being homosexual. Other critics have thought that Enfield thinks that Hyde is the illegitimate son of a "taboo" relationship and is threatening to expose this (Luckhurst, p.185)

Discussion point

How and why did rich people become the victims of blackmail in Victorian times?

Black Mail House is what I call the place with the door, in consequence. Though even that, you know, is far from explaining all," he added, and with the words fell into a vein **(a method)** of musing **(thinking out aloud)**.

From this he was recalled by Mr. Utterson asking rather suddenly: "And you don't know if the drawer of the cheque lives there?"

"A likely place, isn't it?" returned Mr. Enfield. "But I happen to have noticed his address; he lives in some square or other."

"And you never asked about the—place with the door?" said Mr. Utterson.

"No, sir: I had a delicacy," was the reply. "I feel very strongly about putting questions; it partakes **(participates in/belongs to)** too much of the style of the Day of Judgment **(end of the world)**. You start a question, and it's like starting a stone. You sit quietly on the top of a hill; and away the stone goes, starting others; and presently some bland old bird (the last you would have thought of) is knocked on the head in his own back garden and the family have to change their name. No sir, I make it a rule of mine: the more it looks like Queer Street **(something very odd: some critics feel that this is a reference to the thought that Enfield thinks Jekyll is being blackmailed for being "queer" or homosexuality; the term "queer" was possibly slang for being homosexual then, although there is no proof for this)**, the less I ask."

"A very good rule, too," said the lawyer.

"But I have studied the place for myself," continued Mr. Enfield. "It seems scarcely a house. There is no other door, and nobody goes in or out of that one but, once in a great while, the gentleman of my adventure. There are three windows looking on the court on the first floor; none below; the windows are always shut but they're clean. And then there is a chimney which is generally smoking; so somebody must live there. And yet it's not so sure; for the buildings are so packed together about the court, that it's hard to say where one ends and another begins."

The pair walked on again for a while in silence; and then "Enfield," said Mr. Utterson, "that's a good rule of yours."

"Yes, I think it is," returned Enfield.

"But for all that," continued the lawyer, "there's one point I want to ask: I want to ask the name of that man who walked over the child."

"Well," said Mr. Enfield, "I can't see what harm it would do. It was a man of the name of Hyde."

"Hm," said Mr. Utterson. "What sort of a man is he to see?"

"He is not easy to describe. There is something wrong with his appearance; something displeasing, something down-right detestable **(hateful)**. I never saw a man I so disliked, and yet I scarce know why. He must be deformed somewhere; he gives a strong feeling of deformity **(being deformed/mis-shapen)**, although I couldn't specify the point. He's an extraordinary looking man, and yet I really can name nothing out of the way. No, sir; I can make no hand of it; I can't describe him. And it's not want of memory; for I declare I can see him this moment."

> **Simple explanation:** Hyde looks deformed but it is difficult to explain why. He gives people the "creeps".
> **Analysis:** After the practical mystery of where Hyde gets his money from, we are faced with a more intractable one for a reader: his physical appearance. In many of the filmed versions of the novel, Hyde is an out-and-out monster, deformed and grotesque, and yet, in the novel itself, it is clear that this is not the case. Enfield says: "he gives a strong feeling of deformity, although I couldn't specify the point". In other words, there is nothing actually physically wrong with his appearance; it is much more to do with the way his inner soul is played out on his face rather than any noticeable "deformity". He has a "detestable" look. Ultimately, he escapes "description". There is a marvellous irony here: Hyde is beyond describing in words and yet is a character in a novel. Stevenson doesn't actually want to describe him at all, other than he is a small, hairy man. He wants the reader to construct his own vision of inner ugliness; he wants Hyde to infiltrate our imaginations, to disturb us by forcing us to supply our own image of inner ugliness. For me, Hyde looks like some people I know whose angry, sneering sense of superiority is spread all across their faces.
> ### Discussion Point
> Why does Stevenson never describe Hyde in detail?

Mr. Utterson again walked some way in silence and obviously under a weight of consideration **(thought)**. "You are sure he used a key?" he inquired **(asked)** at last.

"My dear sir..." began Enfield, surprised out of himself.

"Yes, I know," said Utterson; "I know it must seem strange. The fact is, if I do not ask you the name of the other party, it is because I know it already. You see, Richard, your tale has gone home. If you have been inexact in any point you had better correct it."

"I think you might have warned me," returned the other with a touch of sullenness. "But I have been pedantically **(precisely)** exact **(correct)**, as you call it. The fellow had a key; and what's more, he has it still. I saw him use it not a week ago."

Mr. Utterson sighed deeply but said never a word; and the young man presently resumed. "Here is another lesson to say nothing," said he. "I am ashamed of my long tongue **(talking too much)**. Let us make a bargain never to refer to this again."

"With all my heart," said the lawyer. "I shake hands on that, Richard."

Summary – fill in the blanks (answers are at the back)

Mr Utterson is a boring but "loveable" lawyer who people get help from when they are in ----. He is friends with a cousin, Enfield, and goes on regular walks with him on Sundays. One Sunday, they pass a dirty ---- in a poor area. Enfield tells Utterson a story about the door and the man who lives behind it. He says he saw a small, revolting man ---- -- a small --- of eight at 3am in the morning. A crowd, led by Enfield, confronted the man and forced him to pay --- in compensation. The man gave them a cheque which we learn at the very end of the chapter was signed by ----- ----, a very ----- person: no one believed that the cheque was ----- but later found out it was. Utterson is worried that Jekyll is being -------- by Mr Hyde.

Comprehension questions

What type of person is Utterson? Why do "downgoing men" seek him out?

Why do Enfield and Utterson go for a walk together every Sunday?

What was of interest about the door that Enfield tells the story about? What did it look like?

What did Enfield witness regarding Hyde and the small girl?

Why and how did the crowd manage to get Hyde to write the girl's family a cheque? What was odd about the cheque?

What is strange about Mr Hyde according to Enfield?

Analytical questions

Our first encounter with Hyde is an "eye-witness" account from Enfield. Why do you think Stevenson chose to introduce Hyde in this way?

What adjectives and imagery are used to describe Hyde?

Evaluative questions

How successful is this opening to the novel? Discuss the parts of the chapter that must have affected its first readers very deeply.

Creative response tasks

Imagine you are Utterson. Write his diary after this chapter has happened.

Write a story about a violent incident you have witnessed or have heard about that has affected you deeply.

You can watch some YouTube videos I made about this chapter of the book here:
Part One:
http://www.youtube.com/watch?v=PpOXi8PSwVI
Part Two:
http://www.youtube.com/watch?v=5UuF8-BYbHk
Part Three:
http://www.youtube.com/watch?v=tuTG95q9rSk

POSSIBLE ANSWERS in brief & bold

Comprehension questions

What type of person is Utterson? Why do "downgoing men" seek him out? **Utterson is a lawyer, and a loyal friend who can be trusted by respectable men who are in trouble or facing a scandal.**

Why do Enfield and Utterson go for a walk together every Sunday? **They are related and enjoyed each other's company even though they don't talk much.**

What was of interest about the door that Enfield tells the story about? What did it look like? **The door is very scruffy and dirty and in a poor area. It was the door that a violent man opened.**

What did Enfield witness regarding Hyde and the small girl? **Hyde trampled on a small girl of eight at three in the morning.**

Why and how did the crowd manage to get Hyde to write the girl's family a cheque? What was odd about the cheque? **The crowd told Hyde that they would make a "scandal" of the situation if he did not give the girl's family some money. The cheque was odd because it was signed by a very respectable man – who we later learn is Dr Jekyll.**

What is strange about Mr Hyde according to Enfield? **Hyde appears deformed in some sort of way, but it is difficult express why he is so unpleasant in words.**

Analytical questions

Our first encounter with Hyde is an "eye-witness" account from Enfield. Why do you think Stevenson chose to introduce Hyde in this way? **Stevenson's central aim at this section is to build up both a sense of mystery and horror regarding Hyde. The story is a very disturbing one because only a deeply unpleasant man would trample upon a girl of eight: this incident generates a real sense of horror regarding the character. The reader thinks if Hyde can trample upon a girl of eight, then what else can he do? Stevenson also makes Hyde deeply mysterious in a number of ways, which also contributes to the suspense. Lots of unanswered questions come into the reader's mind: how and why is Hyde writing cheques signed by a respectable man?**

Why does he live in such a grotty place if he is wealthy? can no one describe him properly?
What adjectives and imagery are used to describe Hyde? **Hyde is described as "cool" and "ugly": both these adjectives have a disturbing effect upon the reader because of their context. Despite the fact that Hyde has just trampled on a small girl, he is "cool": in other words, he is not emotional or remorseful in any fashion. His physical appearance also makes him seem very unpleasant: he is "ugly" and there is a "strong feeling of deformity" about him. It is interesting to note that no one can describe exactly what he looks like. Enfield talks of him being a "damned Juggernaut": he seems to have superhuman powers and strength despite being so small.**

Evaluative questions
How successful is this opening to the novel? Discuss the parts of the chapter that most have affected its first readers very deeply. **The chapter is great at provoking the reader's curiosity in Hyde and his relationship with Dr Jekyll. Stevenson uses the figure of Utterson to create this curiosity: it is Utterson, Jekyll's friend, who guesses that there is a connection between the two men. Utterson's caring nature gives the story a sympathetic character, which is important.**

2 Search for Mr Hyde

YouTube reading:
http://www.youtube.com/watch?v=6L2GVGT7joU
Thematic questions
When and why do people become very interested in other people's lives?
Why do people "spy" on each other?
When have you met someone you really don't like on first sight? Why did you not like them? What was it about their appearance that you didn't like?

That evening Mr. Utterson came home to his bachelor house in sombre spirits and sat down to dinner without relish. It was his custom of a Sunday, when this meal was over, to sit close by the fire, a volume of some dry **(boring)** divinity **(holy book)** on his reading desk, until the clock of the neighbouring church rang out the hour of twelve, when he would go soberly and gratefully to bed. On this night however, as soon as the cloth was taken away **(dinner was finished)**, he took up a candle and went into his business room. There he opened his safe, took from the most private part of it a document endorsed **(backed up)** on the envelope as Dr. Jekyll's Will and sat down with a clouded brow to study its contents. The will was holograph **(a manuscript handwritten by the person named as its author)**, for Mr. Utterson though he took charge of it now that it was made, had refused to lend the least assistance in the making of it; it provided **(made out)** not only that, in case of the decease **(death)** of Henry Jekyll, M.D. **(Doctor of Medicine)**, D.C.L. **(Doctor of Civil Law)**, L.L.D. **(Doctor of Laws)**, F.R.S. **(Fellow of the Royal Society)**, etc., all his possessions were to pass into the hands of his "friend and benefactor **(a person who gives money or other help to a person or cause)** Edward Hyde," but that in case of Dr. Jekyll's "disappearance or unexplained absence for any period exceeding **(more than)** three calendar months," the said Edward Hyde should step into the said Henry Jekyll's shoes without further delay and free from any burthen **(debt/load)** or obligation **(duty)** beyond the payment of a few small sums to the members of the doctor's household.

> **Simple explanation:** Utterson is worried because Jekyll's will gives all his money and property to Hyde if he dies or disappears.
> **Analysis:** The novel contains a number of descriptions of secret places: we have already seen a description of Hyde's door, and now we find a description of Utterson's safe, which contains the bizarre will of Henry Jekyll – and no doubt many other secrets of his clients. Utterson, the normally unflappable, sensible Utterson, is perturbed by the will because in it, the respectable, garlanded Jekyll, gives all his estate to Edward Hyde. The mystery deepens: why would Jekyll give his money to someone that Utterson knows is the brute who attacked the girl? Stevenson cleverly plays on a motif that appears a great deal in Victorian novels: that of the will. Already there is a sense that Jekyll is aware that he will die soon and has made some sort of provision for it.
> **Discussion Point**
> How does the will create a sense of mystery and suspense?

This document had long been the lawyer's eyesore **(something horrible to look at, causing sore eyes)**. It offended (made him feel outraged) him both as a lawyer and as a lover of the sane and customary sides of life, to whom the fanciful was the immodest. And hitherto **(until this time/point)** it was his ignorance of Mr. Hyde that had swelled **(enlarged/grow big)** his indignation **(anger/sense of outrage)**; now, by a sudden turn, it was his knowledge. It was already bad enough when the name was but a name of which he could learn no more. It was worse when it began to be clothed upon with detestable **(hateful)** attributes **(features)**; and out of the shifting, insubstantial mists that had so long baffled **(confused)** his eye, there leaped up the sudden, definite presentment **(feeling/vision)** of a fiend **(devil)**.

"I thought it was madness," he said, as he replaced the obnoxious **(horrible/offensive)** paper in the safe, "and now I begin to fear it is disgrace."

With that he blew out his candle, put on a greatcoat, and set forth in the direction of Cavendish Square **(right next to Harley Street, which is famous for its doctors etc.)**, that citadel **(city/fortress)** of medicine, where his friend, the great Dr. Lanyon, had his house and received his crowding patients. "If anyone knows, it will be Lanyon," he had thought.

The solemn butler knew and welcomed him; he was subjected to no stage of delay, but ushered direct from the door to the dining-room where Dr. Lanyon sat alone over his wine. This was a hearty, healthy, dapper **(well-dressed)**, red-faced gentleman, with a shock of hair prematurely **(before his time)** white, and a boisterous **(lively)** and decided **(confident)** manner **(way of behaving)**. At sight of Mr. Utterson, he sprang up from his chair and welcomed him with both hands. The geniality **(friendliness)**, as was the way of the man, was somewhat theatrical to the eye; but it reposed **(was built on)** on genuine feeling. For these two were old friends, old mates both at school and college, both thorough respecters of themselves and of each other, and what does not always follow, men who thoroughly enjoyed each other's company.

After a little rambling talk, the lawyer led up to the subject which so disagreeably **(nastily)** preoccupied **(took up)** his mind.

"I suppose, Lanyon," said he, "you and I must be the two oldest friends that Henry Jekyll has?"

"I wish the friends were younger," chuckled Dr. Lanyon. "But I suppose we are. And what of that? I see little of him now."

"Indeed?" said Utterson. "I thought you had a bond of common interest."

"We had," was the reply. "But it is more than ten years since Henry Jekyll became too fanciful **(dreamy)** for me. He began to go wrong, wrong in mind; and though of course I continue to take an interest in him for old sake's sake, as they say, I see and I have seen devilish little of the man. Such unscientific balderdash

(nonsense)," added the doctor, flushing suddenly purple, "would have estranged **(caused a falling out)** Damon and Pythias." **(the ultimate loyal friends)**

> **Simple explanation:** Utterson visits Dr Lanyon who is a successful doctor in central London. Lanyon has fallen out with Dr Jekyll over a difference of opinion about science. Utterson does not regard this as very serious.
>
> **Analysis:** The appearance of the superior Lanyon, with his air of pomposity and arrogance, gives us a sense of the social world that Jekyll inhabits. Whereas Utterson is essentially a 'loner', we are aware that Lanyon enjoys all the fruits of being an important member of the scientific community. Lanyon's dismissal of Jekyll's "fanciful" science as "balderdash" is ironic in the light of what happens at the end of the novel because he discovers to the cost of his life that it isn't balderdash at all. Damon and Pythias were characters in Greek mythology who were two inseparable friends. When Pythias was sentenced to death, Damon offered to take his place. Neither wanted to live if it meant that the other died. In such a way, Lanyon is saying that even Damon would have fallen out with Pythias if he had heard the nonsense that Jekyll peddles as science. This prompts the question as to what exactly Jekyll was doing with his experiments to provoke such an extreme reaction in Pythias?
>
> ### Discussion Point
> What do you think of Stevenson's presentation of Lanyon? In what ways does he seem to be a bit of a hypocrite?

This little spirit of temper was somewhat of a relief to Mr. Utterson. "They have only differed on some point of science," he thought; and being a man of no scientific passions (except in the matter of conveyancing **(to do with the legal aspects of property)**), he even added: "It is nothing worse than that!" He gave his friend a few seconds to recover his composure **(calm)**, and then approached the question he had come to put. "Did you ever come across a protégé **(a person who is guided and supported by an older and more experienced or influential person)** of his—one Hyde?" he asked.

"Hyde?" repeated Lanyon. "No. Never heard of him. Since my time."

That was the amount of information that the lawyer carried back with him to the great, dark bed on which he tossed to and fro, until the small hours of the morning began to grow large. It was a night of little ease to his toiling **(working too hard)** mind, toiling in mere darkness and besieged **(stormed/hit)** by questions.

Six o'clock struck on the bells of the church that was so conveniently near to Mr. Utterson's dwelling, and still he was digging at the problem. Hitherto it had touched him on the intellectual side alone; but now his imagination also was engaged, or rather enslaved; and as he lay and tossed in the gross **(horrible)** darkness of the night and the curtained room, Mr. Enfield's tale went by before his mind in a scroll of lighted pictures. He would be aware of the great field of lamps of a nocturnal **(night-time)** city; then of the figure of a man walking swiftly; then of a child running from the doctor's; and then these met, and that human Juggernaut **(heavy vehicle)** trod the child down and passed on regardless of her screams. Or else he would see a room in a rich house, where his friend lay asleep, dreaming and smiling at his dreams; and then the door of that room would be opened, the curtains of the bed plucked apart, the sleeper recalled, and lo! there would stand by his side a figure to whom power was given, and even at that dead hour, he must rise and do its bidding **(do what was asked)**. The figure in these two phases haunted the lawyer all night; and if at any time he dozed over, it was but to see it glide more stealthily **(secretly)** through sleeping houses, or move the more swiftly and still the more swiftly, even to dizziness, through wider labyrinths **(mazes)** of lamplighted city, and at every street corner crush a child and leave her screaming. And still the figure had no face by which he might know it; even in his dreams, it had no face, or one that baffled **(confused him)** him and melted before his eyes; and thus it was that there sprang up and grew apace in the lawyer's mind a singularly **(very/uniquely)** strong, almost an inordinate **(very great/without limit)**, curiosity to behold **(see)** the features of the real Mr. Hyde.

> **Simple explanation:** Utterson has two dreams in which a faceless figure tramples on a girl and then another where the faceless figure visits Dr Jekyll when he is sleeping and makes him do what he wants him to do.
>
> **Analysis:** Utterson's dream is important for a number of reasons. It is probably very similar to the dream that Stevenson had when he first found the inspiration to write the novel. Moreover, the dream highlights some of the key themes of the novel: the secrecy with which the Juggernaut appears, its face never being seen, its sneaking into a 'rich

house', its unstoppable nature, the way in which it compels its subjects to "do its bidding". Thus the Juggernaut is an embodiment of all our subconscious desires, the things we would rather repress but can't, the hidden part of ourselves. Furthermore, the dream is scary because it is about our most innermost places of safety being penetrated by a monster: our homes, our bedrooms, our beds.

Discussion Point

Why is Utterson's dream so chilling?

If he could but once set eyes on him, he thought the mystery would lighten and perhaps roll altogether away, as was the habit of mysterious things when well examined. He might see a reason for his friend's strange preference or bondage **(enslavement)** (call it which you please) and even for the startling clause of the will. At least it would be a face worth seeing: the face of a man who was without bowels **(stomach)** of mercy: a face which had but to show itself to raise up, in the mind of the unimpressionable **(unable to be affected by anything)** Enfield, a spirit of enduring **(long-lasting)** hatred.

From that time forward, Mr. Utterson began to haunt the door in the by-street of shops. In the morning before office hours, at noon when business was plenty, and time scarce, at night under the face of the fogged city moon, by all lights and at all hours of solitude or concourse **(crowdedness)**, the lawyer was to be found on his chosen post.

"If he be Mr. Hyde," he had thought, "I shall be Mr. Seek."

> **Simple explanation:** Utterson waits by Hyde's door day and night in order to track him down.
>
> **Analysis:** This is a particularly suspenseful moment in the novel, with the "fogged city moon" watching down on Utterson as he waits and waits for the appearance of the mysterious Mr Hyde. The novel is, at this point, a grotesque detective novel. Indeed, many people have, along with Edgar Allen Poe, credited Stevenson with inventing the genre with the way he structures this narrative. It is, as well as a compulsive psychological horror story, a great detective narrative.
>
> **Discussion Point**
>
> How does Stevenson create suspense here?

And at last his patience was rewarded. It was a fine dry night; frost in the air; the streets as clean as a ballroom floor; the lamps, unshaken by any wind, drawing a regular pattern of light and shadow. By ten o'clock, when the shops were closed the by-street was very solitary and, in spite of the low growl of London from all round, very silent. Small sounds carried far; domestic **(household)** sounds out of the houses were clearly audible **(to be heard)** on either side of the roadway; and the rumour of the approach of any passenger preceded **(went before)** him by a long time. Mr. Utterson had been some minutes at his post, when he was aware of an odd light footstep drawing near. In the course of his nightly patrols, he had long grown accustomed **(used to)** to the quaint **(odd)** effect with which the footfalls of a single person, while he is still a great way off, suddenly spring out distinct from the vast hum and clatter of the city. Yet his attention had never before been so sharply and decisively **(very clearly)** arrested **(noticed)**; and it was with a strong, superstitious prevision **(premonition/vision)** of success that he withdrew into the entry of the court.

The steps drew swiftly nearer, and swelled out suddenly louder as they turned the end of the street. The lawyer, looking forth from the entry, could soon see what manner of man he had to deal with. He was small and very plainly dressed and the look of him, even at that distance, went somehow strongly against the watcher's inclination. But he made straight for the door, crossing the roadway to save time; and as he came, he drew a key from his pocket like one approaching home.

Mr. Utterson stepped out and touched him on the shoulder as he passed. "Mr. Hyde, I think?"

Mr. Hyde shrank back with a hissing intake of the breath. But his fear was only momentary; and though he did not look the lawyer in the face, he answered coolly enough: "That is my name. What do you want?"

"I see you are going in," returned the lawyer. "I am an old friend of Dr. Jekyll's—Mr. Utterson of Gaunt Street—you must have heard of my name; and meeting you so conveniently, I thought you might admit me."

"You will not find Dr. Jekyll; he is from home," replied Mr. Hyde, blowing in the key. And then suddenly, but still without looking up, "How did you know me?" he asked.

"On your side," said Mr. Utterson "will you do me a favour?"

"With pleasure," replied the other. "What shall it be?"

"Will you let me see your face?" asked the lawyer.

Mr. Hyde appeared to hesitate, and then, as if upon some sudden reflection, fronted about with an air of defiance **(disobedience)**; and the pair stared at each other pretty fixedly for a few seconds. "Now I shall know you again," said Mr. Utterson. "It may be useful."

"Yes," returned Mr. Hyde, "It is as well we have met; and apropos, you should have my address." And he gave a number of a street in Soho.

"Good God!" thought Mr. Utterson, "can he, too, have been thinking of the will?" But he kept his feelings to himself and only grunted in acknowledgment of the address.

"And now," said the other, "how did you know me?"

"By description," was the reply.

"Whose description?"

"We have common friends," said Mr. Utterson.

"Common friends," echoed Mr. Hyde, a little hoarsely. "Who are they?"

"Jekyll, for instance," said the lawyer.

"He never told you," cried Mr. Hyde, with a flush of anger. "I did not think you would have lied."

"Come," said Mr. Utterson, "that is not fitting language."

The other snarled aloud into a savage **(wild/beast-like/animal-like)** laugh; and the next moment, with extraordinary quickness, he had unlocked the door and disappeared into the house.

> **Simple explanation:** Utterson talks to Hyde who, after being annoyed, is pleased that Utterson knows where he lives. Utterson thinks that this means Hyde knows about the will. Hyde accuses Utterson of lying when he says that Jekyll told him about Hyde.
>
> **Analysis:** One of the pleasures of re-reading the novel is the way in which the reader realises that Hyde is interpreting Utterson's words very differently from the lawyer himself. There are multiple ironies: the fact that Utterson believes that they have "common friends" and that Hyde knows for certain that Utterson has lied because he is Jekyll. Furthermore, Hyde almost gives himself away by saying "I did not think you would have lied": in other words, Jekyll is surprised to find that Utterson is lying. This is Jekyll speaking: re-reading the novel one is made aware that Jekyll is very much present in Hyde and that, far from there being a switch in personality, it is more that Jekyll's repressed side is allowed full flower in Hyde. The "savage laugh" is the laugh of a man who loves not being recognised, of being someone else entirely.

Discussion Point
Why is this moment ironic and suspenseful, especially on second reading?

The lawyer stood awhile when Mr. Hyde had left him, the picture of disquietude **(being upset)**. Then he began slowly to mount the street, pausing every step or two and putting his hand to his brow like a man in mental perplexity **(confusion)**. The problem he was thus debating as he walked, was one of a class that is rarely solved. Mr. Hyde was pale and dwarfish, he gave an impression of deformity without any nameable **(ability to be named)** malformation **(mis-shapenness)**, he had a displeasing smile, he had borne himself to the lawyer with a sort of murderous mixture of timidity **(being afraid)** and boldness, and he spoke with a husky, whispering and somewhat broken voice; all these were points against him, but not all of these together could explain the hitherto unknown disgust, loathing and fear with which Mr. Utterson regarded him. "There must be something else," said the perplexed gentleman. "There is something more, if I could find a name for it. God bless me, the man seems hardly human! Something troglodytic **(like a cave man: in Victorian times it also meant someone who lived in a very poor area or slum)**, shall we say? or can it be the old story of Dr. Fell **(a reference to a nursery rhyme: "I do not like thee Dr. Fell/The reason why I cannot tell)** ? or is it the mere radiance **(shining)** of a foul soul that thus transpires **(coming to be known)** through, and transfigures **(transforms/changes)**, its clay continent **(human body)**? The last, I think; for, O my poor old Harry Jekyll, if ever I read Satan's signature upon a face, it is on that of your new friend."

> **Simple explanation:** Hyde disgusts Utterson who thinks Hyde doesn't seem human, more of a devil.
> **Analysis:** We have here another description of Hyde, but as with Enfield's account, Utterson's perceptions of him are very subjective: we learn little of substance about his appearance other than he is small and that he smiles, speaking with a husky voice. Notice too how Utterson describes him as 'troglodytic': troglodytes were cave-dwellers who were very much on Victorians' minds because Darwin's theory of evolution had pointed out that all of us were descended from them. In other words, Hyde is a form of 'primitive' man, an embodiment of the fears of Victorian Britain. On first reading we have the suspense of Utterson's

worry for his friend, then on second reading we realise that Utterson's interpretation has real ironies: he is speaking of his friend himself. His friend has become Satan.

Discussion Point

What in your view are the traits of Satan, the devil? If you were to describe him, how would you describe him? Does Hyde have the signature of Satan upon him as Utterson thinks?

Round the corner from the by-street, there was a square of ancient, handsome houses, now for the most part decayed from their high estate and let in flats and chambers to all sorts and conditions of men; map-engravers, architects, shady lawyers and the agents of obscure enterprises. One house, however, second from the corner, was still occupied entire; and at the door of this, which wore a great air of wealth and comfort, though it was now plunged in darkness except for the fanlight, Mr. Utterson stopped and knocked. A well-dressed, elderly servant opened the door.

"Is Dr. Jekyll at home, Poole?" asked the lawyer.

"I will see, Mr. Utterson," said Poole, admitting the visitor, as he spoke, into a large, low-roofed, comfortable hall paved with flags **(flagstones)**, warmed (after the fashion of a country house) by a bright, open fire, and furnished with costly cabinets **(cupboards)** of oak. "Will you wait here by the fire, sir? or shall I give you a light in the dining-room?"

"Here, thank you," said the lawyer, and he drew near and leaned on the tall fender **(a metal barrier/protection against a fire)**. This hall, in which he was now left alone, was a pet fancy of his friend the doctor's; and Utterson himself was wont to speak of it as the pleasantest room in London. But tonight there was a shudder in his blood; the face of Hyde sat heavy on his memory; he felt (what was rare with him) a nausea and distaste of life; and in the gloom of his spirits, he seemed to read a menace in the flickering of the firelight on the polished cabinets and the uneasy starting of the shadow on the roof. He was ashamed of his relief, when Poole presently returned to announce that Dr. Jekyll was gone out.

"I saw Mr. Hyde go in by the old dissecting room, Poole," he said. "Is that right, when Dr. Jekyll is from home?"

"Quite right, Mr. Utterson, sir," replied the servant. "Mr. Hyde has a key."

Simple explanation: Utterson goes round to the front of the house where Dr Jekyll lives and sees that the house looks wealthy and comfortable. Utterson feels sick and depressed but is pleased when he finds out Jekyll is not at home because he is feeling so low.

Analysis: Stevenson's feel for the symbolic is wonderful here. Hyde has the key! The key to Jekyll's innermost chamber, to his laboratory of secrets, to his dissecting room. Hyde has, in metaphorical terms, dissected Jekyll's character, cut off the extraneous elements, leaving the inner core of malevolence, of lust, of rage.

Discussion Point

How does Stevenson deepen the mystery here? Why is it symbolic that Hyde has the key to the dissecting room?

"Your master seems to repose a great deal of trust in that young man, Poole," resumed the other musingly.

"Yes, sir, he does indeed," said Poole. "We have all orders to obey him."

"I do not think I ever met Mr. Hyde?" asked Utterson.

"O, dear no, sir. He never dines here," replied the butler. "Indeed we see very little of him on this side of the house; he mostly comes and goes by the laboratory."

"Well, good-night, Poole."

"Good-night, Mr. Utterson."

And the lawyer set out homeward with a very heavy heart. "Poor Harry Jekyll," he thought, "my mind misgives me he is in deep waters! He was wild when he was young; a long while ago to be sure; but in the law of God, there is no statute of limitations **(a statute or law prescribing a period of limitation for the bringing of actions of certain kinds)**. Ay, it must be that; the ghost of some old sin, the cancer of some concealed **(hidden)** disgrace: punishment coming, PEDE CLAUDO **(Latin for "on limping foot" and effectively means "punishment comes limping")**, years after memory has forgotten and self-love condoned **(accept bad behaviour)** the fault." And the lawyer, scared by the thought, brooded **(thought intensely)** awhile on his own past, groping in all the corners of memory, least by chance some Jack-in-the-Box of an old iniquity **(evil/wrong-doing)** should leap to light there. His past was fairly blameless; few men could read the rolls of their life with less apprehension **(worry/fear)**; yet he was humbled **(cause (someone) to feel less important or proud)** to the dust by the many ill things he had done, and raised up again into a sober and fearful gratitude **(the quality of being thankful; readiness to show appreciation for and to return kindness)** by the many he had come so near to doing yet avoided. And then by a return on his former subject, he conceived a spark of hope. "This Master Hyde, if he were studied," thought he, "must have secrets of his own; black secrets, by the look of him; secrets compared to which poor Jekyll's worst would be like sunshine. Things cannot continue as they are. It turns me cold to think of this creature stealing like a thief to Harry's bedside; poor Harry, what a wakening! And the danger of it; for if this Hyde suspects the existence of the will, he may grow impatient to inherit. Ay, I must put my shoulders to the wheel—if Jekyll will but let me," he added, "if Jekyll will only let me." For once more he saw before his mind's eye, as clear as transparency, the strange clauses of the will.

Simple explanation: Utterson learns from Jekyll's butler, Poole, that Hyde has a key to Jekyll's laboratory and that the servants have orders to obey Hyde.

Analysis: Stevenson creates suspense on first reading by making the reader wonder whether Hyde will murder Jekyll. On second reading, this reflection gains more power. It makes us realise that far from stealing like a thief to Harry's bedside, Hyde has been invited there; Jekyll has embraced him. Then a further mystery opens up for the reader on a second reading: what are the real reasons for Jekyll to embrace Hyde? We also see Stevenson developing the character of Utterson. The lawyer has been pulled out of his emotionally retarded shell by the mystery: he is beginning to become really emotionally engaged. He is depressed by the thought of his friend being so affected. As a result of Utterson's anxieties, we begin to worry too for Jekyll. Vital to the novel's success is our dismay at the corruption of Jekyll: it is a corruption that all of us could fall into.

Discussion Point

How does Stevenson create suspense here? How does he develop the character of Utterson?

Summary -- fill in the blanks (answers are at the back)

The lawyer Utterson is troubled by the --- that Henry Jekyll has written because it hands over everything to ----- --- if Jekyll dies or disappears for more than three months. Utterson visits Dr. Lanyon, a friend of Jekyll's, to find out more, but discovers that Lanyon has ----- --- with Jekyll over the "unscientific" experiments Jekyll has been conducting. That night, Utterson suffers from nightmares. In one nightmare, he sees the figure of the man who trampled on the girl, and in another nightmare, the same figure approaches the sleeping Jekyll and makes Jekyll do what he wants. This figure has no ----. On waking, Utterson is determined to find out what Hyde looks like so he spends his spare time standing by the door where Hyde lives. Eventually, one night, Hyde arrives and Utterson asks to look at his face: Hyde shows him it and then gives Utterson his -----. Utterson realizes that Hyde is thinking about the will and is frightened for Jekyll. When he goes to visit Jekyll, we realize something Utterson has known for a while that the house that Hyde lives in is actually the laboratory attached to the back of Jekyll's house. Utterson finds that Jekyll is out, and learns from the butler, Poole, that Hyde has a --- to Jekyll's laboratory and the servants have orders to --- him. Utterson leaves feeling very worried that Hyde is blackmailing Jekyll.

Comprehension questions
Why is Utterson so upset about Jekyll's will?
Why does Utterson visit Lanyon? Why has Lanyon lost interest in Jekyll as a scientist?
What is Utterson worried about and what does he dream about?
What steps does Utterson take to find Mr Hyde?
Why does Hyde accuse Utterson of lying to him?
Why does Utterson visit Jekyll immediately after seeing Hyde?
Why is Utterson even more worried about Jekyll at the end of the chapter?
Analytical questions
How does Stevenson generate suspense in this chapter?
How does Stevenson create a Gothic atmosphere in his description of the streets of London and Utterson's dreams?
Evaluative questions
How successful is Stevenson in creating a mood of mystery in this chapter?
Creative response tasks
Write Utterson's diary entry for this chapter, detailing his encounters with Lanyon, with Mr Hyde, and his worries for Henry Jekyll.

Write a story or poem about a nightmare that comes true, calling it "Nightmare".

You can watch a YouTube video I made about this section of the book here:
http://www.youtube.com/watch?v=qD8w12CIJQc

POSSIBLE ANSWERS in brief & bold

Comprehension questions

Why is Utterson so upset about Jekyll's will? **Because he has left all his estate (money and property) to Hyde if he dies or disappears for more than three months.**

Why does Utterson visit Lanyon? Why has Lanyon lost interest in Jekyll as a scientist? **Utterson wants to find out why Lanyon has fallen out with Jekyll, and wants to know if it has anything to do with him knowing something unpleasant about Jekyll. However, he finds out, to his relief, that they have fallen out over a difference of opinion about science; Lanyon believes Jekyll is involved in "unscientific balderdash".**

What is Utterson worried about and what does he dream about? **He is very worried about his good friend Jekyll being blackmailed by Hyde, and possibly being harmed by him.**

What steps does Utterson take to find Mr Hyde? **Utterson waits by Hyde's door day and night.**

Why does Hyde accuse Utterson of lying to him? **Utterson says that Jekyll has told him about Hyde. Hyde knows this is a lie because of course Hyde is Jekyll, and Jekyll has, of course, said nothing about Hyde to Utterson.**

Why does Utterson visit Jekyll immediately after seeing Hyde? **First because Hyde's apartment is actually part of Jekyll's house: it is the back of Jekyll's very large house. This means it is easy for him to see Jekyll. Second because he is very worried about his friend being in trouble in some way.**

Why is Utterson even more worried about Jekyll at the end of the chapter? **He is extremely worried that Jekyll will come to harm; that Hyde will hurt Jekyll in some terrible way. Both his dream and his meeting with Hyde have persuaded him of this. Hyde's apparent interest in Utterson knowing where he lives has made Utterson think that Hyde knows about the will; since he now knows where Hyde lives, he will be more easily able to give the will to Hyde. He can see Hyde thinking this.**

Analytical questions

How does Stevenson generate suspense in this chapter? **Stevenson generates suspense by making Utterson look in such a determined way for Hyde: there is an element of a "hunt" here -- and a mystery. We really want to know what will happen when Utterson meets Hyde. When he does, the meeting is very tense: Hyde seems very anti-social except when he appears to be thinking about the will. This leads the reader to think that**

Hyde may well be planning for Jekyll to die soon so that he can inherit his money. The reader thinks that maybe Hyde is planning Jekyll's murder. The dialogue between Utterson and Hyde is brief and tense. Stevenson's descriptions in the chapter are highly suspenseful: the description of the dreams Utterson has of the faceless figures are genuinely horrific and based on Stevenson's own dreams.

How does Stevenson create a Gothic atmosphere in his description of the streets of London and Utterson's dreams? **The London that Stevenson describes is a "Gothic" London full of darkness and fog, which appears to be both literal and metaphorical. The characters in the novel are immersed in darkness or evil, and the fog could suggest their moral confusion as well.**

Evaluative questions

How successful is Stevenson in creating a mood of mystery in this chapter? **Stevenson's ability to tell a fascinating, fast-paced mystery story as well as his facility to describe London and Utterson's nightmares make this a highly successful chapter. Above all, it is his characterisation of Hyde which makes the story so gripping: Hyde is only shown in "little bursts" but what we do see is very disturbing. This is a man who appears capable of murder and even worse.**

3 Dr Jekyll was quite at ease

YouTube reading:
http://www.youtube.com/watch?v=poBMLbgXOWs
Thematic questions
What makes someone a "pedant" – a person who nit-picks over tiny details? Do you know any pedants? What are they like?
Do you know anyone who has had friends who have been a "bad influence? What was the situation?
Has anyone made you promise anything that you have felt uncomfortable about?

A fortnight later, by excellent good fortune **(luck)**, the doctor gave one of his pleasant dinners to some five or six old cronies **(friends)**, all intelligent, reputable **(with good reputations/respectable)** men and all judges of good wine; and Mr. Utterson so contrived that he remained behind after the others had departed. This was no new arrangement, but a thing that had befallen many scores **(a group or set of twenty or about twenty)** of times. Where Utterson was liked, he was liked well. Hosts loved to detain the dry lawyer, when the light-hearted and loose-tongued **(talking without worrying about the consequences)** had already their foot on the threshold; they liked to sit a while in his unobtrusive **(unnoticed)** company, practising for solitude **(being alone)**, sobering their minds in the man's rich silence after the expense and strain **(music)** of gaiety. To this rule, Dr. Jekyll was no exception; and as he now sat on the opposite side of the fire—a large, well-made, smooth-faced man of fifty, with something of a stylish cast perhaps, but every mark of capacity and kindness—you could see by his looks that he cherished for Mr. Utterson a sincere and warm affection.

Dr Jekyll's character (margin note)

"I have been wanting to speak to you, Jekyll," began the latter. "You know that will of yours?"

A close observer might have gathered that the topic was distasteful; but the doctor carried it off gaily. "My poor Utterson," said he, "you are unfortunate in such a client. I never saw a man so distressed as you were by my will; unless it were that hide-bound pedant **(someone who is obsessed by minor points of detail but misses the overall point of something, a nit-picker)**, Lanyon, at what he called my scientific heresies **(a belief against the rules of the church)**. O, I know he's a good fellow—you needn't frown—an excellent fellow, and I always mean to see more of him; but a hide-bound pedant for all that; an ignorant, blatant **(obvious)** pedant. I was never more disappointed in any man than Lanyon."

"You know I never approved of it," pursued Utterson, ruthlessly disregarding the fresh topic.

"My will? Yes, certainly, I know that," said the doctor, a trifle sharply. "You have told me so."

"Well, I tell you so again," continued the lawyer. "I have been learning something of young Hyde."

The large handsome face of Dr. Jekyll grew pale to the very lips, and there came a blackness about his eyes. "I do not care to hear more," said he. "This is a matter I thought we had agreed to drop."

"What I heard was abominable **(horrible/terrifying)**," said Utterson.

"It can make no change. You do not understand my position," returned the doctor, with a certain incoherency **(not making sense)** of manner. "I am painfully situated **(positioned/placed/in a difficult situation)**, Utterson; my position is a very strange—a very strange one. It is one of those affairs that cannot be mended by talking."

"Jekyll," said Utterson, "you know me: I am a man to be trusted. Make a clean breast **(start anew)** of this in confidence **(without worrying things will be revealed)**; and I make no doubt I can get you out of it."

> **Simple explanation:** Utterson questions Jekyll about Hyde and his connection with him. Jekyll appears disturbed. Utterson says that if Jekyll is being blackmailed, he should trust Utterson and tell him what is going on.
>
> **Analysis:** As with so many moments in the novel, this scene gains more poignancy and mystery on second reading. We realise that Jekyll has a chance to confess to Utterson about what is going on here, and that Utterson might possibly understand, but he decides not to. This is because he is too attached to Hyde. He enjoys being Hyde and Jekyll! His split personality brings him great pleasure. At the heart of Jekyll there is inarticulacy, an unwillingness and inability to talk through the issues at stake. In this sense, Jekyll is like all deeply repressed people, unable and unwilling to discuss any difficult issues. It is this reluctance to talk which is at the heart of his repression; Hyde lives and thrives on his silence. In this sense, Stevenson is very much a forerunner of Freud in the way he suggests that our most damaging aspects of personality exist in the areas that are often not talked about.
>
> **Discussion Point**
>
> Why do you think Jekyll won't talk to Utterson here?

"My good Utterson," said the doctor, "this is very good of you, this is downright **(very)** good of you, and I cannot find words to thank you in. I believe you fully; I would trust you before any man alive, ay, before myself, if I could make the choice; but indeed it isn't what you fancy; it is not as bad as that; and just to put your good heart at rest, I will tell you one thing: the moment I choose, I can be rid of Mr. Hyde. I give you my hand upon that; and I thank you again and again; and I will just add one little word, Utterson, that I'm sure you'll take in good part: this is a private matter, and I beg of you to let it sleep."

> **Simple explanation:** Jekyll says he can get rid of Hyde at any time he wants: in other words, he is NOT being blackmailed by him.

Analysis: Jekyll's insistence that Utterson keeps Hyde a "private matter" is very important. Jekyll is clearly worried for his reputation if it be known that he associates with Hyde. On second reading, we realise that Jekyll is very much enjoying being Hyde at this point and is confident that he can dismiss him when he wants. In other words, Jekyll is deluding himself that he is not Hyde really. While worried that Utterson will embarrass him by revealing his connection with Hyde, Jekyll is clearly confident that all will be well. We realise that Jekyll is an awful and hideous hypocrite: he has probably committed some crimes in the name of Hyde but shows no remorse or repentance. He gives no vow to give up Hyde. Far from it, he is clearly intending to continue his double existence until he sees fit to dismiss Hyde.

Discussion point
Why is Jekyll's complacency so disturbing on second reading?

Utterson reflected a little, looking in the fire.

"I have no doubt you are perfectly right," he said at last, getting to his feet.

"Well, but since we have touched upon this business, and for the last time I hope," continued the doctor, "there is one point I should like you to understand. I have really a very great interest in poor Hyde. I know you have seen him; he told me so; and I fear he was rude. But I do sincerely take a great, a very great interest in that young man; and if I am taken away, Utterson, I wish you to promise me that you will bear with him and get his rights for him. I think you would, if you knew all; and it would be a weight off my mind if you would promise."

"I can't pretend that I shall ever like him," said the lawyer.

"I don't ask that," pleaded Jekyll, laying his hand upon the other's arm; "I only ask for justice; I only ask you to help him for my sake, when I am no longer here."

Utterson heaved an irrepressible **(unable to be stopped)** sigh. "Well," said he, "I promise."

Summary -- fill in the blanks (answers are at the back)
A fortnight (two weeks) later, Jekyll has a ---- party. Utterson remains behind so that he can speak to Jekyll about why he doesn't like Jekyll's will; he tells Jekyll that he can be ---- and urges Jekyll to tell him if he is being -------. Jekyll tells him that it isn't blackmail and that he can get rid

of -- ---- at any time he wishes. He asks Utterson to drop the matter and make sure that he will help Hyde get what is in the will – i.e. everything Jekyll owns -- if he, Jekyll, ----- or ---.

Comprehension questions
Why does Jekyll think Lanyon is a pedant?
What does Jekyll make Utterson promise? Why is Utterson uneasy about the promise?
What is Jekyll's state of mind at this point do you think?
Analytical questions
How does Stevenson present Jekyll in this chapter? How does he create a sense of mystery around the character?
Evaluative questions
How successful is Stevenson in creating a sense of mystery in this chapter?
Creative response tasks
Write a story or poem about a friend who is a good person but befriends a bully who is a bad influence, calling the story "Bad Influence".

Write Utterson's diary for this chapter.

POSSIBLE ANSWERS in brief & bold

Comprehension questions
Why does Jekyll think Lanyon is a pedant? **Jekyll thinks that Lanyon is "nit-picking" when he criticises Jekyll's scientific experiments and ideas.**
What does Jekyll make Utterson promise? Why is Utterson uneasy about the promise? **He makes him promise that he will do his best for Hyde if he dies or disappears: in other words make sure Hyde enjoys the contents of the will. Utterson does not like Hyde and is worried that Jekyll may be murdered by Hyde in order to get the contents of the will.**
What is Jekyll's state of mind at this point do you think? **On the surface, Jekyll appears to be "normal" in that he is socialising and seeing people. However, the moment that Utterson questions him about Hyde a "paleness comes to his lips and blackness about the eyes". He is obviously very worried in some kind of way about Hyde, but won't explain exactly what his worries are.**

Analytical questions
How does Stevenson present Jekyll in this chapter? How does he create a sense of mystery around the character? **Stevenson presents Jekyll as someone who appears on the surface to be happy, but clearly is in a disturbed state of mind deep down. We see how unnerved he becomes when he is asked about Hyde: he becomes "pale"**

there is "blackness about his eyes". The description of the "blackness" is interesting because it suggests a much darker side to Jekyll. When we hear about Jekyll saying that he has a great interest in Hyde, we feel rather sickened because we know that Jekyll is friends with a man who trampled on a little girl. And we are fascinated too: what hold does Hyde have over Jekyll?

Evaluative questions
How successful is Stevenson in creating a sense of mystery in this chapter? **The mystery is generated by the reader trying to guess the relationship between Hyde and Jekyll. Even when we know the solution to the mystery, the book is enjoyable to re-read because we see more clearly just how "conflicted" Jekyll is about Hyde. He is clearly pleased to have a friend who he can get rid of at any time, but he is also worried that Hyde may take over him: this is why he has written the will. The pleasure in reading the book for the first time is the pleasure in trying to find out the mystery; the pleasure on second reading is the pleasure of working out Jekyll's complex psychological relationship with his "dark side", with his Mr Hyde.**

4 The Carew Murder Case

YouTube reading:
http://www.youtube.com/watch?v=tbNXB3wdHAw
Thematic questions
Why do you think people commit murder? What types of people commit murder? Are they inherently evil or has something in their past life "led them astray"?
Why do thugs assault people in the street? What makes them do this?

Nearly a year later, in the month of October, 18—, London was startled by a crime of singular **(unique/great)** ferocity **(fierceness/violence)** and rendered **(made)** all the more notable **(well known)** by the high position **(high social position/importance)** of the victim. The details were few and startling. A maid servant living alone in a house not far from the river, had gone upstairs to bed about eleven. Although a fog rolled over the city in the small hours, the early part of the night was cloudless, and the lane, which the maid's window overlooked, was brilliantly lit by the full moon. It seems she was romantically given, for she sat down upon her box **(seat)**, which stood immediately under the window, and fell into a dream of musing **(dreaming/thinking)**. Never (she used to say, with streaming tears, when she narrated that experience), never had she felt more at peace with all men or thought more kindly of the world. And as she so sat she became aware of an aged beautiful gentleman with white hair, drawing near along the lane; and advancing to meet him, another and very small gentleman, to whom at first she paid less attention. When they had come within speech (which was just under the maid's eyes) the older man bowed and accosted **(greeted)** the other with a very pretty manner of politeness. It did not seem as if the subject of his address were of great importance; indeed, from his pointing, it some times appeared as if he were only inquiring his way; but the moon shone on his face as he spoke, and the girl was pleased to watch it, it seemed to breathe such an innocent and old-world kindness of disposition **(character)**, yet with something high too, as of a well-founded self-content **(feeling happy with life)**. Presently **(after a while)** her eye wandered to the other, and she was surprised to recognise in him a certain Mr. Hyde, who had once visited her master and for whom she had conceived a dislike. He had in his hand a heavy cane, with which he was trifling **(playing)**; but he answered never a word, and seemed to listen with an ill-contained impatience. And then all of a sudden he broke out in a great flame of anger, stamping with his foot, brandishing **(threatening with/waving about)** the cane, and carrying on (as the maid described it) like a madman. The old gentleman took a step back, with the air of one very much surprised and a trifle **(a little)** hurt; and at that Mr. Hyde broke out of all bounds and clubbed him to the earth. And next moment, with ape-like fury, he was trampling his victim under foot and hailing down a storm of blows, under which the bones were audibly **(could be heard)** shattered and the body jumped upon the roadway. At the horror of these sights and sounds, the maid fainted.

> **Simple explanation:** A year later, in October, a maid sees Mr Hyde brutally murder a polite, lovely old man, jumping on him until his bones break. The maid can hear the old man's bones break.
>
> **Analysis:** It is a year after the end of the last chapter, and a maidservant witnesses the terrible murder of Sir Danvers Carew, who is an "aged and beautiful gentleman", of kind

temperament, who becomes embroiled in an argument with Hyde, who suddenly breaks out in a "flame of anger". At the heart of Hyde there is a "fire", an unquenchable rage: in this sense, he is a fore-runner to the "Angry Young Men" of the 1950s and 60s who people British fiction. Like them, he attacks establishment figures like Carew not because anything they've done but for what they symbolise: they are embodiments of the repressed world of emotions which keep people like Hyde from ever expressing themselves. Stevenson uses some of his most descriptive prose to describe the murder: the sound of the crunching bones, the "storm of blows", the "jumping" on the body. In such a way, he creates a horrific scene: an innocent old man being clubbed to death. Hyde chooses his victims amongst the defenseless: children and old men.

Discussion Point

How does Stevenson create a sense of horror here?

It was two o'clock when she came to herself and called for the police. The murderer was gone long ago; but there lay his victim in the middle of the lane, incredibly mangled **(damaged)**. The stick with which the deed had been done, although it was of some rare and very tough and heavy wood, had broken in the middle under the stress of this insensate **(unfeeling)** cruelty; and one splintered half had rolled in the neighbouring gutter—the other, without doubt, had been carried away by the murderer. A purse and gold watch were found upon the victim: but no cards or papers, except a sealed and stamped envelope, which he had been probably carrying to the post, and which bore the name and address of Mr. Utterson.

This was brought to the lawyer the next morning, before he was out of bed; and he had no sooner seen it and been told the circumstances, than he shot out a solemn lip. "I shall say nothing till I have seen the body," said he; "this may be very serious. Have the kindness to wait while I dress." And with the same grave **(serious)** countenance **(face)** he hurried through his breakfast and drove to the police station, whither **(to where)** the body had been carried. As soon as he came into the cell, he nodded.

"Yes," said he, "I recognise him. I am sorry to say that this is Sir Danvers Carew."

"Good God, sir," exclaimed the officer, "is it possible?" And the next moment his eye lighted up with professional ambition. "This will make a deal of noise," he said. "And perhaps you can help us to the man." And he briefly narrated what the maid had seen, and showed the broken stick.

> **Simple explanation:** A letter addressed to Mr Utterson is found on the murdered old man.
> **Analysis:** Notice how Stevenson explores a theme of the book here: that of hypocrisy. The police officer almost seems pleased that Carew has been murdered, that he is a respected member of society, because it means he could professionally advance his reputation if he solves the case. Notice also how the murder of Carew contrasts with the assault on the child at the beginning of the novel: unlike before, when the assault was covered up with hush money, Carew's murder will be properly investigated because of his social position.
> ### Discussion point
> How does Stevenson explore the theme of hypocrisy here?

Mr. Utterson had already quailed **(shivered)** at the name of Hyde; but when the stick was laid before him, he could doubt no longer; broken and battered as it was, he recognized it for one that he had himself presented many years before to Henry Jekyll.

"Is this Mr. Hyde a person of small stature?" he inquired.

"Particularly small and particularly wicked-looking, is what the maid calls him," said the officer.

Mr. Utterson reflected; and then, raising his head, "If you will come with me in my cab," he said, "I think I can take you to his house."

It was by this time about nine in the morning, and the first fog of the season. A great chocolate-coloured pall lowered over heaven, but the wind was continually charging and routing **(sending away)** these embattled vapours; so that as the cab crawled from street to street, Mr. Utterson beheld a marvellous number of degrees and hues **(colours)** of twilight; for here it would be dark like the back-end of evening; and there would be a glow of a rich, lurid **(unpleasantly bright)** brown, like the light of some strange conflagration **(fire)**; and here, for a moment, the fog would be quite broken up, and a haggard shaft of daylight would glance in between the swirling wreaths. The dismal quarter of Soho **(an area in central London known for bad behaviour, e.g. prostitution, gambling etc., as well as its alleyways and seedy streets)** seen under these changing glimpses, with its muddy ways, and slatternly **(scruffy)** passengers, and its lamps, which had never been extinguished

97

(put out) or had been kindled **(lit)** afresh to combat this mournful reinvasion of darkness, seemed, in the lawyer's eyes, like a district of some city in a nightmare. The thoughts of his mind, besides, were of the gloomiest dye **(colour)**; and when he glanced at the companion of his drive, he was conscious of some touch of that terror of the law and the law's officers, which may at times assail **(go after)** the most honest.

As the cab drew up before the address indicated, the fog lifted a little and showed him a dingy **(grotty)** street, a gin palace **(a cheap pub/bar)**, a low **(cheap)** French eating house, a shop for the retail of penny numbers and twopenny salads, many ragged children huddled in the doorways, and many women of many different nationalities passing out, key in hand **(for women to carry their own house key was a sign that they were independent from men and were lower class, and probably prostitutes because all respectable women were expected to have a husband who carried their house key for them)** , to have a morning glass; and the next moment the fog settled down again upon that part, as brown as umber **(dark yellowish-brown)**, and cut him off from his blackguardly **(wicked/evil)** surroundings. This was the home of Henry Jekyll's favourite; of a man who was heir to a quarter of a million sterling **(pounds)**.

An ivory-faced and silvery-haired old woman opened the door. She had an evil face, smoothed by hypocrisy **(pretending to be someone you are not)**: but her manners were excellent. Yes, she said, this was Mr. Hyde's, but he was not at home; he had been in that night very late, but he had gone away again in less than an hour; there was nothing strange in that; his habits were very irregular **(odd/unpredictable)**, and he was often absent **(away)**; for instance, it was nearly two months since she had seen him till yesterday.

"Very well, then, we wish to see his rooms," said the lawyer; and when the woman began to declare it was impossible, "I had better tell you who this person is," he added. "This is Inspector Newcomen of Scotland Yard."

A flash of odious joy appeared upon the woman's face. "Ah!" said she, "he is in trouble! What has he done?"

Mr. Utterson and the inspector exchanged glances. "He don't seem a very popular character," observed the latter. "And now, my good woman, just let me and this gentleman have a look about us."

In the whole extent of the house, which but for the old woman remained otherwise empty, Mr. Hyde had only used a couple of rooms; but these were furnished **(decorated and supplied with furniture etc.)** with luxury **(rich things)** and good taste. A closet **(cupboard)** was filled with wine; the plate was of silver, the napery **(household linen)** elegant; a good picture hung upon the walls, a gift (as Utterson supposed) from Henry Jekyll, who was much of a connoisseur **(expert)**; and the carpets were of many plies **(types)** and agreeable in colour. At this moment, however, the rooms bore every mark of having been recently and hurriedly ransacked **(burgled/rifled through)**; clothes lay about the floor, with their pockets inside out; lock-fast drawers stood open; and on the hearth **(fireplace)** there lay a pile of grey ashes, as though many papers had been burned. From these embers the inspector disinterred **(got out)** the butt end of a green cheque book, which had resisted the action of the fire; the other half of the stick was found behind the door; and as this clinched his suspicions, the officer declared himself delighted. A visit to the bank, where several thousand pounds were found to be lying to the murderer's credit, completed his gratification **(pleasure)**.

"You may depend upon it, sir," he told Mr. Utterson: "I have him in my hand. He must have lost his head, or he never would have left the stick or, above all, burned the cheque book. Why, money's life to the man. We have nothing to do but wait for him at the bank, and get out the handbills."

This last, however, was not so easy of accomplishment **(achievement)**; for Mr. Hyde had numbered few familiars **(friends/people who knew him)**—even the master of the servant maid had only seen him twice; his family could nowhere be traced; he had never been photographed; and the few who could describe him differed widely, as common observers will. Only on one point were they agreed; and that was the haunting sense of unexpressed **(unsaid)** deformity with which the fugitive **(runaway)** impressed his beholders **(people who look)**.

> **Simple explanation:** Utterson identifies the dead body as Sir Danvers Carew, a MP, and also recognizes the broken walking stick as Jekyll's. He takes the police to Hyde's house in Soho, where a housekeeper lets them in. They find the other half of the broken stick there and a burnt cheque book. The police believe that all they have to do is wait at the bank until Hyde comes to draw out money. But Hyde never appears again.
> **Analysis:** The fact that Hyde can't be traced or described creates much of the suspense in the novel, especially with re-reading. Possibly, Hyde is all of us: he is our repressed,

inarticulate rage, our hidden desires, our "unexpressed" deformities. The reason why people can't describe him is because they can't describe their own dark sides. Thus the novel is about being "inarticulate", about not being able to describe the very thing that most threatens us all: our destructive instincts.

Discussion point

Why can't people describe Hyde?

Summary -- fill in the blanks (answers are at the back)

A year later, a maid is sitting at her window during the early hours of the morning when she witnesses Mr Hyde, someone she knows, beat a polite, old gentleman to ---- with a stick, which ----. She faints and then when she wakes up contacts the police who find a letter addressed to--- ---- on the old man. Called on early that morning by the police, Utterson identifies the body at the police station as Sir Danvers Carew, one of his ----. Utterson then recognizes the broken stick as ----- ----. Inspector Newcomen and he visit Hyde's run-down flat and find the ----- ---- there, and a burnt ----. The inspector believes that all they have to do is wait at the --- for Hyde to draw out money because he has no way getting any otherwise. However, Hyde wasn't --- again.

Comprehension questions

What were the circumstances of the murder of Sir Danvers Carew? How was he killed?
Why was Utterson contacted?
What incriminating evidence was found in Hyde's rooms?
Why is Hyde now a hunted man?

Analytical questions

How does Stevenson convey a sense of horror and mystery in this chapter?
Look at Stevenson's descriptions of London and Hyde's flat: how does he generate a Gothic atmosphere here?

Evaluative questions

How successful is Stevenson in making Hyde seem genuinely evil?

Creative response tasks

Write the newspaper article about the murder of Carew.
Continue Utterson's diary for this chapter of the novel, detailing his thoughts on the murder and his discovery of the incriminating evidence in Jekyll's flat.
Write a story or poem called "The Murder".

You can watch a YouTube video I made about the chapter here:
http://www.youtube.com/watch?v=sk5jBmSVn_8

POSSIBLE ANSWERS in brief & bold

Comprehension questions

What were the circumstances of the murder of Sir Danvers Carew? How was he killed? **He was killed in October on a night which was cloudless and there was a full moon. Mr Hyde approached Sir Danvers Carew, exchanged a few words, which did not seem very important, and then lost his temper, clubbing the kind old man to death. He hit him so hard that the maid who witnessed the attack heard the old man's bones shatter. After witnessing the attack, the maid fainted and woke up at 2am, when she saw Hyde's broken stick lying near the old man. It was then that she contacted the police.**

Why was Utterson contacted? **Utterson was approached because when Sir Danver's clothes were searched, a letter addressed to him was found: Utterson was Sir Danver's lawyer.**

What incriminating evidence was found in Hyde's rooms? **The other half of the broken stick.**

Why is Hyde now a hunted man? **Because he murdered a very important politician, Sir Danvers Carew. Notice how people were less bothered about finding him after the attack on the girl, possibly because she was of a lower class than Sir Danvers.**

Analytical questions

How does Stevenson convey a sense of horror and mystery in this chapter? **Stevenson takes great care in describing the murder of Sir Danvers in a number of different ways. First, it is important that a maid witnesses the murder: she is an innocent by-stander and this gives her description more poignancy. Second, she knows Hyde because he visited her master: why? Third, the maid's description is genuinely horrific: it appears that Hyde has attacked a man who described as being very "kindly" and "beautiful" with "white hair" for what appears to be no reason at all. The metaphor used to describe his anger is effective; the maid describes how he broke out in a "great flame of anger". This suggests both the power and horror of Hyde: he is a man who burns with anger. He is genuinely psychotic. Then Sir Danvers' bones are described as "audibly" shattering: in other words, the maid heard his bones crunch as he was smashed by Hyde's stick, which breaks from the violence of the attack.**

Look at Stevenson's descriptions of London and Hyde's flat: how does he generate a Gothic atmosphere here? **Stevenson creates a very Gothic atmosphere firstly by his descriptions of the fog and the darkness. Even though it is the morning, there is still darkness which is created by the fog: "a great chocolate-coloured pall" covers the whole of the city. This metaphor is particularly effective because a "pall" is a cloth spread over a coffin. In other words, it feels like the city itself is a coffin, which contains the dead body of the people. The daylight is described as "haggard": tired, wearied and ugly. Women who have their own "keys" wander about the area where Hyde lives: in Stevenson's day, women who had their own keys were probably prostitutes. The area has a "gin palace": this was a place to get very cheap, strong alcohol. "Ragged" children, who are probably homeless, "huddle in the doorways". This is a city of your worst nightmares: full of vice, of poverty, of unfairness, soaked in fog and a feeling of death.**

Evaluative questions

How successful is Stevenson in making Hyde seem genuinely evil? **Hyde's evil is evoked by the way he murders Carew. He appears to have murdered him for absolutely no reason at all. He is a man consumed by evil, which burns like a "great flame" within him. He seems to enjoy "trampling" upon people: this is a particularly cowardly method of attack. He only seems to pick upon people weaker than himself and seems to enjoy murdering Carew. He is a sadist: he enjoys seeing people suffer. Thus we can see that Stevenson is extremely successful in evoking Hyde's evil nature: we see him doing very evil things, and what is more we see him enjoying his evil deeds. He appears totally out of control. For me, his real evil comes from the fact that he only picks on weak people: he is a psychotic bully.**

5 Incident of the letter

YouTube reading:
http://www.youtube.com/watch?v=Bv1nrLUD47Q
Thematic questions
When have you seen a friend or relative in distress? How you know the cause of their distress?
When has a friend tried to reassure you that they are fine when they are not?
When have you lied or been lied to?

Have you know anyone who has forged a note/letter, or pretended to be someone else? Why do you think people pretend to be other people?

It was late in the afternoon, when Mr. Utterson found his way to Dr. Jekyll's door, where he was at once admitted by Poole, and carried down by the kitchen offices and across a yard which had once been a garden, to the building which was indifferently **(unconcerned)** known as the laboratory or dissecting **(cutting up)** rooms. The doctor had bought the house from the heirs of a celebrated **(famous)** surgeon; and his own tastes being rather chemical than anatomical **(to do with bodies)**, had changed the destination of the block at the bottom of the garden. It was the first time that the lawyer had been received in that part of his friend's quarters **(rooms)**; and he eyed the dingy, windowless structure with curiosity, and gazed round with a distasteful sense of strangeness as he crossed the theatre, once crowded with eager students and now lying gaunt **(unused)** and silent, the tables laden with chemical apparatus **(equipment)**, the floor strewn **(littered)** with crates and littered with packing straw, and the light falling dimly through the foggy cupola **(a dome which forms a roof)**. At the further end, a flight of stairs mounted to a door covered with red baize **(woollen material)**; and through this, Mr. Utterson was at last received into the doctor's cabinet. It was a large room fitted round with glass presses, furnished, among other things, with a cheval-glass **(a tall mirror fitted at its middle to an upright frame so that it can be tilted)** and a business table, and looking out upon the court by three dusty windows barred with iron. The fire burned in the grate; a lamp was set lighted on the chimney shelf, for even in the houses the fog began to lie thickly; and there, close up to the warmth, sat Dr. Jekyll, looking deathly sick.

> **Simple explanation:** Utterson visits Jekyll and finds that his laboratory hasn't been used in a long time and that Jekyll looks very ill.
> **Analysis:** Utterson now begins to delve deeper and deeper into the mystery of Jekyll and Hyde. Symbolically, he enters a part of the house he has never been in before. There is an air of abandonment about the operating theatre – once crowded with students. The cupola is "foggy" and the quarters are "windowless": there is a deep sense of secrecy, of covering things up, of confusion and fogginess. Entering through another door, he enters the Jekyll's lair: the place where Hyde was created. It is symbolically barred with iron

and rapt in fog. Jekyll is now deadly sick, and quite unlike the happy, complacent person Utterson spoke to about Hyde a year before. There is the stink of corruption about the place: the sense of a sordid hiding place.

Discussion Point

How does Stevenson create suspense here?

He did not rise to meet his visitor, but held out a cold hand and bade him welcome in a changed voice.

"And now," said Mr. Utterson, as soon as Poole had left them, "you have heard the news?"

The doctor shuddered. "They were crying it in the square," he said. "I heard them in my dining-room."

"One word," said the lawyer. "Carew was my client, but so are you, and I want to know what I am doing. You have not been mad enough to hide this fellow?"

"Utterson, I swear to God," cried the doctor, "I swear to God I will never set eyes on him again. I bind my honour to you that I am done with him in this world. It is all at an end. And indeed he does not want my help; you do not know him as I do; he is safe, he is quite safe; mark **(listen to)** my words, he will never more be heard of."

The lawyer listened gloomily; he did not like his friend's feverish manner. "You seem pretty sure of him," said he; "and for your sake, I hope you may be right. If it came to a trial, your name might appear."

"I am quite sure of him," replied Jekyll; "I have grounds for certainty that I cannot share with any one. But there is one thing on which you may advise me. I have—I have received a letter; and I am at a loss whether I should show it to the police. I should like to leave it in your hands, Utterson; you would judge wisely, I am sure; I have so great a trust in you."

"You fear, I suppose, that it might lead to his detection?" asked the lawyer.

"No," said the other. "I cannot say that I care what becomes of Hyde; I am quite done with him. I was thinking of my own character, which this hateful business has rather exposed."

Utterson ruminated **(thought)** awhile **(for a while)**; he was surprised at his friend's selfishness, and yet relieved by it. "Well," said he, at last, "let me see the letter."

The letter was written in an odd, upright hand and signed "Edward Hyde": and it signified, briefly enough, that the writer's benefactor **(a person who gives money/does good)**, Dr.

Jekyll, whom he had long so unworthily repaid for a thousand generosities, need labour under no alarm for his safety, as he had means of escape on which he placed a sure dependence. The lawyer liked this letter well enough; it put a better colour on the intimacy **(friendship)** than he had looked for; and he blamed himself for some of his past suspicions.

"Have you the envelope?" he asked.

"I burned it," replied Jekyll, "before I thought what I was about. But it bore no postmark. The note was handed in."

"Shall I keep this and sleep upon it?" asked Utterson.

"I wish you to judge for me entirely," was the reply. "I have lost confidence in myself."

"Well, I shall consider," returned the lawyer. "And now one word more: it was Hyde who dictated the terms in your will about that disappearance?"

The doctor seemed seized with a qualm **(shudder/fit)** of faintness; he shut his mouth tight and nodded.

"I knew it," said Utterson. "He meant to murder you. You had a fine escape."

"I have had what is far more to the purpose," returned the doctor solemnly: "I have had a lesson—O God, Utterson, what a lesson I have had!" And he covered his face for a moment with his hands.

> **Simple explanation:** Jekyll shows Utterson a letter written by Hyde which says that Hyde has escaped and that he was unworthy of Jekyll's generosity.
>
> **Analysis:** On second reading, we realise that Jekyll is still absolving himself of the blame for the murder, even though he is clearly very guilty about what he has done. He merely feels he has had a "lesson", that he has learnt something, rather than feeling what he has done is beyond the pale.
>
> ### Discussion Point
> How does Stevenson convey Jekyll's despair here?

On his way out, the lawyer stopped and had a word or two with Poole. "By the bye," said he, "there was a letter handed in to-day: what was the messenger like?" But Poole was positive nothing had come except by post; "and only circulars by that," he added.

This news sent off the visitor with his fears renewed. Plainly the letter had come by the laboratory door; possibly, indeed, it had been written in the cabinet; and if that were so, it must be differently judged, and handled with the more caution. The newsboys, as he went, were crying themselves hoarse along the footways **(pavement/streets)**: "Special edition. Shocking murder of an M.P." That was the funeral oration **(speech)** of one friend and client; and he could not help a certain apprehension **(fear/worry)** lest the good name of another should be sucked down in the eddy **(whirlpool/current in dangerous waters)** of the scandal. It was, at least, a ticklish **(difficult)** decision that he had to make; and self-reliant as he was by habit, he began to cherish a longing for advice. It was not to be had directly; but perhaps, he thought, it might be fished for.

Presently after, he sat on one side of his own hearth, with Mr. Guest, his head clerk, upon the other, and midway between, at a nicely calculated distance from the fire, a bottle of a particular old wine that had long dwelt unsunned in the foundations of his house. The fog still slept on the wing above the drowned city, where the lamps glimmered like carbuncles **(a big boil/abscess full of pus)**; and through the muffle and smother of these fallen clouds, the procession of the town's life was still rolling in through the great arteries **(muscly tubes that carry blood/main roads)** with a sound as of a mighty wind. But the room was gay with firelight. In the bottle the acids were long ago resolved; the imperial **(strong)** dye had softened with time, as the colour grows richer in stained windows; and the glow of hot autumn afternoons on hillside vineyards, was ready to be set free and to disperse the fogs of London. Insensibly **(without knowing it)** the lawyer melted **(gave way)**. There was no man from whom he kept fewer secrets than Mr. Guest; and he was not always sure that he kept as many as he meant. Guest had often been on business to the doctor's; he knew Poole; he could scarce have failed to hear of Mr. Hyde's familiarity about the house; he might draw conclusions: was it not as well, then, that he should see a letter which put that mystery to right? and above all since Guest, being a great student and critic of handwriting, would consider the step natural and obliging? The clerk, besides, was a man of counsel; he could scarce read so strange a document without dropping a remark; and by that remark Mr. Utterson might shape his future course.

"This is a sad business about Sir Danvers," he said.

"Yes, sir, indeed. It has elicited **(produced)** a great deal of public feeling," returned Guest. "The man, of course, was mad."

"I should like to hear your views on that," replied Utterson. "I have a document here in his handwriting; it is between ourselves, for I scarce know what to do about it; it is an ugly business at the best. But there it is; quite in your way: a murderer's autograph."

Guest's eyes brightened, and he sat down at once and studied it with passion. "No sir," he said: "not mad; but it is an odd hand."

"And by all accounts a very odd writer," added the lawyer.

Just then the servant entered with a note.

"Is that from Dr. Jekyll, sir?" inquired the clerk. "I thought I knew the writing. Anything private, Mr. Utterson?"

"Only an invitation to dinner. Why? Do you want to see it?"

"One moment. I thank you, sir;" and the clerk laid the two sheets of paper alongside and sedulously compared their contents. "Thank you, sir," he said at last, returning both; "it's a very interesting autograph."

There was a pause, during which Mr. Utterson struggled with himself. "Why did you compare them, Guest?" he inquired suddenly.

"Well, sir," returned the clerk, "there's a rather singular resemblance; the two hands are in many points identical: only differently sloped."

"Rather quaint," said Utterson.

"It is, as you say, rather quaint **(odd)**," returned Guest.

"I wouldn't speak of this note, you know," said the master.

"No, sir," said the clerk. "I understand."

But no sooner was Mr. Utterson alone that night, than he locked the note into his safe, where it reposed from that time forward. "What!" he thought. "Henry Jekyll forge for a murderer!" And his blood ran cold in his veins.

> **Simple explanation:** Utterson learns from a servant that no letter was delivered to Jekyll that day, and he learns from a handwriting expert that Hyde's letter was actually written by Jekyll.
>
> **Analysis:** Stevenson develops the theme of corruption by making Utterson think that Jekyll has forged for a murderer. Notice how the servant is more perceptive than his master in seeing that Hyde's handwriting is the same as Jekyll's. Utterson is careful to keep everything a secret, locking the note in the safe. Secrecy is all. He wishes to hide Jekyll's corruption, his dirty secret, from the world. In such a way, Utterson is presented as being similar to Jekyll.
>
> ### Discussion Point
>
> Why does Utterson lock the note away in the safe? What do you think of Stevenson's presentation of Utterson here?

Summary -- fill in the blanks (answers are at the back)

Utterson visits Henry Jekyll who, looking ---- ---, tells him that he has finished with ----. He shows Utterson a letter written by Hyde which says that Hyde has ---- and won't be caught. Hyde says that he is ---- of Jekyll's generosity. Utterson is pleased to read the letter, but then learns from Poole the butler that no one has delivered a ---- to the house. He shows the letter to a -------- expert, Mr Guest, who says that the letter is written in Jekyll's hand-writing, only the slope of the writing is different. Utterson is horrified that Jekyll would ---- a letter for a murderer.

Comprehension questions
What does the state of Jekyll's laboratory tell us about his state of mind?
What does the letter to Jekyll from Hyde say?
Why does Utterson believe Jekyll forged the letter?
Analytical questions
How does Stevenson reveal Jekyll's state of mind in this chapter? Think about his use of dialogue, the descriptions of the laboratory, and the plot twist that the letter is a forgery.
Evaluative questions
How successful is Stevenson in generating mystery and suspense in the chapter?
Creative response tasks
Write a story or poem called "The Forgery".

Write Utterson's diary for this chapter, discussing his feelings about seeing his friend Henry Jekyll and his concern when he finds out the letter is a forgery.

You can watch a YouTube video I made about this section here: http://www.youtube.com/watch?v=AS7-NztAoTk

POSSIBLE ANSWERS in brief & bold

Comprehension questions
What does the state of Jekyll's laboratory tell us about his state of mind? **That he is neglectful of his previous interests: all of his scientific equipment is unused. This suggests he is probably depressed because he is not pursuing his favourite past-time: science.**
What does the letter to Jekyll from Hyde say? **Hyde says that he has escaped and can't be caught, and that he will not return.**
Why does Utterson believe Jekyll forged the letter? **First, he learns from a servant that no one delivered the letter. Second, his friend Mr Guest, who is a hand-writing expert, notices that Hyde's handwriting in the letter is identical to Jekyll's, except that it is differently sloped.**

Analytical questions

How does Stevenson reveal Jekyll's state of mind in this chapter? Think about his use of dialogue, the descriptions of the laboratory, and the plot twist that the letter is a forgery. **Through his description of the abandoned and disused laboratory, he reveals that Jekyll is no longer pursing his passion, science, this suggests that Jekyll is depressed. When he talks to Jekyll, it is obvious that he is in a state of shock, but convinced that Hyde won't trouble him again. Stevenson's use of dialogue is effective in conveying Jekyll's sense of shock. However, the revelation that Jekyll has possibly forged the letter suggests that Jekyll is deceitful for some reason. This narrative "twist" is very effective in making the reader think that Jekyll is hiding some terrible secret, and is not to be trusted.**

Evaluative questions

How successful is Stevenson in generating mystery and suspense in the chapter? **Stevenson's characterisation of Jekyll as a cunning but shocked person is highly effective for a number of reasons. First, it creates mystery: we, as readers, are desperate to know the solution to the mystery. Second, it is highly successful in constructing a picture of a highly complex personality: Jekyll is not a "straight-forward" person at all, and this provokes our interest in the story further.**

6 Remarkable Incident of Dr Lanyon

YouTube reading:
http://www.youtube.com/watch?v=ypCi_vCJjrU

Thematic questions
Have you ever been in shock? What has happened to you?
Have you ever seen anyone in shock?
Have you ever met anyone who has changed a great deal since when you first met them? What was your reaction?

Time ran on; thousands of pounds were offered in reward, for the death of Sir Danvers was resented as a public injury; but Mr. Hyde had disappeared out of the ken **(knowledge)** of the police as though he had never existed. Much of his past was unearthed, indeed, and all disreputable **(disgraceful/creating a poor**

reputation): tales came out of the man's cruelty, at once so callous and violent; of his vile life, of his strange associates **(people he knew)**, of the hatred that seemed to have surrounded his career; but of his present whereabouts, not a whisper. From the time he had left the house in Soho on the morning of the murder, he was simply blotted out **(erased/got rid of)**; and gradually, as time drew on, Mr. Utterson began to recover from the hotness of his alarm, and to grow more at quiet with himself. The death of Sir Danvers was, to his way of thinking, more than paid for by the disappearance of Mr. Hyde. Now that that evil influence had been withdrawn, a new life began for Dr. Jekyll. He came out of his seclusion **(being alone)**, renewed relations with his friends, became once more their familiar guest and entertainer; and whilst he had always been known for charities, he was now no less distinguished for religion **(gave money to charities and religious causes)**. He was busy, he was much in the open air, he did good; his face seemed to open and brighten, as if with an inward consciousness **(awareness)** of service **(doing your duty/doing good)**; and for more than two months, the doctor was at peace.

On the 8th of January Utterson had dined at the doctor's with a small party; Lanyon had been there; and the face of the host had looked from one to the other as in the old days when the trio **(three people)** were inseparable **(could not be separated)** friends. On the 12th, and again on the 14th, the door was shut against the lawyer. "The doctor was confined to the house," Poole said, "and saw no one." On the 15th, he tried again, and was again refused; and having now been used for the last two months to see his friend almost daily, he found this return of solitude **(being alone)** to weigh upon his spirits. The fifth night he had in Guest to dine with him; and the sixth he betook himself to Dr. Lanyon's.

There at least he was not denied admittance **(entry)**; but when he came in, he was shocked at the change which had taken place in the doctor's appearance. He had his death-warrant **(certain to die)** written legibly **(clearly)** upon his face. The rosy man had grown pale; his flesh had fallen away; he was visibly balder and older; and yet it was not so much these tokens of a swift physical decay that arrested the lawyer's notice, as a look in the eye and quality of manner that seemed to testify to some deep-seated terror of the mind. It was unlikely that the doctor should fear death; and yet that was what Utterson was tempted to suspect. "Yes," he thought; "he is a doctor, he must know his own state and that his days are counted; and the knowledge is more than he can bear." And yet when Utterson remarked on his ill-looks, it was with an air of great firmness that Lanyon declared himself a doomed **(destined to die)** man.

"I have had a shock," he said, "and I shall never recover. It is a question of weeks. Well, life has been pleasant; I liked it; yes, sir, I used to like it. I sometimes think if we knew all, we should be more glad to get away."

"Jekyll is ill, too," observed Utterson. "Have you seen him?"

But Lanyon's face changed, and he held up a trembling hand. "I wish to see or hear no more of Dr. Jekyll," he said in a loud, unsteady voice. "I am quite done with that person; and I beg that you will spare me any allusion **(reference/mention)** to one whom I regard as dead."

> **Simple explanation:** Dr Jekyll entertains guests, including Lanyon and Utterson, and does good works, but then shuts himself away from Utterson suddenly. Utterson visits Lanyon to find out what is going on and finds Lanyon about to die. Lanyon says that he never wants to have anything to do with Jekyll again.
>
> **Analysis:** How changed Lanyon is since we last saw him! He is no longer the slick, superficial, brash, arrogant man about town, the know-it-all doctor. He is an utterly broken man, about to die. The crucial sentence he says, which is so haunting on second reading is: "I sometimes think if we knew all we should be more glad to get away." The pronouncement is mysterious – like so much in the book – but we do have a sense that Lanyon is speaking for all mankind here: if we knew the truth about ourselves, we'd all want to "get away" – to die. He then further enhances the mystery by declaring he regards Jekyll as dead. He is clearly frightened by Jekyll: we realise on second reading this is because Jekyll is too like him. Stevenson keeps up the narrative tension by having Lanyon tell us that after he has died the truth will come out. It is fascinating that Lanyon can't tell the truth while he is still alive. On second reading, we realise that Lanyon knows the truth about Jekyll at this point, and cannot face speaking or thinking about the horror of it all.
>
> ### Discussion Point
>
> What is Lanyon so afraid of? Why does he regard Jekyll as dead? What do you think of Stevenson's presentation of Lanyon here? Why can't Lanyon tell the truth while he is still alive?

"Tut-tut," said Mr. Utterson; and then after a considerable pause, "Can't I do anything?" he inquired. "We are three very old friends, Lanyon; we shall not live to make others."

"Nothing can be done," returned Lanyon; "ask himself."

"He will not see me," said the lawyer.

"I am not surprised at that," was the reply. "Some day, Utterson, after I am dead, you may perhaps come to learn the right and wrong of this. I cannot tell you. And in the meantime, if you can sit and talk with me of other things, for God's sake, stay and do so; but if you cannot keep clear of this accursed topic, then in God's name, go, for I cannot bear it."

As soon as he got home, Utterson sat down and wrote to Jekyll, complaining of his exclusion **(being prevented from seeing someone)** from the house, and asking the cause of this unhappy break with Lanyon; and the next day brought him a long answer, often very pathetically **(sadly)** worded, and sometimes darkly mysterious in drift **(in tone or meaning)**. The quarrel with Lanyon was incurable. "I do not blame our old friend," Jekyll wrote, "but I share his view that we must never meet. I mean from henceforth to lead a life of extreme seclusion **(being alone)**; you must not be surprised, nor must you doubt my friendship, if my door is often shut even to you. You must suffer me to go my own dark way. I have brought on myself a punishment and a danger that I cannot name. If I am the chief of sinners, I am the chief of sufferers also. I could not think that this earth contained a place for sufferings and terrors so unmanning; and you can do but one thing, Utterson, to lighten this destiny, and that is to respect my silence."

> **Simple explanation:** Jekyll writes to Utterson telling him that he intends never to see anyone again and that he is terrified of something, but doesn't say what this is.
>
> **Analysis:** Jekyll and Lanyon both wish to remain silent on the reasons for their falling out – and neither wish to meet again. These men's response to the crisis is silence, no discussion, no negotiation, no exploration of the issues, because they are too horrifying to contemplate. On second reading, the reader probably finds Jekyll utterly contemptible here. The line: "If am the chief of sinners, I am the chief of sufferers also." Overwhelmingly, Jekyll feels sorry for himself: there is not much sense of repentance, only a confession that he is the "chief of sinners".

Discussion Point
How do our perceptions of Jekyll change on first and second readings?

Utterson was amazed; the dark influence of Hyde had been withdrawn, the doctor had returned to his old tasks and amities; a week ago, the prospect had smiled with every promise of a cheerful and an honoured age; and now in a moment, friendship, and peace of mind, and the whole tenor **(way)** of his life were wrecked **(destroyed)**. So great and unprepared a change pointed to madness; but in view of Lanyon's manner and words, there must lie for it some deeper ground **(bigger reason)**.

A week afterwards Dr. Lanyon took to his bed, and in something less than a fortnight he was dead. The night after the funeral, at which he had been sadly affected, Utterson locked the door of his business room, and sitting there by the light of a melancholy **(sad)** candle, drew out and set before him an envelope addressed by the hand and sealed with the seal of his dead friend. "PRIVATE: for the hands of G. J. Utterson ALONE, and in case of his predecease to be destroyed unread," so it was emphatically superscribed; and the lawyer dreaded to behold the contents. "I have buried one friend to-day," he thought: "what if this should cost me another?" And then he condemned the fear as a disloyalty, and broke the seal. Within there was another enclosure, likewise sealed, and marked upon the cover as "not to be opened till the death or disappearance of Dr. Henry Jekyll." Utterson could not trust his eyes. Yes, it was disappearance; here again, as in the mad will which he had long ago restored to its author, here again were the idea of a disappearance and the name of Henry Jekyll bracketted. But in the will, that idea had sprung from the sinister suggestion of the man Hyde; it was set there with a purpose all too plain and horrible. Written by the hand of Lanyon, what should it mean? A great curiosity came on the trustee, to disregard the prohibition and dive at once to the bottom of these mysteries; but professional honour and faith to his dead friend were stringent obligations; and the packet slept in the inmost corner of his private safe.

It is one thing to mortify **(subdue/to stop or repress a desire with a real effort)** curiosity, another to conquer it; and it may be doubted if, from that day forth, Utterson desired the society of his surviving friend with the same eagerness. He thought of him kindly; but his thoughts were disquieted **(disturbed)** and fearful. He went to call indeed; but he was perhaps relieved to be denied admittance **(entry)**; perhaps, in his heart, he preferred to speak with Poole upon the doorstep and surrounded by the air and sounds of the open city, rather than to be admitted into that house of voluntary **(willing/chosen to do something of your own free will)** bondage **(slavery)**, and to sit and speak with its inscrutable recluse. Poole had, indeed, no very pleasant news to communicate. The doctor, it appeared, now more than ever confined himself to the cabinet **(small room/large cupboard)** over the laboratory, where he would sometimes even sleep; he was out of spirits, he had grown very silent, he did not read; it seemed as if he had something on his mind. Utterson became so used to the unvarying **(unchanging)** character **(nature)** of these reports, that he fell off little by little in the frequency of his visits.

Summary -- fill in the blanks (answers are at the back)

Time passes but Hyde is not ----. Jekyll starts seeing people, doing --- works and holds a dinner party which ---- and ---- come to. A few days later though, when Utterson calls, Jekyll won't see ----. Utterson visits Lanyon and sees that Lanyon is sick and will --- soon. Lanyon won't talk about Jekyll, who he regards as ----. Utterson writes to Jekyll to ---- about not seeing him. Jekyll writes back and telling him that he does not blame Lanyon for treating him in this way and that he has brought a ---- upon himself. A few weeks later Lanyon dies, giving Utterson an envelope. When he opens it, he finds another envelope only to be opened ---- Jekyll disappears or dies. Utterson tries to see Jekyll again, but the butler ---- to let him in.

Comprehension questions

Dr Jekyll enters a new phase of life at the beginning of the chapter: what does he do that was different from before?

Then he refuses to see Utterson: why do you think – look at "Henry Jekyll's full statement of the case" for the answer?

How has Lanyon changed when Utterson visits him?

What letter does Utterson receive from Lanyon and what instructions come with it?

Analytical questions

How does Stevenson develop Lanyon's character in this chapter?

Evaluative questions

How successfully does Stevenson arouse the reader's curiosity in this chapter?

Creative response tasks

Write Utterson's diary for this chapter, explaining what he thinks and feels at Jekyll and Lanyon's behaviour.

Stevenson writes of Hyde at the beginning of the chapter: "Much of his past was unearthed, indeed, and all disreputable **(disgraceful/creating a poor reputation)**: tales came out of the man's cruelty, at once so callous and violent; of his vile life, of his strange associates **(people he knew)**, of the hatred that seemed to have surrounded his career". Write a series of newspaper articles about what Hyde has done.

Write a poem or story called "The Shock".

You can watch a YouTube video I made about this section here:
http://www.youtube.com/watch?v=VDO-vorkfUc

POSSIBLE ANSWERS in brief & bold

Comprehension questions

Dr Jekyll enters a new phase of life at the beginning of the chapter: what does he do that was different from before? **He does "good", i.e. charitable works. He also socialises like he used to, inviting Utterson and Lanyon to dinner.**

Then he refuses to see Utterson: why do you think – look at "Henry Jekyll's full statement of the case" for the answer? **We learn in Jekyll's narrative that he has been turning into Hyde without wishing to: this is the reason that he won't see anyone.**

How has Lanyon changed when Utterson visits him? **He has his "death warrant" written on his face, in other words, he is going to die.**

What letter does Utterson receive from Lanyon and what instructions come with it? **He receives a letter addressed to him but he is told that he must not open it until Jekyll has disappeared or died.**

Analytical questions

How does Stevenson develop Lanyon's character in this chapter? **Stevenson has been very careful to "develop" his characterisation of Lanyon in this chapter because he reveals him to be a very different man from the beginning of the book, where Lanyon was presented as a smug person who was utterly confident that Jekyll was pursuing "unscientific balderdash" and would have nothing to do with him and his projects. He was certain of himself and his views. In this chapter, we see a man who has had all of his views about life shattered and changed: he has lost his confidence and is about to die. He has changed very dramatically.**

Evaluative questions
How successfully does Stevenson arouse the reader's curiosity in this chapter? **The change in Lanyon provokes the reader's curiosity because it is so extreme. We, as readers, wonder: how can such a confident and successful man change so dramatically? What has happened to cause his death?**

7 Incident at the window

YouTube reading:
http://www.youtube.com/watch?v=0c7Y7uwntgw
Thematic questions
Are there times when you find it difficult to talk to people and
you'd prefer to be alone?
What kinds of people like to be alone and away from other people?
Why are they this way?

It chanced **(happened)** on Sunday, when Mr. Utterson was on
his usual walk with Mr. Enfield, that their way lay once again
through the by-street; and that when they came in front of the
door, both stopped to gaze on it.

"Well," said Enfield, "that story's at an end at least. We shall
never see more of Mr. Hyde."

"I hope not," said Utterson. "Did I ever tell you that I once saw
him, and shared your feeling of repulsion
(disgust/revulsion/hating something)?"

"It was impossible to do the one without the other," returned
Enfield. "And by the way, what an ass you must have thought me,
not to know that this was a back way to Dr. Jekyll's! It was partly
your own fault that I found it out, even when I did."

"So you found it out, did you?" said Utterson. "But if that be so,
we may step into the court and take a look at the windows. To tell
you the truth, I am uneasy about poor Jekyll; and even outside, I
feel as if the presence of a friend might do him good."

The court was very cool and a little damp, and full of premature
(before its time) twilight, although the sky, high up overhead,
was still bright with sunset. The middle one of the three windows
was half-way open; and sitting close beside it, taking the air with
an infinite **(without end)** sadness of mien
(character/atmosphere), like some disconsolate **(unhappy)**
prisoner, Utterson saw Dr. Jekyll.

"What! Jekyll!" he cried. "I trust you are better."

"I am very low, Utterson," replied the doctor drearily
(miserably/sadly), "very low. It will not last long, thank God."

"You stay too much indoors," said the lawyer. "You should be
out, whipping up the circulation **(getting the blood flowing by
walking)** like Mr. Enfield and me. (This is my cousin—Mr.
Enfield—Dr. Jekyll.) Come now; get your hat and take a quick turn
with us."

"You are very good," sighed the other. "I should like to very much; but no, no, no, it is quite impossible; I dare not. But indeed, Utterson, I am very glad to see you; this is really a great pleasure; I would ask you and Mr. Enfield up, but the place is really not fit."

"Why, then," said the lawyer, good-naturedly, "the best thing we can do is to stay down here and speak with you from where we are."

"That is just what I was about to venture to propose," returned the doctor with a smile. But the words were hardly uttered, before the smile was struck out of his face and succeeded **(followed)** by an expression of such abject **(great)** terror and despair, as froze the very blood of the two gentlemen below. They saw it but for a glimpse for the window was instantly thrust down; but that glimpse had been sufficient, and they turned and left the court without a word. In silence, too, they traversed **(travelled down/crossed)** the by-street; and it was not until they had come into a neighbouring thoroughfare **(street)**, where even upon a Sunday there were still some stirrings of life, that Mr. Utterson at last turned and looked at his companion. They were both pale; and there was an answering horror in their eyes.

"God forgive us, God forgive us," said Mr. Utterson.

But Mr. Enfield only nodded his head very seriously, and walked on once more in silence.

> **Simple explanation:** Utterson and Enfield are on one of their Sunday walks when they see Jekyll sitting at his laboratory window. He talks to them but then suddenly appears terrified and disappears.
> **Analysis:** Jekyll locks himself away from everyone. One Sunday afternoon, the lawyer Utterson and Mr Enfield stop at the back door of Jekyll's laboratory. To their surprise, they see Jekyll who is seems pleased to see them. But then, as we see in the passage above, an expression of "abject terror and despair" comes upon him and the window is "thrust down". However, the two men glimpse the face clearly very disturbed by what they have seen. On second reading, we realise that Jekyll has suddenly changed into Hyde again and has to hide himself away. The two men almost glimpse this, gaining a sense of Jekyll's degradation.
> ### Discussion point
> How does Stevenson create a sense of horror here?
>
> ### Summary
> Utterson and Enfield pass by the door where Enfield saw Hyde --- after he trampled the girl. Enfield has now worked

out that it is the door to the laboratory that connects to ----
house. Enfield says that they will never --- Hyde again. They
look up and see Jekyll at the window looking very ----. They
ask him to come out for a ---- with them but he says he can't.
Then a look of --- seizes him and he disappears. The two
men walk on in ----.

Comprehension questions
What does Enfield discover about Hyde's rooms that he didn't know?
Why do you think Utterson hadn't already told him this information?
What are Jekyll's mood and emotions like in this chapter?
Analytical questions
How does Stevenson use description and dialogue to create a sense of
drama and impending doom in this chapter?
Evaluative questions
How successful is this chapter in provoking the reader's curiosity?
Creative response tasks
Write a poem or short story about a brief but chilling meeting with a
friend who is in a bad way, calling it "My Sad Friend".

Write Enfield's diary for this chapter in which he talks about his
friendship with Utterson and his thoughts on Jekyll and Hyde.

You can watch a YouTube video I made about this section
here:
http://www.youtube.com/watch?v=VDO-vorkfUc

POSSIBLE ANSWERS in brief & bold

Comprehension questions
What does Enfield discover about Hyde's rooms that he didn't know? **He
realises that Hyde's living quarters are actually the back part of
Dr Jekyll's house.**
Why do you think Utterson hadn't already told him this information?
**Utterson is a very "discreet" person: he does not reveal his
friend's secrets or troubles to anyone. Thus we see him as
someone who can be trusted and doesn't gossip.**
What are Jekyll's mood and emotions like in this chapter? **Jekyll is
revealed as being in a state of "abject terror" when he finishes
talking to Enfield and Utterson: he is terrified in the most
extreme fashion.**

Analytical questions
How does Stevenson use description and dialogue to create a sense of
drama and impending doom in this chapter? **The description of
Jekyll sitting in such a dejected way at the window creates a
sense of impending doom because we see that hhe feels that he
has no future prospects. He appears to be without hope: he**

can't even go out for a walk with his friends. Then when his mood shifts from one of depression to "abject terror" we have a sense that something terrible is going to happen to Jekyll.

Evaluative questions
How successful is this chapter in provoking the reader's curiosity? **Stevenson's manages to carry on creating a deep and profound of mystery in this chapter because, on first reading, we don't know what is troubling Jekyll or what is making his mood swing so sharply. As far as we are concerned, Hyde has disappeared and therefore Jekyll possibly doesn't need to worry about him. The shift from depression to "abject terror" is particularly perplexing. Why has he suddenly shut the window on his friends? What has happened to him to make him suddenly feel this way? The chapter, like the previous one, provokes many questions in the reader's mind.**

8 The Last Night

YouTube readings:
Part One: http://www.youtube.com/watch?v=RnTusZVnZNs
Part Two: http://www.youtube.com/watch?v=aGQakr19q8w
Thematic questions
What are the major confrontations you have had in your life?
Has there ever been a time when you have had to confront a friend or relative over their behavior? If so, what happened? If not, think about why some people encounter these times in their lives?

Mr. Utterson was sitting by his fireside one evening after dinner, when he was surprised to receive a visit from Poole.

"Bless me, Poole, what brings you here?" he cried; and then taking a second look at him, "What ails you?" he added; "is the doctor ill?"

"Mr. Utterson," said the man, "there is something wrong."

"Take a seat, and here is a glass of wine for you," said the lawyer. "Now, take your time, and tell me plainly what you want."

"You know the doctor's ways, sir," replied Poole, "and how he shuts himself up. Well, he's shut up again in the cabinet **(small room)**; and I don't like it, sir—I wish I may die if I like it. Mr. Utterson, sir, I'm afraid."

"Now, my good man," said the lawyer, "be explicit. What are you afraid of?"

"I've been afraid for about a week," returned Poole, doggedly disregarding the question, "and I can bear it no more."

The man's appearance amply bore out his words; his manner was altered for the worse; and except for the moment when he had first announced his terror, he had not once looked the lawyer in the face. Even now, he sat with the glass of wine untasted on his knee, and his eyes directed to a corner of the floor. "I can bear it no more," he repeated.

"Come," said the lawyer, "I see you have some good reason, Poole; I see there is something seriously amiss. Try to tell me what it is."

"I think there's been foul play **(bad behaviour/criminal behaviour)**," said Poole, hoarsely.

"Foul play!" cried the lawyer, a good deal frightened and rather inclined to be irritated in consequence. "What foul play! What does the man mean?"

"I daren't say, sir," was the answer; "but will you come along with me and see for yourself?"

Mr. Utterson's only answer was to rise and get his hat and greatcoat; but he observed with wonder the greatness of the relief that appeared upon the butler's face, and perhaps with no less, that the wine was still untasted when he set it down to follow.

It was a wild, cold, seasonable night of March, with a pale moon, lying on her back as though the wind had tilted her, and flying wrack of the most diaphanous **(light, delicate, and translucent)** and lawny texture. The wind made talking difficult, and flecked the blood into the face. It seemed to have swept the streets unusually bare of passengers, besides; for Mr. Utterson thought he had never seen that part of London so deserted. He could have wished it otherwise; never in his life had he been conscious of so sharp a wish to see and touch his fellow-creatures; for struggle as he might, there was borne in upon his mind a crushing anticipation **(belief that something will happen)** of calamity **(disaster)**. The square, when they got there, was full of wind and dust, and the thin trees in the garden were lashing themselves along the railing. Poole, who had kept all the way a pace or two ahead, now pulled up in the middle of the pavement, and in spite of the biting weather, took off his hat and mopped his brow with a red pocket-handkerchief. But for all the hurry of his coming, these were not the dews of exertion that he wiped away, but the moisture of some strangling anguish; for his face was white and his voice, when he spoke, harsh and broken.

"Well, sir," he said, "here we are, and God grant there be nothing wrong."

"Amen, Poole," said the lawyer.

Thereupon the servant knocked in a very guarded manner; the door was opened on the chain; and a voice asked from within, "Is that you, Poole?"

"It's all right," said Poole. "Open the door."

The hall, when they entered it, was brightly lighted up; the fire was built high; and about the hearth the whole of the servants, men and women, stood huddled together like a flock of sheep. At the sight of Mr. Utterson, the housemaid broke into hysterical whimpering; and the cook, crying out "Bless God! it's Mr. Utterson," ran forward as if to take him in her arms.

"What, what? Are you all here?" said the lawyer peevishly. "Very irregular, very unseemly; your master would be far from pleased."

"They're all afraid," said Poole.

Blank silence followed, no one protesting; only the maid lifted her voice and now wept loudly.

"Hold your tongue!" Poole said to her, with a ferocity of accent that testified to his own jangled nerves; and indeed, when the girl had so suddenly raised the note of her lamentation **(sorrow)**, they had all started and turned towards the inner door with faces of dreadful expectation. "And now," continued the butler, addressing the knife-boy, "reach me a candle, and we'll get this through hands at once" **(this phrase is Scottish for we'll deal with this).** And then he begged Mr. Utterson to follow him, and led the way to the back garden.

"Now, sir," said he, "you come as gently as you can. I want you to hear, and I don't want you to be heard. And see here, sir, if by any chance he was to ask you in, don't go."

Mr. Utterson's nerves, at this unlooked-for termination **(end)**, gave a jerk that nearly threw him from his balance; but he recollected his courage and followed the butler into the laboratory building through the surgical theatre, with its lumber of crates and bottles, to the foot of the stair. Here Poole motioned him to stand on one side and listen; while he himself, setting down the candle and making a great and obvious call on his resolution **(decision)**, mounted the steps and knocked with a somewhat uncertain hand on the red baize of the cabinet door.

"Mr. Utterson, sir, asking to see you," he called; and even as he did so, once more violently signed to the lawyer to give ear.

A voice answered from within: "Tell him I cannot see anyone," it said complainingly.

"Thank you, sir," said Poole, with a note of something like triumph in his voice; and taking up his candle, he led Mr. Utterson back across the yard and into the great kitchen, where the fire was out and the beetles were leaping on the floor.

"Sir," he said, looking Mr. Utterson in the eyes, "Was that my master's voice?"

"It seems much changed," replied the lawyer, very pale, but giving look for look.

"Changed? Well, yes, I think so," said the butler. "Have I been twenty years in this man's house, to be deceived about his voice? No, sir; master's made away with **(he has been taken away or killed)**; he was made away with eight days ago, when we heard him cry out upon the name of God; and who's in there instead of him, and why it stays there, is a thing that cries to Heaven, Mr. Utterson!"

> **Simple explanation:** One evening, Utterson is visited by Poole who says that something bad has happened to his master. Utterson goes with Poole to Jekyll's house and finds the servants all frightened in the hallway. Poole takes him to the door of Jekyll's room, his "cabinet", and hears someone, not sounding like Dr Jekyll, saying that he can't see anyone.
>
> **Analysis:** There is something frightening about someone locking himself in a room and refusing to come out and only speaking in strangulated phrases through the door. Once again, on second reading we feel a sense of corruption: the Jekyll we knew has fallen very low indeed, his subconscious, in the form of Hyde, is now becoming manifest all the time. The narrative is really becoming very tense now: Utterson has in his possession a letter from Lanyon which is not to be opened until the death or disappearance of Henry Jekyll. The reader is desperate to know what is in the letter: but Utterson, being the faithful lawyer that he is, does not open it, keeping the letter sealed shut until Jekyll has disappeared. Likewise, the door is locked. The reader has reached an impasse, a locking away of secrets, which we know will be overcome soon.
>
> ### Discussion Point
> How does Stevenson maintain the narrative tension here?

"This is a very strange tale, Poole; this is rather a wild tale my man," said Mr. Utterson, biting his finger. "Suppose it were as you suppose, supposing Dr. Jekyll to have been—well, murdered what could induce **(persuade)** the murderer to stay? That won't hold water **(doesn't make sense)**; it doesn't commend itself to reason."

"Well, Mr. Utterson, you are a hard man to satisfy, but I'll do it yet," said Poole. "All this last week (you must know) him, or it, whatever it is that lives in that cabinet, has been crying night and day for some sort of medicine and cannot get it to his mind. It was sometimes his way—the master's, that is—to write his orders on a sheet of paper and throw it on the stair. We've had nothing else this week back; nothing but papers, and a closed door, and the very meals left there to be smuggled in when nobody was looking. Well, sir, every day, ay, and twice and thrice in the same day, there have been orders and complaints, and I have been sent flying to all the wholesale chemists in town. Every time I brought the stuff back, there would be another paper telling me to return it, because it was not pure, and another order to a different firm. This drug is wanted bitter bad, sir, whatever for."

"Have you any of these papers?" asked Mr. Utterson.

> **Simple explanation:** Utterson learns from Poole that Jekyll has been writing to chemists asking for drugs, but he never seems to have enough or the right sort of drug.
> **Analysis:** Jekyll is behaving like a drug addict, demanding chemicals from the wholesale chemists in town. Notice how Stevenson creates a sense of mystery here by revealing Jekyll's need for a "pure" drug. We don't know quite why Jekyll needs this kind of drug.
> ### Discussion Point
> In what ways do you think the story is a parable about drug addiction?

Poole felt in his pocket and handed out a crumpled note, which the lawyer, bending nearer to the candle, carefully examined. Its contents ran thus: "Dr. Jekyll presents his compliments to Messrs. Maw. He assures them that their last sample is impure and quite useless for his present purpose. In the year 18—, Dr. J. purchased a somewhat large quantity from Messrs. M. He now begs them to search with most sedulous care, and should any of the same quality be left, forward it to him at once. Expense is no consideration. The importance of this to Dr. J. can hardly be exaggerated." So far the letter had run composedly enough, but here with a sudden splutter of the pen, the writer's emotion had broken loose. "For God's sake," he added, "find me some of the old."

"This is a strange note," said Mr. Utterson; and then sharply, "How do you come to have it open?"

"The man at Maw's was main angry, sir, and he threw it back to me like so much dirt," returned Poole.

"This is unquestionably the doctor's hand, do you know?" resumed the lawyer.

"I thought it looked like it," said the servant rather sulkily; and then, with another voice, "But what matters hand of write?" he said. "I've seen him!"

"Seen him?" repeated Mr. Utterson. "Well?"

"That's it!" said Poole. "It was this way. I came suddenly into the theatre from the garden. It seems he had slipped out to look for this drug or whatever it is; for the cabinet door was open, and there he was at the far end of the room digging among the crates. He looked up when I came in, gave a kind of cry, and whipped upstairs into the cabinet. It was but for one minute that I saw him, but the hair stood upon my head like quills. Sir, if that was my master, why had he a mask upon his face? If it was my master, why did he cry out like a rat, and run from me? I have served him long enough. And then..." The man paused and passed his hand over his face.

> **Simple explanation:** Poole has seen someone who is much shorter than Jekyll wearing a mask looking for something in the laboratory – the old dissecting room.
> **Analysis:** The horror deepens when we realise that Jekyll or Hyde is wearing a mask. Again, we have more images of secrecy, of hiding bodily corruption, of covering up moral decay. Jekyll, who was once so arrogant and content, is now reduced to scuttling around like a frightened rat in his own home. The loyal servant Poole's reaction of passing a hand over his face is moving: he is aware that something terrible has happened. Something will mean nothing is ever the same again.
> ### Discussion Point
> Why is Jekyll wearing a mask? What is the effect of him wearing the mask?

"These are all very strange circumstances," said Mr. Utterson, "but I think I begin to see daylight. Your master, Poole, is plainly seized with one of those maladies that both torture and deform the sufferer; hence, for aught I know, the alteration of his voice; hence the mask and the avoidance of his friends; hence his eagerness to find this drug, by means of which the poor soul retains **(believes)** some hope of ultimate recovery—God grant that he be not deceived! There is my explanation; it is sad enough, Poole, ay, and appalling to consider; but it is plain and natural, hangs well together, and delivers us from all exorbitant **(very great)** alarms."

"Sir," said the butler, turning to a sort of mottled **(blotchy)** pallor **(paleness)**, "that thing was not my master, and there's the truth. My master"—here he looked round him and began to whisper—"is a tall, fine build of a man, and this was more of a dwarf." Utterson attempted to protest. "O, sir," cried Poole, "do you think I do not know my master after twenty years? Do you think I do not know where his head comes to in the cabinet door, where I saw him every morning of my life? No, sir, that thing in the mask was never Dr. Jekyll—God knows what it was, but it was never Dr. Jekyll; and it is the belief of my heart that there was murder done."

> **Simple explanation:** Poole believes that Jekyll has been murdered by Mr Hyde.
> **Analysis:** Finally, Poole bursts out with what he thinks is the truth. We realise on second reading that there was no murder: gradually Jekyll's true nature is being revealed.
> ### Discussion Point
> How does Stevenson create a real sense of psychological horror here?

"Poole," replied the lawyer, "if you say that, it will become my duty to make certain. Much as I desire to spare your master's feelings, much as I am puzzled by this note which seems to prove him to be still alive, I shall consider it my duty to break in that door."

"Ah, Mr. Utterson, that's talking!" cried the butler.

"And now comes the second question," resumed Utterson: "Who is going to do it?"

"Why, you and me, sir," was the undaunted reply.

"That's very well said," returned the lawyer; "and whatever comes of it, I shall make it my business to see you are no loser."

"There is an axe in the theatre," continued Poole; "and you might take the kitchen poker for yourself."

The lawyer took that rude but weighty instrument into his hand, and balanced it. "Do you know, Poole," he said, looking up, "that you and I are about to place ourselves in a position of some peril **(danger)**?"

"You may say so, sir, indeed," returned the butler.

"It is well, then that we should be frank," said the other. "We both think more than we have said; let us make a clean breast. This masked figure that you saw, did you recognise it?"

"Well, sir, it went so quick, and the creature was so doubled up, that I could hardly swear to that," was the answer. "But if you mean, was it Mr. Hyde?—why, yes, I think it was! You see, it was much of the same bigness; and it had the same quick, light way with it; and then who else could have got in by the laboratory door? You have not forgot, sir, that at the time of the murder he had still the key with him? But that's not all. I don't know, Mr. Utterson, if you ever met this Mr. Hyde?"

"Yes," said the lawyer, "I once spoke with him."

"Then you must know as well as the rest of us that there was something queer **(odd)** about that gentleman—something that gave a man a turn—I don't know rightly how to say it, sir, beyond this: that you felt in your marrow kind of cold and thin."

"I own I felt something of what you describe," said Mr. Utterson.

"Quite so, sir," returned Poole. "Well, when that masked thing like a monkey jumped from among the chemicals and whipped into the cabinet, it went down my spine like ice. O, I know it's not evidence, Mr. Utterson; I'm book-learned enough for that; but a man has his feelings, and I give you my bible-word it was Mr. Hyde!"

"Ay, ay," said the lawyer. "My fears incline to the same point. Evil, I fear, founded—evil was sure to come—of that connection. Ay truly, I believe you; I believe poor Harry is killed; and I believe his murderer (for what purpose, God alone can tell) is still lurking in his victim's room. Well, let our name be vengeance **(revenge)**. Call Bradshaw."

The footman came at the summons, very white and nervous.

"Put yourself together, Bradshaw," said the lawyer. "This suspense, I know, is telling upon all of you; but it is now our intention to make an end of it. Poole, here, and I are going to force our way into the cabinet **(small room)**. If all is well, my shoulders are broad enough to bear the blame. Meanwhile, lest anything should really be amiss, or any malefactor seek to escape by the back, you and the boy must go round the corner with a pair of good sticks and take your post at the laboratory door. We give you ten minutes, to get to your stations."

As Bradshaw left, the lawyer looked at his watch. "And now, Poole, let us get to ours," he said; and taking the poker under his arm, led the way into the yard. The scud had banked over the moon, and it was now quite dark. The wind, which only broke in puffs and draughts into that deep well of building, tossed the light of the candle to and fro about their steps, until they came into the shelter of the theatre, where they sat down silently to wait. London hummed solemnly **(in a formal & dignified fashion)** all around; but nearer at hand, the stillness was only broken by the sounds of a footfall moving to and fro along the cabinet floor.

"So it will walk all day, sir," whispered Poole; "ay, and the better part of the night. Only when a new sample comes from the chemist, there's a bit of a break. Ah, it's an ill **(bad)** conscience **(a person's sense of right and wrong)** that's such an enemy to rest! Ah, sir, there's blood foully shed in every step of it! But hark again, a little closer—put your heart in your ears, Mr. Utterson, and tell me, is that the doctor's foot?"

The steps fell lightly and oddly, with a certain swing, for all they went so slowly; it was different indeed from the heavy creaking tread of Henry Jekyll. Utterson sighed. "Is there never anything else?" he asked.

Poole nodded. "Once," he said. "Once I heard it weeping!"

"Weeping? how that?" said the lawyer, conscious of a sudden chill of horror.

"Weeping like a woman or a lost soul," said the butler. "I came away with that upon my heart, that I could have wept too."

But now the ten minutes drew to an end.

> **Simple explanation:** After not believing Poole, Utterson changes his mind and believes that Jekyll has been murdered. Poole talks about how he hears Hyde constantly pacing up and down, and, at times, weeping.
>
> **Analysis:** One of the ways that Stevenson creates a sense of horror is not only through his powerful use of visual imagery – the locked doors, the apparatus in the laboratory, the foggy London streets – but through his use of sound. The "husky" voice of Hyde, the "audible shattering" of Carew's bones, and the sound of the footsteps here, which fall "lightly and oddly, with a certain swing". It is unmistakably the loping, almost merry steps of Hyde, who has taken over Jekyll almost entirely. However, we realise, on second reading, that there is something of Jekyll left: the self-pitying part. He is heard "weeping like a woman or a lost soul". Thus, we see how the novel grows in richness the more you read it.

Discussion Point
Why and how does Stevenson use sound in this novel?

Poole disinterred **(got out)** the axe from under a stack of packing straw; the candle was set upon the nearest table to light them to the attack; and they drew near with bated **(lessened/reduced)** breath to where that patient foot was still going up and down, up and down, in the quiet of the night. "Jekyll," cried Utterson, with a loud voice, "I demand to see you." He paused a moment, but there came no reply. "I give you fair warning, our suspicions are aroused, and I must and shall see you," he resumed; "if not by fair means, then by foul—if not of your consent, then by brute force!"

"Utterson," said the voice, "for God's sake, have mercy!"

"Ah, that's not Jekyll's voice—it's Hyde's!" cried Utterson. "Down with the door, Poole!"

Poole swung the axe over his shoulder; the blow shook the building, and the red baize door leaped against the lock and hinges. A dismal screech, as of mere animal terror, rang from the cabinet. Up went the axe again, and again the panels crashed and the frame bounded; four times the blow fell; but the wood was tough and the fittings were of excellent workmanship; and it was not until the fifth, that the lock burst and the wreck of the door fell inwards on the carpet.

The besiegers **(people who besiege or attack a particular place)**, appalled **(dismayed/horrified)** by their own riot **(bad behaviour)** and the stillness that had succeeded **(followed)**, stood back a little and peered in. There lay the cabinet before their eyes in the quiet lamplight, a good fire glowing and chattering on the hearth, the kettle singing its thin strain, a drawer or two open, papers neatly set forth on the business table, and nearer the fire, the things laid out for tea; the quietest room, you would have said, and, but for the glazed presses full of chemicals, the most commonplace that night in London.

Right in the middle there lay the body of a man sorely contorted **(twisted or bent out of shape)** and still twitching. They drew near on tiptoe, turned it on its back and beheld the face of Edward Hyde. He was dressed in clothes far too large for him, clothes of the doctor's bigness; the cords of his face still moved with a semblance **(trace)** of life, but life was quite gone: and by the crushed phial in the hand and the strong smell of kernels **(sweet-smelling nuts – the deadly poison cyanide gives off this smell)** that hung upon the air, Utterson knew that he was looking on the body of a self-destroyer **(suicide victim)**.

"We have come too late," he said sternly, "whether to save or punish. Hyde is gone to his account; and it only remains for us to find the body of your master."

> **Simple explanation:** Poole breaks down the door with an axe and finds a quiet room, which looks normal, except for the fact that Hyde is lying dead in Jekyll's larger clothes.
> **Analysis:** The brilliance of the novel is that it repays re-reading. On the first reading, the mystery deepens because we think that Hyde has murdered Jekyll and then possibly killed himself. On second reading, we realise that there has indeed been a terrible battle between Jekyll and Hyde, which Jekyll has won because he has managed to kill Hyde – we know from Jekyll's subsequent narrative that Hyde has desperately wanted to life, that indeed he is the embodiment of the survival of the fittest, the will to power. But there is a sense that Hyde has won because he has totally hijacked the body of Jekyll.
> ### Discussion point
> Why does the novel grow in meaning on a second reading?

The far greater proportion **(part)** of the building was occupied by the theatre, which filled almost the whole ground storey and was lighted from above, and by the cabinet, which formed an upper story at one end and looked upon the court. A corridor joined the theatre to the door on the by-street; and with this the cabinet communicated separately by a second flight of stairs. There were besides a few dark closets and a spacious cellar. All these they now thoroughly examined. Each closet **(cupboard)** needed but a glance, for all were empty, and all, by the dust that fell from their doors, had stood long unopened. The cellar, indeed, was filled with crazy lumber **(wooden logs cut for a fire)**, mostly dating from the times of the surgeon who was Jekyll's predecessor **(the person who came before)**; but even as they opened the door they were advertised of the uselessness of further search, by the fall of a perfect mat of cobweb which had for years sealed up the entrance. Nowhere was there any trace of Henry Jekyll dead or alive.

Poole stamped on the flags **(flagstones/floor)** of the corridor. "He must be buried here," he said, hearkening to the sound.

"Or he may have fled," said Utterson, and he turned to examine the door in the by-street. It was locked; and lying near by on the flags, they found the key, already stained with rust.

"This does not look like use," observed the lawyer.

"Use!" echoed Poole. "Do you not see, sir, it is broken? much as if a man had stamped on it."

"Ay," continued Utterson, "and the fractures, too, are rusty." The two men looked at each other with a scare. "This is beyond me, Poole," said the lawyer. "Let us go back to the cabinet."

They mounted the stair in silence, and still with an occasional awestruck **(amazed)** glance at the dead body, proceeded more thoroughly to examine the contents of the cabinet. At one table, there were traces of chemical work, various measured heaps of some white salt being laid on glass saucers, as though for an experiment in which the unhappy man had been prevented.

"That is the same drug that I was always bringing him," said Poole; and even as he spoke, the kettle with a startling noise boiled over.

This brought them to the fireside, where the easy-chair was drawn cosily up, and the tea things stood ready to the sitter's elbow, the very sugar in the cup. There were several books on a shelf; one lay beside the tea things open, and Utterson was amazed to find it a copy of a pious **(holy)** work, for which Jekyll had several times expressed a great esteem **(respect and admiration)**, annotated **(add notes to a text or diagram giving explanation or comment)**, in his own hand with startling **(surprising)** blasphemies **(unholy talk/swear words)**.

> **Simple explanation:** They can't find Jekyll anywhere.
> **Analysis:** Stevenson's imagination is chilling here. Perhaps more spooky than the discovery of Hyde's dead body in the over-sized clothes of Jekyll is the description of the dead man's things: the noise of the kettle boiling over, the sugar waiting for the cup of tea, and the "pious" book scrawled with blasphemies. On second reading, we realise that Jekyll had been trying to make himself comfortable and was attempting to guide himself in a religious and pious direction when suddenly he was overwhelmed by Hyde and realised that he had to kill himself. The blasphemies indicate Hyde's childish nature, his rebellion against the strictures of conventional Christianity, his wish to step outside normal moral boundaries into the realm of unfettered desire, unchained emotions.
>
> ### Discussion Point
> Why is the description of the dead man's thing so effective here?

Next, in the course of their review of the chamber, the searchers came to the cheval-glass **(a tall mirror fitted at its middle to an upright frame so that it can be tilted)**, into whose depths they looked with an involuntary **(done against someone's will)** horror. But it was so turned as to show them nothing but the rosy glow playing on the roof, the fire sparkling in a hundred repetitions along the glazed front of the presses, and their own pale and fearful countenances **(faces)** stooping to look in.

"This glass has seen some strange things, sir," whispered Poole.

"And surely none stranger than itself," echoed the lawyer in the same tones. "For what did Jekyll"—he caught himself up at the word with a start, and then conquering the weakness—"what could Jekyll want with it?" he said.

"You may say that!" said Poole.

Next they turned to the business table. On the desk, among the neat array of papers, a large envelope was uppermost, and bore, in the doctor's hand, the name of Mr. Utterson. The lawyer unsealed it, and several enclosures fell to the floor. The first was a will, drawn in the same eccentric terms as the one which he had returned six months before, to serve as a testament in case of death and as a deed of gift in case of disappearance; but in place of the name of Edward Hyde, the lawyer, with indescribable **(unable to be described/incredible)** amazement read the name of Gabriel John Utterson. He looked at Poole, and then back at the paper, and last of all at the dead malefactor **(person who does evil)** stretched upon the carpet.

"My head goes round," he said. "He has been all these days in possession; he had no cause to like me; he must have raged to see himself displaced **(got rid of/erased from the will)**; and he has not destroyed this document."

He caught up the next paper; it was a brief note in the doctor's hand and dated at the top. "O Poole!" the lawyer cried, "he was alive and here this day. He cannot have been disposed of **(got rid of)** in so short a space; he must be still alive, he must have fled! And then, why fled? and how? and in that case, can we venture **(guess/dare)** to declare this suicide? O, we must be careful. I foresee **(see in the future)** that we may yet involve your master in some dire catastrophe **(disaster)**."

"Why don't you read it, sir?" asked Poole.

"Because I fear," replied the lawyer solemnly. "God grant I have no cause for it!" And with that he brought the paper to his eyes and read as follows:

"My dear Utterson,—When this shall fall into your hands, I shall have disappeared, under what circumstances I have not the penetration **(insight/cleverness)** to foresee, but my instinct and all the circumstances of my nameless situation tell me that the end is sure and must be early. Go then, and first read the narrative which Lanyon warned me he was to place in your hands; and if you care to hear more, turn to the confession of

"Your unworthy and unhappy friend,

"HENRY JEKYLL."

"There was a third enclosure?" asked Utterson.

"Here, sir," said Poole, and gave into his hands a considerable packet sealed in several places.

The lawyer put it in his pocket. "I would say nothing of this paper. If your master has fled or is dead, we may at least save his credit. It is now ten; I must go home and read these documents in quiet; but I shall be back before midnight, when we shall send for the police."

They went out, locking the door of the theatre behind them; and Utterson, once more leaving the servants gathered about the fire in the hall, trudged back to his office to read the two narratives in which this mystery was now to be explained.

Summary -- fill in the blanks (answers are at the back)

One evening Utterson is visited by Poole who tells Utterson that he thinks there has been some "--- ---" regarding Dr Jekyll. Utterson goes with Poole to Jekyll's house and finds all the servants cowering in the ----. Poole and Utterson go quietly through the laboratory to the "cabinet" or small room where they knock. A ---- voice says that he cannot see anyone. Poole then tells him that he thinks Jekyll was "---- - --- ----" eight days before, and that the strange voice has spent much time demanding drugs, the orders for which are written on pieces of paper and pushed under the door. Utterson reads one of these notes, and thinks that Jekyll is - --. Poole then tells him that he has caught a glimpse of the "thing" and saw it was much --- than Jekyll. Utterson decides to break down the door and send two servants around the back to stop Hyde escaping. Utterson says to the creature in the laboratory that he will break down the door if Jekyll doesn't open it, to which a strange voice says "---- ---- !". When they break down the door, they find Hyde is ---- in Jekyll's large clothes and has just ---- himself by drinking poison. They find no sign of ----. On the business table, they find a will the same as the one that Jekyll wrote for Hyde except that ------ name has replaced Hyde's, and they find a note that asks Utterson to read ----- account and another letter, which is the "------" of Henry Jekyll.

Comprehension questions

Why does Poole ask for help? What is his mood?
What is the weather like?
Why are all the servants afraid?
What has Poole had to do for his master during these past few weeks?
What do Jekyll's notes to the chemist reveal about his state of mind?
What has Jekyll being doing these past few weeks? Why does Poole call him "it"?
Why and how do they break down the door?
When they break into the "cabinet" what do they find?
What evidence is there that Hyde has killed himself?
What evidence is there that Jekyll has been there very recently?

Analytical questions

How and why does Stevenson use the "pathetic fallacy" in this chapter?
How does Stevenson make this chapter so dramatic and yet manages to prolong the mystery?

Evaluative questions

How successful is Stevenson is creating an atmosphere of horror?

Creative response tasks

Write a story or poem called "The Disappearance" in which you describe the room of someone who has disappeared.

Write Poole's diary entry for this chapter, and other chapters where relevant. In the diary, get Poole to describe his relationship with Jekyll and his thoughts about his master.

You can watch a YouTube video I made about this section here:
http://www.youtube.com/watch?v=HQMt54K_vgw

POSSIBLE ANSWERS in brief & bold

Comprehension questions

Why does Poole ask for help? What is his mood? **He asks for help from Utterson because he suspects that there has been "foul play": he is very worried for the safety of his master.**
What is the weather like? **It is a clear night with a full moon and "diaphanous" or transparent clouds. It is very windy.**
Why are all the servants afraid? **They think something terrible has happened to Dr Jekyll and don't know what to do.**
What has Poole had to do for his master during these past few weeks? **He has had to take notes to the chemist which demand drugs which are "pure".**

What do Jekyll's notes to the chemist reveal about his state of mind? **He shows that he is very agitated because he has scribbled on the notes that he must have pure drugs using the phrase "for God's sake" in wild handwriting.**

What has Jekyll being doing these past few weeks? Why does Poole call him "it"? **Jekyll has shut himself away and won't see anyone, even his servants. Poole believes that Jekyll has been "made away with" – either kidnapped or killed – and that Hyde, who he calls "it", is living there.**

Why and how do they break down the door? **They believe Jekyll has been murdered. They break down the door with an axe.**

When they break into the "cabinet" what do they find? **They find a very "normal" or commonplace set up: a kettle on the oven, a fire in the grate, and papers on a business desk. The only strange thing initially they see are the chemicals in their "presses". Then they discover the dead body of Hyde in the larger clothes of Jekyll, twitching in the last throes of life.**

What evidence is there that Hyde has killed himself? **There is a "crush phial" in his hand which has contained poison.**

What evidence is there that Jekyll has been there very recently? **They find a letter written by him that day.**

Analytical questions

How and why does Stevenson use the "pathetic fallacy" in this chapter? **The wind is very "wild" and strong and it is a clear night with a full moon: the wind possibly could suggest the violence of Edward Hyde.**

How does Stevenson make this chapter so dramatic and yet manages to prolong the mystery? **The chapter is punctuated by a number of gripping incidents. First, Poole's appearance at Utterson's door is dramatic because it is so unusual for the butler to leave Jekyll's house without his master's permission. The story he tells is wild and incomplete: he says that there has been "foul play" but we don't know exactly what "foul play" there has been. The reader begins to wonder whether Jekyll has been murdered or kidnapped by Hyde? Poole's mood adds to the tension: he is clearly in a state of near panic, which is unusual for this butler who is normally so calm. Second, Stevenson's descriptions of the places and the weather add to the dramatic tension because he describes a clear windy night with a full moon: this setting suggests that something supernatural is afoot. Other descriptions of the house, the laboratory and Jekyll's quiet room with the dead body of Hyde in it are very evocative. They provoke many questions which don't have answers: why is Hyde dead and not Jekyll? Stevenson's description of the servants huddled in the doorway adds to the sense of crisis and bemusement: why are they so frightened?**

Why don't they know what is going on? Then, Stevenson piles on the mystery when we listen to Poole's full explanation: he believes that Jekyll has been murdered by Hyde, but we wonder how the notes to the chemist, written in Jekyll's hand, have been written. Further tension is created by the strange, strangulated sound of Jekyll's voice pleading with Utterson to leave him alone. Stevenson's description of the breaking down of the door is incredibly powerful: he describes the violence with which Poole attacks the door in vivid imagery, deploying dynamic verbs to evoke a sense of violence. The door "leapt" off its hinges: this personification of the door adds to the sense of drama; even the door is in shock! Then the ensuing description of the quiet laboratory and the small body of Hyde twitching in the big clothes of Jekyll provide a nice contrast to the violence of the attack on the door. There is something horrifying and pitiable about the description of Hyde's body twitching in the huge clothes of Jekyll. It is also deeply mysterious: how and why has this happened? The mystery is furthered when we learn about the will being made out to Utterson and the fact that Jekyll himself is nowhere to be seen.

Evaluative questions

How successful is Stevenson is creating an atmosphere of horror? **The horror is generated not by description of lots of "blood and gore" but by the fact that we begin to realise that something truly terrifying has happened to both Hyde and Jekyll. Hyde who had seemed so indestructible is now lying dead in the huge clothes of Jekyll. Further horror is generated by the servants' reactions to Hyde and Jekyll: Poole, normally so calm, is in a state of total panic, while the other servants seemed to have completely imploded, huddling as they do in the doorway. Stevenson is successful in creating a sense of horror in the way he develops the mystery and forces us to think so hard about what has happened to Jekyll. The horror comes from us thinking about how this once respected man, who was so in command of his life, has been brought down so low: demanding drugs all the time and falling victim to the machinations of Hyde.**

9 Dr Lanyon's narrative

YouTube reading:
http://www.youtube.com/watch?v=iciliuhdvkA

Thematic questions

Think carefully about the topic of "transformation". Draw a spider-diagram of all the films/books/times where there is an interesting transformation, e.g. men turning into werewolves, people dressing up, changes in mood and personality. Why do you think "transformation" is such a major theme in this book and other texts?

Think about the times when you have had your beliefs changed or challenged. Why and how did it happen? Think about people like religious people/scientists who change their opinions, e.g. lose their faith/gain faith.

On the ninth of January, now four days ago, I received by the evening delivery a registered envelope, addressed in the hand of my colleague and old school companion, Henry Jekyll. I was a good deal surprised by this; for we were by no means in the habit of correspondence **(writing to each other)**; I had seen the man, dined with him, indeed, the night before; and I could imagine nothing in our intercourse **(conversation)** that should justify formality (behaving according to strict rules) of registration. The contents increased my wonder; for this is how the letter ran:

"10th December, 18—.

"Dear Lanyon,—You are one of my oldest friends; and although we may have differed at times on scientific questions, I cannot remember, at least on my side, any break in our affection **(friendship)**. There was never a day when, if you had said to me, `Jekyll, my life, my honour, my reason, depend upon you,' I would not have sacrificed my left hand to help you. Lanyon my life, my honour, my reason, are all at your mercy; if you fail me to-night, I am lost. You might suppose, after this preface, that I am going to ask you for something dishonourable to grant. Judge for yourself.

"I want you to postpone **(put off)** all other engagements **(meetings)** for to-night—ay, even if you were summoned to the bedside of an emperor; to take a cab, unless your carriage should be actually at the door; and with this letter in your hand for consultation, to drive straight to my house. Poole, my butler, has his orders; you will find him waiting your arrival with a locksmith. The door of my cabinet is then to be forced: and you are to go in alone; to open the glazed press (letter E) on the left hand, breaking the lock if it be shut; and to draw out, with all its contents as they stand, the fourth drawer from the top or (which is the same thing) the third from the bottom. In my extreme distress of mind, I have a morbid **(unhealthy)** fear of misdirecting **(giving you the wrong directions)** you; but even if I am in error, you may know the right drawer by its contents: some powders, a phial **(test-tube)** and a paper book. This drawer I beg of you to carry back with you to Cavendish Square exactly as it stands.

"That is the first part of the service: now for the second. You should be back, if you set out at once on the receipt of this, long before midnight; but I will leave you that amount of margin, not only in the fear of one of those obstacles **(things blocking the way)** that can neither be prevented nor foreseen, but because an hour when your servants are in bed is to be preferred for what will then remain to do. At midnight, then, I have to ask you to be alone in your consulting room, to admit with your own hand into the house a man who will present himself in my name, and to place in his hands the drawer that you will have brought with you from my cabinet. Then you will have played your part and earned my gratitude completely. Five minutes afterwards, if you insist upon an explanation, you will have understood that these arrangements are of capital **(very great)** importance; and that by the neglect of one of them, fantastic as they must appear, you might have charged your conscience **(your sense of right and wrong)** with my death or the shipwreck of my reason.

Simple explanation: Dr Lanyon is telling the story by writing to Utterson. This is the letter Utterson was told not to read until Jekyll had died or disappeared. So this is Lanyon's story. One day, Lanyon receives a letter from Jekyll asking him to get a drawer full of drugs from his room. He should bring them back to his house and wait to meet someone who will pick them up at midnight.

Analysis: Stevenson now backtracks and provides us with Lanyon's story. The writer has not revealed the solution to the mystery, although we have had some strong clues. Stevenson plays around with time in the novel here to create a sense of tragic irony: the reader is aware that everything is going to end with Jekyll's disappearance and possible death, but we don't know how. Here, we are reading Jekyll's urgent orders to Lanyon, with a promise to reveal all if he wants to hear it. Jekyll has to rely upon a fellow scientist in order to prop up the "shipwreck of his reason".

Discussion Point

Why does Stevenson put Lanyon's narrative at this point, when he could have placed it earlier on in the novel?

"Confident as I am that you will not trifle (play) with this appeal **(plea/request/order)**, my heart sinks and my hand trembles at the bare thought of such a possibility. Think of me at this hour, in a strange place, labouring **(working/thinking)** under a blackness of distress that no fancy **(imagination)** can exaggerate, and yet well aware that, if you will but punctually serve me, my troubles will roll away like a story that is told. Serve me, my dear Lanyon and save

"Your friend,

"H.J.

"P.S.—I had already sealed this up when a fresh terror struck upon my soul. It is possible that the post-office may fail me, and this letter not come into your hands until to-morrow morning. In that case, dear Lanyon, do my errand **(task)** when it shall be most convenient for you in the course of the day; and once more expect my messenger at midnight. It may then already be too late; and if that night passes without event, you will know that you have seen the last of Henry Jekyll."

Upon the reading of this letter, I made sure my colleague was insane; but till that was proved beyond the possibility of doubt, I felt bound to do as he requested. The less I understood of this farrago, the less I was in a position to judge of its importance; and an appeal so worded could not be set aside without a grave responsibility. I rose accordingly from table, got into a hansom, and drove straight to Jekyll's house. The butler was awaiting my arrival; he had received by the same post as mine a registered letter of instruction, and had sent at once for a locksmith and a carpenter. The tradesmen came while we were yet speaking; and we moved in a body to old Dr. Denman's surgical theatre, from which (as you are doubtless aware) Jekyll's private cabinet is most conveniently entered. The door was very strong, the lock excellent; the carpenter avowed **(said)** he would have great trouble and have to do much damage, if force were to be used; and the locksmith was near despair. But this last was a handy **(good with his hands)** fellow, and after two hour's work, the door stood open. The press marked E was unlocked; and I took out the drawer, had it filled up with straw and tied in a sheet, and returned with it to Cavendish Square.

Here I proceeded to examine its contents. The powders were neatly enough made up, but not with the nicety of the dispensing chemist; so that it was plain **(clear)** they were of Jekyll's private manufacture **(made them himself)**: and when I opened one of the wrappers I found what seemed to me a simple crystalline salt of a white colour. The phial **(test-tube)**, to which I next turned my attention, might have been about half full of a blood-red liquor, which was highly pungent **(very strong smelling)** to the sense of smell and seemed to me to contain phosphorus **(glowing, poisonous chemical)** and some volatile ether **(could easily catch fire)**. At the other ingredients I could make no guess. The book was an ordinary version book and contained little but a series of dates. These covered a period of many years, but I observed that the entries ceased nearly a year ago and quite abruptly **(very suddenly)**. Here and there a brief remark was appended **(added)** to a date, usually no more than a single word: "double" occurring perhaps six times in a total of several hundred entries; and once very early in the list and followed by several marks of exclamation, "total failure!!!" All this, though it whetted **(caused)** my curiosity, told me little that was definite. Here were a phial of some salt, and the record of a series of experiments that had led (like too many of Jekyll's investigations) to no end of practical usefulness. How could the presence of these articles in my house affect either the honour, the sanity, or the life of my flighty **(silly, uncontrolled)** colleague? If his messenger could go to one place, why could he not go to another? And even granting some impediment **(problem/obstacle)**, why was this gentleman to be received by me in secret? The more I reflected the more convinced I grew that I was dealing with a case of cerebral **(brain)** disease; and though I dismissed my servants to bed, I loaded an old revolver, that I might be found in some posture **(bodily shape)** of self-defence.

Twelve o'clock had scarce rung out over London, ere the knocker sounded very gently on the door. I went myself at the summons, and found a small man crouching against the pillars of the portico.

"Are you come from Dr. Jekyll?" I asked.

He told me "yes" by a constrained **(forced)** gesture; and when I had bidden **(asked)** him enter, he did not obey me without a searching backward glance into the darkness of the square. There was a policeman not far off, advancing with his bull's eye open; and at the sight, I thought my visitor started and made greater haste **(speed/hurry)**.

These particulars struck me, I confess, disagreeably **(unpleasantly)**; and as I followed him into the bright light of the consulting room, I kept my hand ready on my weapon. Here, at last, I had a chance of clearly seeing him. I had never set eyes on him before, so much was certain. He was small, as I have said; I was struck besides with the shocking expression of his face, with his remarkable combination of great muscular activity and great apparent debility (physical weakness) of constitution **(bodily strength)**, and—last but not least—with the odd, subjective **(personal)** disturbance caused by his neighbourhood. This bore some resemblance to incipient (beginning to happen) rigour **(energy)**, and was accompanied by a marked sinking **(lessening)** of the pulse. At the time, I set it down to some idiosyncratic **(peculiar/individual)**, personal distaste, and merely wondered at the acuteness **(strength)** of the symptoms; but I have since had reason to believe the cause to lie much deeper in the nature of man, and to turn on some nobler hinge than the principle of hatred.

> **Simple explanation:** Lanyon meets Hyde at midnight and finds that his pulse slows down and that he feels uncomfortable around him.
> **Analysis:** Of all the people who meet Hyde, Lanyon has the most scientific reaction to him. Here we see him realising that his own pulse slows down in the presence of Hyde and that Hyde has a very real physical effect upon him. He reflects later on that the "distaste" he feels for Hyde has a "cause to life much deeper in the nature of man", in other words all men would have the same reaction to Hyde because of some atavistic, primal reason. Some critics such as Robert Mighall have argued that Stevenson is exploring the idea of Hyde being a "proto-type" man here, an evolutionary throw-back to how we used to be as a species, closer to being an ape than a man and that Stevenson drew upon the ideas of the scientist Francis Galton (Mighall, p. 152) for inspiration when describing Hyde. Galton used photographs to isolate certain physical traits that were indicative of certain elements of the human character, trying to argue that certain physical traits were more "primitive" than others.
> ### Discussion point
> To what extent do you think Hyde is "primitive"?

This person (who had thus, from the first moment of his entrance, struck in me what I can only describe as a disgustful curiosity) was dressed in a fashion that would have made an ordinary person laughable; his clothes, that is to say, although they were of rich and sober fabric **(material)**, were enormously too large for him in every measurement—the trousers hanging on his legs and rolled up to keep them from the ground, the waist of the coat below his haunches **(buttocks and thighs)**, and the collar sprawling wide upon his shoulders. Strange to relate, this ludicrous **(ridiculous/very silly)** accoutrement **(piece of clothing)** was far from moving me to laughter. Rather, as there was something abnormal and misbegotten **(badly made)** in the very essence of the creature that now faced me—something seizing, surprising and revolting—this fresh disparity **(great difference)** seemed but to fit in with and to reinforce it; so that to my interest in the man's nature and character, there was added a curiosity as to his origin, his life, his fortune and status in the world.

These observations, though they have taken so great a space to be set down in, were yet the work of a few seconds. My visitor was, indeed, on fire with sombre **(gloomy/serious)** excitement.

"Have you got it?" he cried. "Have you got it?" And so lively was his impatience that he even laid his hand upon my arm and sought to shake me.

I put him back, conscious at his touch of a certain icy pang **(shiver)** along my blood. "Come, sir," said I. "You forget that I have not yet the pleasure of your acquaintance **(meeting you)**. Be seated, if you please." And I showed him an example, and sat down myself in my customary seat and with as fair an imitation **(copy)** of my ordinary manner to a patient, as the lateness of the hour, the nature of my preoccupations, and the horror I had of my visitor, would suffer me to muster.

"I beg your pardon, Dr. Lanyon," he replied civilly **(politely)** enough.

> **Simple explanation:** Lanyon is disturbed by how desperate Hyde is to take the drugs.
> **Analysis:** As with other encounters with Hyde, this passage pays re-reading after finishing the novel. Then one realises that Hyde has forgotten that he is Hyde and thinks he looks like Jekyll and assumes that Lanyon recognises him. He is then brought up short when Lanyon rather sniffily says he does not recognise him. We definitely hear Jekyll speaking when he begs Lanyon's pardon. However, we realise that the impatience which demands the potion is very much Hyde. In such a way, we realise that Hyde is not different from Jekyll at all: he is Jekyll. Notice Lanyon's reaction is one of having an "icy pang". As with other reactions to Hyde, there is a sense that the pang is one of recognition, that Hyde troubles something in the innermost soul of man.
> **Discussion Point**

What does Stevenson reveal about Hyde and Jekyll at this point in the novel?

"What you say is very well founded; and my impatience has shown its heels to my politeness. I come here at the instance of your colleague, Dr. Henry Jekyll, on a piece of business of some moment; and I understood..." He paused and put his hand to his throat, and I could see, in spite of his collected manner, that he was wrestling against the approaches of the hysteria **(madness)**—"I understood, a drawer..."

But here I took pity on my visitor's suspense, and some perhaps on my own growing curiosity.

"There it is, sir," said I, pointing to the drawer, where it lay on the floor behind a table and still covered with the sheet.

He sprang to it, and then paused, and laid his hand upon his heart: I could hear his teeth grate with the convulsive **(spasmodic/twitching)** action of his jaws; and his face was so ghastly to see that I grew alarmed both for his life and reason.

> **Simple explanation:** Hyde leaps towards the drugs.
> **Analysis:** Increasingly with re-reading, we come to realise that Hyde and Jekyll are tussling with each other when he is Hyde -- and when he is Jekyll. Here, the urgency with which Hyde springs to the potion is Jekyll's urgency to return to his civilised exterior, to get his emotions under control, to suppress the rage and desire within him. It is therefore ironic that Lanyon feels alarmed for his life and reason: these are the very things he is trying to reclaim.
> **Discussion Point**
> Why his thirst for the potion so disturbing?

"Compose yourself," said I.

He turned a dreadful smile to me, and as if with the decision of despair, plucked away the sheet. At sight of the contents, he uttered one loud sob of such immense relief that I sat petrified **(terrified)**. And the next moment, in a voice that was already fairly well under control, "Have you a graduated glass **(piece of laboratory equipment used to measure the volume of a liquid)**?" he asked.

I rose from my place with something of an effort and gave him what he asked.

He thanked me with a smiling nod, measured out a few minims **(drops)** of the red tincture and added one of the powders. The mixture, which was at first of a reddish hue **(colour)**, began, in proportion as the crystals melted, to brighten in colour, to effervesce **(give off bubbles)** audibly **(could be heard)**, and to throw off small fumes of vapour. Suddenly and at the same moment, the ebullition **(bubbling liquid)** ceased and the compound changed to a dark purple, which faded again more slowly to a watery green.

> **Simple explanation:** Hyde makes the potion which bubbles, changes colour and smokes before Lanyon.
> **Analysis:** Stevenson virtually invented the stereotype of the obsessive scientist with his smoking potions and fumes of colour. This is an incredibly "cinematic" scene and has been obviously imitated countless times on film. It was this kind of visually compelling scene that Stevenson excelled in writing: his descriptions have been much copied but never bettered. It must be remembered that the power of this description overwhelmed his audience: they'd never read anything like this before. Even in *Frankenstein*, Mary Shelley had avoided theatrical descriptions of the creation of the monster.
> ### Discussion Point
> Why are Stevenson's descriptions of Jekyll's potions so effective?

My visitor, who had watched these metamorphoses **(magical change)** with a keen eye, smiled, set down the glass upon the table, and then turned and looked upon me with an air of scrutiny **(looking carefully at something)**.

"And now," said he, "to settle what remains. Will you be wise? will you be guided? will you suffer me to take this glass in my hand and to go forth from your house without further parley **(talking)**? or has the greed of curiosity too much command of you? Think before you answer, for it shall be done as you decide. As you decide, you shall be left as you were before, and neither richer nor wiser, unless the sense of service rendered to a man in mortal **(deadly)** distress may be counted as a kind of riches of the soul.

> **Simple explanation:** In fancy language, Hyde asks Lanyon whether he is "greedy" enough – i.e. so desperate to know the truth -- to watch him take the potion.
> **Analysis:** The more florid style of speaking here is very much the style of speech of Jekyll. Stevenson regretted doing this, feeling that it was a stylistic mistake. However, one could see it as effective because it makes clear that Hyde and Jekyll are not split personalities at all, but one and the

same person, and that the naming of himself as Hyde enables Jekyll to play a 'con trick' not only on himself but also the reader, hiding the fact that everything that Hyde does is secretly wished for by Jekyll. Notice how that Jekyll realises that Lanyon is just like him, that the "greed of curiosity too much command" of him.

Discussion Point

Why is Lanyon like Jekyll? Do you think that Stevenson was wise to give Hyde these florid speech patterns which are more like Jekyll?

Or, if you shall so prefer to choose, a new province **(world)** of knowledge and new avenues to fame and power shall be laid open to you, here, in this room, upon the instant; and your sight shall be blasted by a prodigy **(amazing thing)** to stagger **(amaze)** the unbelief of Satan **(the devil)**."

"Sir," said I, affecting **(pretending)** a coolness **(calm)** that I was far from truly possessing, "you speak enigmas, and you will perhaps not wonder that I hear you with no very strong impression of belief. But I have gone too far in the way of inexplicable **(unable to be explained)** services to pause before I see the end."

"It is well," replied my visitor. "Lanyon, you remember your vows: what follows is under the seal of our profession **(this was the Hippocratic oath which doctors must swear to obey: they must not speak about a patient's circumstances in public. In Stevenson's day, it also referred to doctors always supporting each other)** . And now, you who have so long been bound to the most narrow and material views, you who have denied the virtue of transcendental **(spiritual/mystical/magical)** medicine, you who have derided **(mocked/made fun of)** your superiors **(people who are better than you)** —behold!"

> **Simple explanation:** Hyde reminds Lanyon that he must never speak about what he sees because of the promises he made as a doctor: the Hippocratic Oath. He says that Lanyon should watch someone better than him take the drug i.e. Jekyll/Hyde says he is better than Lanyon.
> **Analysis:** Notice how Hyde talks to Lanyon about "our profession": here we see Jekyll's mask slipping because it is Jekyll not Hyde who is a doctor. The possessive pronoun "our" indicates that the "Hyde" mask is dropping in Jekyll's use of language.

He put the glass to his lips and drank at one gulp. A cry followed; he reeled, staggered, clutched at the table and held on, staring with injected eyes, gasping with open mouth; and as I looked there came, I thought, a change—he seemed to swell—his face became suddenly black and the features seemed to melt and alter—and the next moment, I had sprung to my feet and leaped back against the wall, my arms raised to shield me from that prodigy, my mind submerged **(covered)** in terror.

"O God!" I screamed, and "O God!" again and again; for there before my eyes—pale and shaken, and half fainting, and groping before him with his hands, like a man restored from death—there stood Henry Jekyll!

What he told me in the next hour, I cannot bring my mind to set on paper. I saw what I saw, I heard what I heard, and my soul sickened at it; and yet now when that sight has faded from my eyes, I ask myself if I believe it, and I cannot answer. My life is shaken to its roots; sleep has left me; the deadliest terror sits by me at all hours of the day and night; and I feel that my days are numbered, and that I must die; and yet I shall die incredulous **(unbelieving)**. As for the moral turpitude **(evil/wickedness)** that man unveiled **(shown)** to me, even with tears of penitence **(regret/being sorry for what you have done)**, I can not, even in memory, dwell on it without a start of horror.

> **Simple explanation:** Hyde takes the potion and changes into Jekyll before Lanyon, who has decided to watch.
> **Analysis:** Here, finally, Jekyll reveals himself as Hyde. His speech before he transforms into Jekyll is important. He describes his medicine as "transcendental medicine", meaning it is a kind of medicine which is superior both morally and spiritually to the "narrow and material" medicine which Lanyon subscribes to. Here, we begin to get a glimpse that there is a wider purpose to Jekyll's medicine than thrill-seeking. Lanyon is terrified because what he sees is his own "moral turpitude": ultimately the horror for him is the revelation that he too would have done exactly the same thing as Jekyll if given the chance. The revelation and what he has witnessed means that he can't sleep, that he dwells upon the transformation day and night. He has seen what human kind truly is – and he can't bear the force of this knowledge.
> ### Discussion Point
> How does Stevenson make the transformation such an exciting and climatic moment in the novel?

I will say but one thing, Utterson, and that (if you can bring your mind to credit **(believe)** it) will be more than enough. The creature who crept into my house that night was, on Jekyll's own confession, known by the name of Hyde and hunted for in every corner of the land as the murderer of Carew.

HASTIE LANYON

Summary -- fill in the blanks (answers are at the back)

Dr Lanyon talks about how he received a letter from Jekyll telling him to take a specific ---- from his laboratory and return to his house, where a man using Jekyll's name will come and collect the ----. Lanyon does as he was told, and meets at ---- a nasty little man at his door who comes into the laboratory and says that either Lanyon can ---- him take the drug, or not. If he does, he will see something that will "stagger the unbelief of ----". Lanyon then watches Hyde take the drug and turn into ----. He realises that Jekyll is ---- and that he ---- Carew. "The ----- ----" now afflicts him day and night.

Comprehension questions
What does Jekyll's letter to Lanyon order him to do?
What is Lanyon's reaction to Jekyll's letter and the contents of Jekyll's drawer?
What does Lanyon think of Hyde?
Why does Hyde warn Lanyon about if he watches him taking the potion?
What happens to Hyde and why is Lanyon so shocked? Why does the sight of Hyde's transformation cause his death?

Analytical questions
Why is this chapter written in the first person with Lanyon narrating?
How does Stevenson create a sense of drama when Hyde turns into Jekyll? How and why have many writers and film-makers imitated and borrowed from this scene?

Evaluative questions
We learn the answer to the mystery in this chapter. Do you think it is a good solution?

Creative response tasks
Write a story or poem called "The Transformation".

Write Utterson's diary in response to reading this account, discussing his feelings when he learns that Hyde is Jekyll. Is he as shocked as Lanyon?

POSSIBLE ANSWERS in brief & bold

Comprehension questions

What does Jekyll's letter to Lanyon order him to do? **He orders Lanyon to go to his room, or "cabinet", and collect some drugs from a specific drawer, and then return to his house where a man at midnight will collect the drugs for Jekyll.**

What is Lanyon's reaction to Jekyll's letter and the contents of Jekyll's drawer? **Lanyon thinks that Jekyll has probably lost his mind, that he has a "cerebral" or "brain" disease. He decides to arm himself with a revolver to defend himself. He assumes that Jekyll must have lost his mind because of some experiment that has gone wrong: Lanyon is not surprised by this because he has always been suspicious of Jekyll's scientific methods.**

What does Lanyon think of Hyde? **Lanyon finds Hyde unpleasant but also ridiculous because he is dressed in clothes that are far too big for him. He notices that Hyde has a physical effect upon him, making him feel revolted.**

Why does Hyde warn Lanyon about watching him take the potion? **Because what Lanyon will see will "stagger the unbelief of Satan", in other words even the Devil himself would be amazed to see what he is going to see.**

What happens to Hyde and why is Lanyon so shocked? Why does the sight of Hyde's transformation cause his death? **Hyde turns into Jekyll. Lanyon is shocked for two reasons. First, because the transformation proves that Jekyll is a good scientist: he had called what Jekyll did previously "unscientific balderdash". Second, his faith in human nature is shaken: how could someone as respectable as Jekyll change into someone as evil as Hyde?**

Analytical questions

Why is this chapter written in the first person with Lanyon narrating? **Stevenson uses a number of different styles of writing in the book. The first half of the book is largely written in the third person, and is mainly a description of Utterson's quest to help his friend, Jekyll, and discover what his problems really are. The third person narrative style suits the "detective" genre of the writing. However, by having Lanyon tell his story in his own words makes the story all the more believable and emotional. We, the reader, become Lanyon himself as he watches Hyde transform into Jekyll: the first person narration allows us to feel his shock and pain at seeing his friend turn from the monster Hyde into his friend Henry Jekyll.**

How does Stevenson create a sense of drama when Hyde turns into Jekyll? How and why have many writers and film-makers imitated and borrowed from this scene? **Stevenson uses a great deal of "visual imagery" at key points in the book. Certain important scenes** are described in so much detail that we can clearly visualise exactly what is happening. This is particularly the case with the transformation from Hyde to Jekyll.

> He put the glass to his lips and drank at one gulp. A cry followed; he reeled, staggered, clutched at the table and held on, staring with injected eyes, gasping with open mouth; and as I looked there came, I thought, a change—he seemed to swell—his face became suddenly black and the features seemed to melt and alter—and the next moment, I had sprung to my feet and leaped back against the wall, my arms raised to shield me from that prodigy, my mind submerged **(covered)** in terror.
> "O God!" I screamed, and "O God!" again and again; for there before my eyes—pale and shaken, and half fainting, and groping before him with his hands, like a man restored from death—there stood Henry Jekyll!

We see here how Stevenson uses some very powerful verbs to describe the way in which Hyde is affected by drinking the potion: he "reels", "staggers", "clutches", "stares", "gasps". The effect of these verbs is to give the prose a real sense of action: each verb generates a visual image which suggests the pain of Jekyll. We see Hyde "staggering" around like someone who is drunk and has lost his faculty to stand properly; the verb "gasp" suggests that he is suffocating. In the next part, the verbs acquire a psychedelic, magical quality, Hyde's face "melts" and "alters": this is very sinister and possibly horrific to see someone's face melt like wax. Lanyon's reaction adds to the terror: he screams out "O God!" because he has no other response than this. What he is seeing is almost beyond words to convey.

Evaluative questions

We learn the answer to the mystery in this chapter. Do you think it is a good solution? **Some critics believe that the genius of the book is the solution to the mystery, which is both unexpected but obvious. Even when the novel is re-read again and again, it is this solution which intrigues, teases and attracts the reader: this horror story becomes a study of the human condition because of this solution. If Hyde had been another person or a ghost or ghoul, it would have been an ordinary ghost story about an evil person or thing who is the "shadow" of a good man. However, by making Jekyll and Hyde one and the same person, we begin to examine ourselves: do we not too have a "Hyde" within us? What would we do if we could have a Hyde who could do whatever he/she wanted without ever being** caught? The novel thus moves from being a mystery story to a psychological fable which makes the reader ask questions of him or herself. Thus we could say the true horror of the story is that Stevenson has a point which is still true today: all of us have a "Hyde" within us. It comes as no surprise that the phrase a "Jekyll/Hyde character" has entered the language meaning a person who can suddenly switch from being very nice to committing evil.

10 Henry Jekyll's full statement of the case

YouTube reading:
http://www.youtube.com/watch?v=I6XShukmDEE
Thematic questions
If you knew you could "get away" with any crime you wanted, what crimes might you commit? What do you think other people would do in other circumstances?
Do you think human beings are both good and evil? Do you think they have two sides to their natures?
Are humans born good or evil, or do they learn to be that way?
Do humans have many different "personalities", more than two sides, depending upon the situations they are in?
Do you think that stopping people having what they want leads to them wanting it more?

I was born in the year 18— to a large fortune **(money)**, endowed **(given)** besides with excellent parts **(body and mind)**, inclined by nature to industry **(work)**, fond of the respect of the wise and good among my fellowmen, and thus, as might have been supposed, with every guarantee of an honourable **(good)** and distinguished **(successful)** future. And indeed the worst of my faults was a certain impatient gaiety **(happiness, it was also slang in Stevenson's time for men who chased after women)** of disposition **(character)**, such as has made the happiness of many, but such as I found it hard to reconcile **(restore friendly relations between)** with my imperious **(arrogant)** desire to carry my head high, and wear a more than commonly grave **(serious)** countenance **(face)** before the public. Hence it came about that I concealed my pleasures; and that when

wants to be seen as more important

150

(good and evil)

I reached years of reflection, and began to look round me and take stock of my progress and position in the world, I stood already *probably sexual* committed to a profound **(very great)** duplicity **(two-facedness, double-sided, hypocritical)** of me. Many a man would have even blazoned **(talked about proudly)** such irregularities **(bad behaviour)** as I was guilty of; but from the *drug taking gambling* high views that I had set before me, I regarded and hid them with an almost morbid **(deathly)** sense of shame.

Simple explanation: Jekyll grew up in a very rich family. As a young man he enjoyed doing things which were not respectable, and yet he wanted to appear respectable to the world. This led to him becoming two-faced, and having two sides to his nature: a side that presented a "nice" face to the world, and a side which was hidden from most people but enjoyed doing bad things.

Analysis: Stevenson here starts to delve into the psychology of Jekyll by making it clear that the roots of Jekyll's transformation into Hyde lie within his own character. He speaks of having as a young man a "certain impatient gaiety of disposition", in other words he is keen to seek pleasures quickly and without much thought. This is at odds with his desire to appear like a respectable man. This leads him to concealing his pleasures, thus committing him to a "profound duplicity of life" – which means being "two-faced". Even before he became Hyde his life was split into two: the pursuit of pleasure was associated with his secretive life, while the pursuit of respectability was associated with his public life. Thus we can see Stevenson revealing that Jekyll's life is full of opposites, which has pleasure and pain as its two main opposites: the pleasure of secrecy, the pain of respectability, the pleasure of sexual gratification, the pain of repression, the pleasure of violence, the pain of stifled anger. Jekyll is a deeply repressed man before he transforms himself into Hyde.

Discussion point

Why does Stevenson tell us that there was a "profound duplicity" to Jekyll's life before he became Hyde?

he is superior

It was thus rather the exacting **(making high demands)** nature of my aspirations **(hopes/ambitions)** than any particular degradation **(humiliation/shame/being brought down)** in my faults, that made me what I was, and, with even a deeper trench **(affect)** than in the majority **(most)** of men, severed

Francis Gilbert

(cut) in me those provinces **(areas)** of good and ill which divide and compound **(add to)** man's dual **(two-sided/two-faced)** nature **(way of being)**. In this case, I was driven to reflect deeply and inveterately **(for a long time)** on that hard law of life, which lies at the root of religion and is one of the most plentiful springs of distress. Though so profound **(deep, very great)** a double-dealer **(two-faced person)**, I was in no sense a hypocrite **(pretending to someone you are not)**; both sides of me were in dead earnest **(serious)**; I was no more myself when I laid **(put)** aside restraint **(self-control)** and plunged **(dived into)** in shame, than when I laboured **(worked)**, in the eye of day, at the furtherance **(development)** of knowledge or the relief of sorrow and suffering. And it chanced **(happened)** that the direction of my scientific studies, which led wholly towards the mystic **(magical/spiritual)** and the transcendental **(magical)**, reacted and shed a strong light on this consciousness (awareness) of the perennial **(continual)** war among my members **(the different aspects of my personality)**. With every day, and from both sides of my intelligence, the moral and the intellectual, I thus drew steadily nearer to that truth, by whose partial discovery I have been doomed to such a dreadful shipwreck: that man is not truly one, but truly two. I say two, because the state of my own knowledge does not pass beyond that point. Others will follow, others will outstrip me on the same lines; and I hazard **(take)** the guess that man will be ultimately known for a mere polity **(collection)** of multifarious **(many and different)**, incongruous **(badly matched)** and independent denizens **(people)**. I, for my part, from the nature of my life, advanced infallibly **(never making a mistake)** in one direction and in one direction only. It was on the moral side **(the side connected with deciding between good and evil)**, and in my own person, that I learned to recognise the thorough and primitive duality **(the fighting between two things)** of man; I saw that, of the two natures that contended in the field of my consciousness **(mind)**, even if I could rightly be said to be either, it was only because I was radically **(extremely)** both; and from an early date, even before the course of my scientific discoveries had begun to suggest the most naked possibility of such a miracle, I had learned to dwell with pleasure, as a beloved daydream, on the thought of the separation of these elements **(of good and evil)**.

Jeckyl is a hypocrite, trying to tell the truth but failing

at war with himself

his death

splitting apart human psyche

inability to see himself

Simple explanation: Jekyll decides to use his scientific knowledge to find a way of separating off the different sides of the human personality or soul: the good and the bad.

Analysis: The splitting of the two sides of man became a "beloved day-dream" because Jekyll was "radically both". It is interesting to note that he views the duality of man as being "primitive". Once again, we can see how the novel is influenced by the ideas of Darwin here: it was a perception of the time that all men were essentially "apes" at heart, when stripped of their civilised facades. What Jekyll doesn't realise is that this duality is created by a society which prizes "respectability" above all else, which demands that people appear to be pious and good, which has strict moral codes which suppress desire, and indeed label it as sinful.

Discussion point

What do we learn about the society Jekyll lives in here? Why does he have such a day-dream?

[handwritten: Jekyll could enjoy life]

[handwritten: Jekyll's view on life]

If each, I told myself, could be housed in separate identities, life would be relieved of all that was unbearable **(horrible)**; the unjust **(the bad man)** might go his way, delivered from the aspirations **(hopes)** and remorse **(guilt)** of his more upright **(honest)** twin; and the just could walk steadfastly and securely on his upward path, doing the good things in which he found his pleasure, and no longer exposed **(made visible)** to disgrace and penitence **(regret)** by the hands of this extraneous **(irrelevant)** evil. It was the curse of mankind that these incongruous **(ill-fitting)** faggots **(bits of material/earth)** were thus bound together—that in the agonised **(very unhappy)** womb of consciousness **(human mind)**, these polar twins should be continuously struggling. How, then were they dissociated **(separated)**?

[handwritten: bits of him dont fit, are bundled together]

I was so far in my reflections when, as I have said, a side light began to shine upon the subject from the laboratory table. I began to perceive more deeply than it has ever yet been stated, the trembling immateriality **(complete irrelevance requiring no further consideration)**, the mistlike transience **(lasting only for a short while)**, of this seemingly so solid body in which we walk attired **(clothed)**. Certain agents **(drugs)** I found to have the power to shake and pluck back that fleshly vestment, even as a wind might toss the curtains of a pavilion. For two good reasons, I will not enter deeply into this scientific branch of my confession. First, because I have been made to learn that the doom and burthen **(load)** of our life is bound for ever on man's shoulders,

[handwritten: the struggle of good and evil is part of life]

and when the attempt is made to cast it off, it but returns upon us with more unfamiliar and more awful pressure. Second, because, as my narrative will make, alas! too evident, my discoveries were incomplete. Enough then, that I not only recognised my natural body from the mere aura **(atmosphere)** and effulgence **(shining)** of certain of the powers that made up my spirit, but managed to compound **(put together)** a drug by which these powers should be dethroned **(beaten)** from their supremacy **(ruling position)**, and a second form **(way of living)** and countenance **(face)** substituted **(replaced)**, none the less natural to me because they were the expression, and bore the stamp of lower elements in my soul. *[handwritten: admitting Hyde is a natural part of him]*

I hesitated long before I put this theory to the test of practice. I knew well that I risked death; for any drug that so potently controlled and shook the very fortress **(armed castle)** of identity, might, by the least scruple **(little bit)** of an overdose or at the least inopportunity **(inconvenience)** in the moment of exhibition **(being shown)**, utterly blot out that immaterial tabernacle **(home)** which I looked to it to change. But the temptation of a discovery so singular **(unique)** and profound **(great)** at last overcame the suggestions of alarm. I had long since prepared my tincture **(potion)**; I purchased at once, from a firm of wholesale chemists, a large quantity of a particular salt **(chemical)** which I knew, from my experiments, to be the last ingredient required; and late one accursed night, I compounded the elements, watched them boil and smoke together in the glass, and when the ebullition had subsided, with a strong glow of courage, drank off the potion.

The most racking **(painful)** pangs succeeded: a grinding in the bones, deadly nausea, and a horror of the spirit that cannot be exceeded **(be in greater number)** at the hour of birth or death. Then these agonies **(tortures)** began swiftly to subside **(die down)**, and I came to myself as if out of a great sickness. There was something strange in my sensations, something indescribably **(cannot be described)** new and, from its very novelty **(newness)**, incredibly sweet. I felt younger, lighter, happier in body; within I was conscious **(aware)** of a heady recklessness **(giving little thought to danger)**, a current of disordered **(chaotic)** sensual **(sexual, of the senses)** images running like a millrace **(the channel carrying the swift current of water that drives a mill wheel)** in my fancy **(imagination)**, a solution **(disappearance/dissolving)** of the bonds **(ties)** of obligation **(duty)**, an unknown but not an innocent freedom of the soul. I knew myself, at the first breath of this new life, to be more wicked, tenfold more wicked, sold a slave to my original evil **(many Christians at this time believed people were born evil, in a state of original sin, and needed to believe in Christ to stop them from being evil)**; and the thought, in that moment, braced and delighted me like wine. I stretched out my hands, exulting **(rejoicing/feeling very happy)** in the freshness of these sensations **(feelings)**; and in the act, I was suddenly aware that I had lost in stature **(height/body shape)**.

> **Simple explanation:** Jekyll takes the potion and feels younger, smaller, lighter, and a different person.
>
> **Analysis:** Here we come to the essence as to why Jekyll wants to be Hyde. He says: "I knew myself, at the first breath of this new life, to be wicked, tenfold more wicked". It is important to think about what he means by "wicked" here: Hyde is interested only pursuing his desires and suppresses no emotions. The transformation "delighted me like wine". Here we get the sense that there is something intoxicating and drug-like about the transformation. The master stroke for Stevenson was to make Jekyll lose his stature and become the small, wiry Hyde.
>
> **Discussion Point**
>
> What is the appeal of the transformation for Jekyll?

There was no mirror, at that date, in my room; that which stands beside me as I write, was brought there later on and for the very purpose of these transformations **(changes)**. The night however, was far gone into the morning—the morning, black as it was, was nearly ripe for the conception **(beginning)** of the day—the inmates **(inhabitants, prisoners)** of my house were locked in the most rigorous **(great)** hours of slumber **(sleep)**; and I determined **(decided)**, flushed as I was with hope and triumph, to venture **(go out)** in my new shape as far as to my bedroom. I crossed the yard, wherein the constellations **(stars)** looked down upon me, I could have thought, with wonder, the first creature of that sort that their unsleeping vigilance **(watchfulness)** had yet disclosed **(revealed/shown)** to them; I stole through the corridors, a stranger in my own house; and coming to my room, I saw for the first time the appearance of Edward Hyde.

I must here speak by theory alone, saying not that which I know, but that which I suppose to be most probable. The evil side of my nature, to which I had now transferred the stamping **(violent)** efficacy **(the ability to produce a desired or intended** result), was less robust **(strong)** and less developed than the good which I had just deposed **(got rid of)**. Again, in the course of my life, which had been, after all, nine tenths a life of effort, virtue and control, it had been much less exercised and much less exhausted. And hence, as I think, it came about that Edward Hyde was so much smaller, slighter and younger than Henry Jekyll. Even as good shone upon the countenance **(face)** of the one, evil was written broadly and plainly on the face of the other. Evil besides (which I must still believe to be the lethal **(deadly)** side of *devolved* man) had left on that body an imprint of deformity and decay. And *opposite of evolution* yet when I looked upon that ugly idol **(an image or representation of a god used as an object of worship)** in the glass **(mirror)**, I was conscious of no repugnance **(disgust)**, rather of a leap of welcome. This, too, was myself. It seemed natural and human. In my eyes it bore a livelier image of the spirit, *Jekyll is divided* it seemed more express and single, than the imperfect and divided countenance I had been hitherto accustomed **(used to)** to call mine. And in so far I was doubtless right. I have observed that when I wore the semblance **(resemblance, likeness)** of Edward Hyde, none could come near to me at first without a visible **(easily seen)** misgiving **(feeling of doubt)** of the flesh **(body)**. This, as I take it, was because all human beings, as we meet them, are commingled **(mixed)** out of good and evil: and Edward Hyde, alone in the ranks of mankind, was pure evil.

Hyde is pure

I lingered but a moment at the mirror: the second and conclusive experiment had yet to be attempted; it yet remained to be seen if I had lost my identity beyond redemption and must flee before daylight from a house that was no longer mine; and hurrying back to my cabinet, I once more prepared and drank the cup, once more suffered the pangs of dissolution **(change)**, and came to myself once more with the character, the stature **(body)** and the face of Henry Jekyll.

That night I had come to the fatal cross-roads. Had I approached my discovery in a more noble spirit, had I risked the experiment while under the empire of generous or pious aspirations **(hopes)**, all must have been otherwise, and from these agonies of death and birth, I had come forth an angel instead of a fiend **(devil)**. The drug had no discriminating **(having or showing refined taste or good judgement)** action; it was neither diabolical **(devil-like)** nor divine **(holy)**; it but shook the doors of the prison house of my disposition **(character)**; and like the captives of Philippi **(in the Bible, Acts 16: 26 Paul and Silas are imprisoned at Philippi)**, that which stood within ran forth. At that time my virtue **(goodness)** slumbered; my evil, kept awake by ambition, was alert and swift to seize the occasion; and the thing that was projected **(shown/represented)** was Edward Hyde.

> **Simple explanation:** Jekyll looks in the mirror and sees someone who is ugly, but he feels delight in him because the person is him. He takes the potion again and turns back into Jekyll.
>
> **Analysis:** This is a vital point. Jekyll makes it clear here that he has changed into Hyde because of his innate nature, and not because the drug turns everyone into Hyde. In other words, the drug's effects depend upon the personalities of those who take it. For Jekyll, it "shook the doors of the prison-house of my disposition", suggesting that Jekyll felt that all his emotions and desires were in a prison house before the drug released them like the "captives of Philippi". This is a reference to a part of the Bible, Acts, and 16:26: when God causes an earthquake at the prison in Philippi, where Paul and Silas are held, "immediately all the doors were opened, and everyone's bands were loosed." Paul and Silas remain behind turning themselves in while the rest of the criminals run free. The reference suggests that like Paul and Silas, part of Jekyll remains in the prison house, while the rest of his "criminal" desires are allowed to be "loosed" or freed. Furthermore, we see how Hyde is actually a projection of Jekyll. In other words, Hyde is Jekyll's evil side made manifest. Thus we see how the novel is very psychological in approach: it is more about the nature of Jekyll's mind than anything else at this point.
>
> ### Discussion point
> What do we learn about Jekyll here?

Hence, although I had now two characters as well as two appearances, one was wholly evil, and the other was still the old Henry Jekyll, that incongruous compound of whose reformation and improvement I had already learned to despair. The movement was thus wholly toward the worse.

Even at that time, I had not conquered my aversions **(dislike/hatred)** to the dryness of a life of study. I would still be merrily disposed **(inclined/feeling in a certain way)** at times; and as my pleasures were (to say the least) undignified **(appearing foolish or evil)**, and I was not only well known and highly considered **(thought of)**, but growing towards the elderly man, this incoherency **(disorganisation)** of my life was daily growing more unwelcome. It was on this side that my new power tempted me until I fell in slavery. I had but to drink the cup, to doff at once the body of the noted professor, and to assume, like a thick cloak, that of Edward Hyde. I smiled at the notion; it seemed to me at the time to be humorous **(funny)**; and I made my preparations with the most studious care. I took and furnished that house in Soho, to which Hyde was tracked by the police; and engaged as a housekeeper a creature whom I knew well to be silent and unscrupulous **(sly/deceitful/dishonest)**. On the other side, I announced to my servants that a Mr. Hyde (whom I described) was to have full liberty **(freedom)** and power about my house in the square; and to parry **(fight off)** mishaps **(problems)**, I even called and made myself a familiar object, in my second character. I next drew up that will to which you so much objected; so that if anything befell **(happened to)** me in the person of Dr. Jekyll, I could enter on that of Edward Hyde without pecuniary **(monetary/of money)** loss. And thus fortified **(strengthened)**, as I supposed, on every side, I began to profit **(do well)** by the strange immunities **(protection from harm)** of my position.

Men have before hired bravos **(tough men)** to transact their crimes, while their own person and reputation sat under shelter **(sheltered/protected)**. I was the first that ever did so for his pleasures. I was the first that could plod in the public eye with a load of genial **(friendly)** respectability, and in a moment, like a schoolboy, strip off these lendings **(borrowed things)** and spring headlong into the sea of liberty **(freedom)**. But for me, in my impenetrable **(impossible to pass through or enter)** mantle **(cloak/clothing)**, the safety was complete. Think of it—I did not even exist! Let me but escape into my laboratory door, give me but a second or two to mix and swallow the draught that I had always standing ready; and whatever he had done, Edward Hyde would pass away like the stain of breath upon a mirror; and there in his stead, quietly at home, trimming the midnight lamp in his study, a man who could afford to laugh at suspicion, would be Henry Jekyll.

The pleasures which I made haste **(hurried)** to seek in my disguise were, as I have said, undignified **(lacking in dignity/embarrassing/humiliating/sinful/wrong)**; I would scarce use a harder term. But in the hands of Edward Hyde, they soon began to turn toward the monstrous. When I would come back from these excursions **(walks/journey)**, I was often plunged into a kind of wonder at my vicarious **(experienced in** *doesn't know himself very well*

the imagination through the feelings or actions of another person) depravity **(evil/wickedness)**. This familiar **(a demon supposedly attending and obeying a witch, often said to assume the form of an animal)** that I called *jekyll in control* out of my own soul, and sent forth alone to do his good pleasure, was a being inherently **(essentially)** malign **(evil)** and villainous **(evil)**; his every act and thought centered on self; drinking pleasure with bestial **(beast-like)** avidity **(interest/enthusiasm)** from any degree of torture to another; *jekyll can't believe* relentless **(never stopping)** like a man of stone. Henry Jekyll *in what* stood at times aghast **(in shock)** before the acts of Edward Hyde; *hyde is* but the situation was apart from ordinary laws, and insidiously *doing* **(causing harm in the way that a bad thing is not noticed)** relaxed the grasp of conscience **(guilt)**. It was Hyde, after all, and *I* Hyde alone, that was guilty. Jekyll was no worse; he woke again to *trying* his good qualities seemingly **(in appearance but not in** *to distance* **reality)** unimpaired **(not weakened or damaged)**; he would *himself* even make haste, where it was possible, to undo the evil done by *blame Hyde* Hyde. And thus his conscience slumbered **(slept)**.

saying he isn't guilty

Simple explanation: Jekyll carefully prepares things so that he can live a life as Hyde: he makes a home with nice furniture for Hyde in Soho, and employs a housekeeper there who will keep all his secrets. He tells his servants to obey Hyde and that they must allow Hyde to do whatever he wants to do. He writes a will in which Hyde inherits all of his money if Jekyll disappears. He delights in doing whatever he wants. Before becoming Hyde, Jekyll had been doing things which he felt he shouldn't be doing, but now he can become Hyde he can do these things without worrying: no-one will know it was Jekyll doing bad things. Hyde was like an animal who took a selfish pleasure in everything he did, without feeling guilt.

Analysis: This is a fascinating section because of what it says – and what it leaves out. Firstly, to consider the subject matter that Jekyll decides not to dwell upon: he does not describe in detail the sex, the beatings, the escapades that Hyde engages upon. For all his way with words, he remains inarticulate upon these matters. This is, in part, an inarticulacy of the age: the Victorians did not describe the sexual act in detail at all. Fascinatingly, Jekyll describes this as "vicarious depravity", in other words, he believes that he is not committing these awful acts because his bodily shape has changed. But, of course, we must remember that it is Jekyll who has committed these deeds. Don't be deceived by his self-serving words! He blames Hyde for his crimes, but, in actual fact, there is no Hyde, there is only a transformed version of Jekyll. However, the doctor is insistent that he has had nothing to do with the crimes: "it was Hyde, after all, and Hyde alone, that was guilty." This allows Jekyll leave his unimpeachable life at home. But there is a sense of guilt in the way Jekyll says: "his conscience slumbered". There is awareness that the fiction of Hyde is a cover-up, a mask, a facade which hides the truly ugly Jekyll.

Discussion Point

What clues does Stevenson give us that Hyde does not really exist and that it is merely a transformed Jekyll who is present?

cant reconcile Hydes depravity with himself

Into the details of the infamy **(famous for being bad/evil)** at which I thus connived **(secretly allow)** (for even now I can scarce grant that I committed it) I have no design of entering; I mean but to point out the warnings and the successive steps with which my chastisement **(punishment)** approached. I met with one accident which, as it brought on no consequence, I shall no more than mention. An act of cruelty to a child aroused **(brought out)** against me the anger of a passer-by, whom I recognised the other day in the person of your kinsman **(family member)**; the doctor and the child's family joined him; there were moments when I feared for my life; and at last, in order to pacify **(calm down)** their too just **(understandable/righteous)** resentment, Edward Hyde had to bring them to the door, and pay them in a cheque drawn in the name of Henry Jekyll. But this danger was easily eliminated **(destroyed)** from the future, by opening an account at another bank in the name of Edward Hyde himself; and when, by sloping my own hand **(handwriting)** backward, I had supplied my double with a signature, I thought I sat beyond the reach of fate. *euphemism - him trying to decieve himself*

Some two months before the murder of Sir Danvers, I had been out for one of my adventures, had returned at a late hour, and woke the next day in bed with somewhat odd sensations **(feelings)**. It was in vain I looked about me; in vain I saw the decent furniture and tall proportions of my room in the square; in vain that I recognised the pattern of the bed curtains and the design of the mahogany frame; something still kept insisting that I was not where I was, that I had not wakened where I seemed to be, but in the little room in Soho where I was accustomed **(used to)** to sleep in the body of Edward Hyde. I smiled to myself, and in my psychological way, began lazily to inquire into the elements of this

confusing perspective

illusion, occasionally, even as I did so, dropping back into a comfortable morning doze. I was still so engaged when, in one of my more wakeful moments, my eyes fell upon my hand. Now the hand of Henry Jekyll (as you have often remarked) was professional in shape and size: it was large, firm, white and comely **(good looking)**. But the hand which I now saw, clearly enough, in the yellow light of a mid-London morning, lying half shut on the bedclothes, was lean, corded **(muscly)**, knuckly, of a dusky **(dark)** pallor (colour) and thickly shaded **(cover)** with a swart **(black)** growth of hair. It was the hand of Edward Hyde.

I must have stared upon it for near half a minute, sunk as I was in the mere stupidity of wonder, before terror woke up in my breast as sudden and startling as the crash of cymbals; and bounding **(jumping up)** from my bed I rushed to the mirror. At the sight that met my eyes, my blood was changed into something exquisitely **(delicately made)** thin and icy. Yes, I had gone to bed Henry Jekyll, I had awakened Edward Hyde. How was this to be explained? I asked myself; and then, with another bound of terror—how was it to be remedied **(cured/put right)**? It was well on in the morning; the servants were up; all my drugs were in the cabinet—a long journey down two pairs of stairs, through the back passage, across the open court and through the anatomical theatre, from where I was then standing horror-struck. It might indeed be possible to cover my face; but of what use was that, when I was unable to conceal **(hide)** the alteration **(change)** in my stature **(height/body shape)**?

> **Simple explanation:** When Hyde first appeared, he was not that strong because Jekyll had always kept the evil side of himself repressed, but now that Hyde is enjoying himself, he becomes stronger. He becomes so strong that one morning, Jekyll, without taking the drug, wakes up as Hyde.
> **Analysis:** Here we see how Hyde is beginning to take over. Jekyll has gone to sleep and woken up as Hyde, finding the "lean, corded knuckly" hand of Hyde in the bed. This is a superb literary touch: this is the hand of the murderer, of the probable rapist, of the profligate, of the psychopath, and yet it is the mind of Jekyll who sees it. Jekyll inhabits the body of Hyde because the truth is dawning upon him: it wasn't Hyde who committed those terrible deeds but Jekyll. The fiction of Hyde is both being stripped away and becoming more powerful. Hyde is being stripped away because Jekyll is being forced to realise that he is Hyde. The invented character of Hyde is becoming more powerful

because he is dominating: the fiction is becoming real permanently.

Discussion point
Why is Hyde taking over Jekyll now? What is so horrific about this invasion?

And then with an overpowering sweetness of relief, it came back upon my mind that the servants were already used to the coming and going of my second self. I had soon dressed, as well as I was able, in clothes of my own size: had soon passed through the house, where Bradshaw stared and drew back at seeing Mr. Hyde at such an hour and in such a strange array; and ten minutes later, Dr. Jekyll had returned to his own shape and was sitting down, with a darkened brow, to make a feint **(pretense)** of breakfasting.

> **Simple explanation:** Hyde dresses in Jekyll's clothes and is seen by a servant Bradshaw, who is scared at seeing him but does not stop him because he is used to seeing Hyde. Hyde takes the potion and turns back into Jekyll.
> **Analysis:** The relief that Jekyll feels is the relief of the criminal who has got away with it; the relief of the person with a secret who has managed to maintain the secret. The reader feels in a strange position: we are relieved too, and yet we feel that what Jekyll is doing is reprehensible or wrong.

Discussion point
Why is Jekyll so relieved? What do you think of Stevenson's presentation of Jekyll here?

Small indeed was my appetite. This inexplicable incident, this reversal of my previous experience, seemed, like the Babylonian finger on the wall, to be spelling out the letters of my judgment **(God's judgment)**; and I began to reflect more seriously than ever before on the issues and possibilities of my double existence.

> **Simple explanation:** Jekyll feels that the fact that he has turned into Hyde in his sleep is a warning that he must stop taking the drug.
> **Analysis:** The reference to the Babylonian finger on the wall is taken from a book in the Bible called Daniel, chapter 5, in which Daniel, who can see the future, foresees the death of King Belshazzar in the way he interprets some supernatural or ghostly writing on a wall created by "fingers of a man's hand" (Daniel 5:5). The full passage can be found

here:
http://www.biblegateway.com/passage/?search=Da
niel+5.
An explanation of the quote can be found on this Wikipedia
page:
http://en.wikipedia.org/wiki/The_writing_on_the
_wall
, together with a copy of Rembrandt's wonderful painting of
this incident. In terms of this passage, we can see that
Jekyll's change into Hyde without taking the potion is the
"writing on the wall" in that it is a warning not to carry on as
he is doing.

Discussion point
Why does Jekyll talk about the Babylonian finger?

That part of me which I had the power of projecting **(pretending
to be someone I wasn't, pretending to be respectable)**,
had lately been much exercised and nourished; it had seemed to
me of late as though the body of Edward Hyde had grown in
stature, as though (when I wore that form) I were conscious of a
more generous tide of blood; and I began to spy a danger that, if
this were much prolonged, the balance of my nature might be
permanently overthrown, the power of voluntary change be
forfeited, and the character of Edward Hyde become irrevocably
mine.

Simple explanation: Jekyll is worried about becoming
Hyde forever because Hyde has grown so much stronger.
Analysis: This is a fascinating reflection by Jekyll who is
saying that because he has allowed Hyde to go out so much
into the world, Hyde has secretly grown stronger inside him
and is threatening to take over. This is idea is different to
the idea of "repression" in the story because it suggests that
if you start doing bad things you'll want to do more and
more of them; in other words because you haven't repressed
your "bad side", it will grow stronger. The novel is puzzling
and contradictory because at some points it promotes the
idea that repression causes people's "dark sides" to appear
in unexpected ways, but it also suggests that if you give your
dark side free reign then it will become stronger.

Discussion point
Why do you think Hyde has become stronger?

The power of the drug had not been always equally displayed. Once, very early in my career, it had totally failed me; since then I had been obliged on more than one occasion to double, and once, with infinite **(very great)** risk of death, to treble **(triple/three times)** the amount; and these rare uncertainties had cast hitherto the sole shadow on my contentment **(happiness)**. Now, however, and in the light of that morning's accident, I was led to remark that whereas, in the beginning, the difficulty had been to throw off the body of Jekyll, it had of late gradually but decidedly transferred itself to the other side. All things therefore seemed to point to this; that I was slowly losing hold of my original and better self, and becoming slowly incorporated **(taken over)** with my second and worse.

Between these two, I now felt I had to choose. My two natures had memory in common, but all other faculties **(intelligences/abilities)** were most unequally shared between them. Jekyll (who was composite **(made up of more than one thing)**) now with the most sensitive apprehensions **(fears)**, now with a greedy gusto **(enthusiasm)**, projected and shared in the pleasures and adventures of Hyde; but Hyde was indifferent **(not caring)** to Jekyll, or but remembered him as the mountain bandit remembers the cavern in which he conceals **(hides)** himself from pursuit **(being hunted)**. Jekyll had more than a father's interest **(care/love)**; Hyde had more than a son's indifference **(not caring)**.

Jekyll loves Hyde
Hyde does not care for Jekyll

Simple explanation: Jekyll has to decide to live a life of pleasure and become Hyde, or live a life of respectability and no pleasure and stay Jekyll.

Analysis: Again, one is tempted to think that Jekyll's interpretation is a false one because it is clear that Hyde is already predominant. It is not so much that there is a choice to be made, but that the veneer of Jekyll is being stripped away and revealing what is underneath, which is Hyde. The huge "iceberg" subconscious of Hyde is now crashing into the fragile ship of Jekyll. The fact that Hyde is so much more powerful is shown by the way he is utterly indifferent to Jekyll: he only remembers him as a "cavern" to hide his banditry in, a cave for a bad man to hide in. Jekyll is a shell.

Discussion Point
Do you think that Jekyll genuinely has a choice to make between the good of Jekyll and the badness of Hyde, or is it more complex than that?

To cast in my lot with Jekyll, was to die to those appetites **(desires)** which I had long secretly indulged **(allow to indulge)** and had of late begun to pamper **(spoil)**. To cast it in with Hyde, was to die to a thousand interests and aspirations **(hopes)**, and to become, at a blow and forever, despised **(hated)** and friendless. The bargain might appear unequal; but there was still another consideration in the scales; for while Jekyll would suffer smartingly in the fires of abstinence **(the practice of restraining oneself from indulging in something, typically alcohol or sex)**, Hyde would be not even conscious of all that he had lost. Strange as my circumstances were, the terms of this debate are as old and commonplace as man; much the same inducements **(a thing that persuades or leads someone to do something)** and alarms cast the die **(to make a choice from which there is no return)** for any tempted and trembling sinner; and it fell out with me, as it falls **(turns out)** with so vast a majority of my fellows, that I chose the better part and was found wanting **(lacking)** in the strength to keep to it.

> **Simple explanation:** Jekyll decides to stay Jekyll forever, but finds that he doesn't have the strength to be good all the time and gives in to sin as a result.
> **Analysis:** Here we realise that Jekyll too weak to stop himself from sinning.
> #### Discussion Point
> How does Stevenson create real tension here?

Yes, I preferred the elderly and discontented **(unhappy)** doctor, surrounded by friends and cherishing **(caring for)** honest hopes; and bade a resolute **(definite)** farewell to the liberty **(freedom)**, the comparative youth, the light step, leaping impulses **(sudden, strong desires)** and secret pleasures, that I had enjoyed in the disguise of Hyde. I made this choice perhaps with some unconscious **(done or existing without one realizing)** reservation **(doubt)**, for I neither gave up the house in Soho, nor destroyed the clothes of Edward Hyde, which still lay ready in my cabinet. For two months, however, I was true to my determination; for two months, I led a life of such severity **(seriousness)** as I had never before attained to, and enjoyed the compensations **(a reward for the loss of something)** of an approving **(agreeing that something is right)** conscience **(sense of right and wrong)**. But time began at last to obliterate **(destroy)** the freshness of my alarm; the praises of conscience began to grow into a thing of course; I began to be tortured with throes **(intense violent pain)** and longings, as of Hyde struggling after freedom; and at last, in an hour of moral weakness, I once again compounded **(made up)** and swallowed the transforming **(that causes change)** draught **(drink)**.

> **Simple explanation:** For two months, Jekyll doesn't take the potion but then he gives in and takes it.
> **Analysis:** Here we have it conclusively: Jekyll wants Hyde back! He needs him to be free; to live his life properly, to be whole again. He views this as weakness, but we, reading the book from the perspective of 21st century, see it very differently: the need for Hyde is the need to express his desires. To this extent, Jekyll is a proto-existentialist: someone who realises that to live properly one has to leave conventional Christian morality behind.
> ### Discussion Point
> Why does Jekyll want to be Hyde again?

I do not suppose that, when a drunkard reasons with himself upon his vice **(wrong-doing)**, he is once out of five hundred times affected by the dangers that he runs through his brutish **(thuggish)**, physical insensibility **(lack of feeling)**; neither had I, long as I had considered my position, made enough allowance for the complete moral **(awareness of good and evil)** insensibility **(lack of feeling)** and insensate **(lacking sense or reason)** readiness **(enthusiasm for/openness)** to evil, which were the leading characters of Edward Hyde. Yet it was by these that I was punished. My devil had been long caged, he came out roaring. I was conscious, even when I took the draught, of a more unbridled **(uncontrolled)**, a more furious **(very angry)** propensity **(tendency to behave)** to ill **(do bad things)**. It must have been this, I suppose, that stirred in my soul that tempest **(storm)** of impatience with which I listened to the civilities **(pleasant, polite words and behaviour)** of my unhappy victim; I declare, at least, before God, no man morally sane could have been guilty of that crime upon so pitiful a provocation **(an action which makes someone angry)**; and that I struck in no more reasonable spirit than that in which a sick child may break a plaything **(toy)**. But I had voluntarily **(by choice)** stripped myself of all those balancing instincts by which even the worst of us continues to walk with some degree of steadiness **(behaving in a calm way)** among temptations; and in my case, to be tempted, however slightly, was to fall.

Instantly the spirit of hell awoke in me and raged. With a transport of glee, I mauled **(destroyed)** the unresisting **(not fighting)** body, tasting delight from every blow; and it was not till weariness **(tiredness)** had begun to succeed **(take over)**, that I was suddenly, in the top fit of my delirium **(madness)**, struck through the heart by a cold thrill of terror. A mist dispersed; I saw my life to be forfeit **(lost)**; and fled from the scene of these excesses **(out of control behaviour)**, at once glorying and trembling, my lust of evil gratified **(given pleasure)** and stimulated, my love of life screwed to the topmost peg **(at its highest point/its greatest moment)**.

> **Simple explanation:** the drug works much more strongly because he hasn't taken it in a while. Jekyll describes how he is delighted to kill Carew in the body of Hyde.
>
> **Analysis:** The way Stevenson presents the murder of Carew is interesting. Perhaps on initial reading we thought there was some real reason for it: for example, that Carew had found out the truth about Hyde. But here it becomes clear that Hyde kills him because he has been pent up too long in Jekyll's mind for too long. In this sense, we realise that Jekyll's experiment has made him psychotic: by repressing his natural instincts for so long, he has turned himself into a murderer. Notice how Jekyll has started to use a language which is not based upon conventional morality at all; he describes the murder as being like a sick child breaking a "plaything".
>
> ### Discussion Point
> Why is this description of the murder even more shocking than the original description?

I ran to the house in Soho, and (to make assurance **(sure)** doubly sure) destroyed my papers; thence **(from there)** I set out through the lamplit streets, in the same divided ecstasy **(joy)** of mind, gloating **(thinking with pleasure)** on my crime, light-headedly devising **(working out)** others in the future, and yet still hastening **(hurrying)** and still hearkening **(listening)** in my wake **(behind me)** for the steps of the avenger **(someone looking for revenge)**. Hyde had a song upon his lips as he compounded **(made)** the draught **(the drink)**, and as he drank it, pledged **(promised)** the dead man. The pangs of transformation had not done tearing him, before Henry Jekyll, with streaming tears of gratitude **(being thankful)** and remorse **(guilt)** had fallen upon his knees and lifted his clasped hands to

God. The veil of self-indulgence **(doing whatever you want)** was rent **(torn/destroyed)** from head to foot. I saw my life as a whole: I followed it up from the days of childhood, when I had walked with my father's hand, and through the self-denying toils **(work)** of my professional life, to arrive again and again, with the same sense of unreality, at the damned horrors of the evening. I could have screamed aloud; I sought with tears and prayers to smother down the crowd of hideous **(horrible)** images and sounds with which my memory swarmed **(moving large numbers like insects)** against me; and still, between the petitions **(formal requests)**, the ugly face of my iniquity **(evil)** stared into my soul. As the acuteness **(strength)** of this remorse **(guilt)** began to die away, it was succeeded by a sense of joy. The problem of my conduct was solved. Hyde was thenceforth **(from now onwards)** impossible; whether I would or not, I was now confined to the better part of my existence; and O, how I rejoiced to think of it! with what willing humility **(being humble/the opposite of pride)** I embraced **(hugged)** anew the restrictions **(rules that stop you doing things)** of natural life! with what sincere **(genuine/real)** renunciation **(giving up certain behaviour)** I locked the door by which I had so often gone and come, and ground the key under my heel!

> **Simple explanation:** Aware that he will be hung if he turns into Hyde again, Jekyll decides to renounce him forever. He is very grateful to escape punishment for the murder of Carew.
>
> **Analysis:** Jekyll's reaction to the murder of Carew is very disturbing. Rather feeling he needs to turn himself in as a felon, he feels that the murder solves a problem, the problem of Hyde. Hyde can no longer exist. He says his "renunciation" is sincere: again the language is religious. He is like a monk renouncing the ungodly life. He uses the imagery of the door again: locking it so that Hyde can no longer come in. He also talks about the "veil of self-indulgence" being "rent from head to foot"; this is a Biblical image, like many in Jekyll's confession, which echoes the Gospel of Luke in which the "veil of the temple" was "rent" after Jesus died. In other words, there is a sense that God is punishing him for his sins.
>
> ### Discussion Point
>
> What do you think of Jekyll's reaction to the murder of Carew?

The next day, came the news that the murder had not been overlooked, that the guilt of Hyde was patent to the world, and that the victim was a man high in public estimation **(judgment)**. It was not only a crime, it had been a tragic folly. I think I was glad to know it; I think I was glad to have my better impulses thus buttressed and guarded by the terrors of the scaffold. Jekyll was now my city of refuge **(place of safety)**; let but Hyde peep out an instant, and the hands of all men would be raised to take and slay **(kill)** him.

I resolved in my future conduct **(behaviour)** to redeem **(compensate for the faults or bad aspects of)** the past; and I can say with honesty that my resolve was fruitful of some good. You know yourself how earnestly, in the last months of the last year, I laboured **(worked)** to relieve suffering; you know that much was done for others, and that the days passed quietly, almost happily for myself. Nor can I truly say that I wearied of this beneficent **(well-meaning/good)** and innocent life; I think instead that I daily enjoyed it more completely; but I was still cursed with my duality **(two-faced: an instance of opposition or contrast between two concepts or two aspects of something)** of purpose; and as the first edge of my penitence **(regret)** wore off, the lower side of me, so long indulged **(treated very well; spoilt)**, so recently chained down, began to growl for licence **(freedom to do what you want)**. Not that I dreamed of resuscitating **(bringing back to life)** Hyde; the bare idea of that would startle **(surprise)** me to frenzy **(madness)**: no, it was in my own person that I was once more tempted to trifle **(play)** with my conscience **(sense of right and wrong)**; and it was as an ordinary secret sinner that I at last fell before the assaults of temptation. Jekyll sinning as Himself

Simple explanation: Jekyll does good works and sees his friends again. However, he does give in to temptation and "sins" not as Hyde but as Jekyll.

Analysis: Of course, Hyde will not go away. Hyde is inextricably part of Jekyll because he is Jekyll. He feels Hyde, his subconscious, growling for "license" – or freedom. He wants his freedom again to express himself. It is like Hyde is a beast, a dog on the leash that needs to be untethered. We see here how Jekyll now gives in to the "assaults of temptation" as Jekyll not as Hyde, and this triggers off his involuntary change into Hyde that follows.

Discussion point

Why is the imagery of the "growling" so important here? What does it tell us about Jekyll's state of mind?

There comes an end to all things; the most capacious **(roomy)** measure **(vessel/cup)** is filled at last; and this brief condescension **(an attitude of patronizing superiority; disdain)** to my evil finally destroyed the balance of my soul. And yet I was not alarmed; the fall seemed natural, like a return to the old days before I had made my discovery. It was a fine, clear, January day, wet under foot where the frost had melted, but cloudless overhead; and the Regent's Park was full of winter chirrupings and sweet with spring odours **(smells)**. I sat in the sun on a bench; the animal within me licking the chops of memory **(remembering things fondly)**; the spiritual side a little drowsed **(sleepy)**, promising subsequent penitence **(doing good things to compensate for the bad things)**, but not yet moved to begin. After all, I reflected, I was like my neighbours; and then I *arrogant* smiled, comparing myself with other men, comparing my active good-will with the lazy cruelty of their neglect. And at the very moment of that vainglorious **(big: feeling self-importance)** thought, a qualm **(shudder)** came over me, a horrid nausea **(feeling sick)** and the most deadly shuddering. These passed away, and left me faint; and then as in its turn faintness subsided **(died away)**, I began to be aware of a change in the temper of my thoughts, a greater boldness, a contempt **(the feeling that a person or a thing is worthless or deserving scorn)** of danger, a solution **(dissolving)** of the bonds **(chains)** of obligation **(duty)**. I looked down; my clothes hung formlessly **(without shape)** on my shrunken limbs; the hand that lay on my knee was corded and hairy. I was once more Edward Hyde. A moment before I had been safe of all men's respect, wealthy, beloved—the cloth laying for me in the dining-room at home; and now I was the common quarry **(hunted animal)** of mankind, hunted, houseless, a known murderer, thrall **(slave)** to the gallows **(the place where people are hung)**.

Simple explanation: Jekyll is in Regent's Park when he finds that he has changed into Hyde, and that his clothes are now too big for him, and he is now a man who is wanted for murder.
Analysis: The imagery here is wonderful, possibly Shakespearean. It recalls Macbeth's line "why do you dress me/ In borrowed robes?". Macbeth, like Jekyll, was a man who appeared very respectable and honorable but

harboured a very dark side which comes at when he murders the king. Shakespeare constantly uses the imagery of ill-fitting clothes to describe Macbeth's position: he is a man whose dark side does not fit the respectable clothes he wears. Here, Stevenson uses similar imagery to describe Jekyll's position: he is a man whose respectable clothes no longer fit.

Discussion Point
Why is the imagery Stevenson uses here so powerful?

My reason wavered, but it did not fail me utterly. I have more than once observed that in my second character, my faculties seemed sharpened to a point and my spirits more tensely elastic **(flexible)**; thus it came about that, where Jekyll perhaps might have succumbed **(given in)**, Hyde rose to the importance of the moment. My drugs were in one of the presses of my cabinet; how was I to reach them? That was the problem that (crushing my temples in my hands) I set myself to solve. The laboratory door I had closed. If I sought to enter by the house, my own servants would consign **(send/condemn)** me to the gallows. I saw I must employ another hand **(person)**, and thought of Lanyon. How was he to be reached? how persuaded? Supposing that I escaped capture in the streets, how was I to make my way into his presence? and how should I, an unknown and displeasing visitor, prevail on the famous physician to rifle **(search through like a burglar)** the study of his colleague, Dr. Jekyll? Then I remembered that of my original character, one part remained to me: I could write my own hand; and once I had conceived **(worked out)** that kindling spark **(first idea)**, the way that I must follow became lighted up from end to end.

Thereupon, I arranged my clothes as best I could, and summoning a passing hansom **(a two-wheeled horse-drawn cab accommodating two inside, with the driver seated behind)**, drove to an hotel in Portland Street, the name of which I chanced to remember. At my appearance (which was indeed comical enough, however tragic a fate these garments **(clothes)** covered) the driver could not conceal his mirth. I gnashed my teeth upon him with a gust of devilish fury; and the smile withered from his face—happily for him—yet more happily for myself, for in another instant I had certainly dragged him from his perch. At the inn, as I entered, I looked about me with so black a countenance **(face)** as made the attendants tremble; not a look did they exchange in my presence; but obsequiously **(in a way that**

shows he is "sucking up" or grovelling) took my orders, led me to a private room, and brought me wherewithal **(where)** to write. Hyde in danger of his life was a creature new to me; shaken with inordinate **(very great)** anger, strung to the pitch of murder, lusting to inflict pain. Yet the creature was astute **(clever)**; mastered **(got control of)** his fury with a great effort of the will; composed his two important letters, one to Lanyon and one to Poole; and that he might receive actual evidence of their being posted, sent them out with directions that they should be registered.

> **Simple explanation:** Hyde goes to a hotel in Portland Street, writes a letter to Lanyon in Jekyll's handwriting, asking for drugs. Lanyon doesn't know what Hyde looks like, and therefore won't report him to the police like his servants would. He writes a letter to Poole to tell him about Lanyon coming to collect the drugs.
> **Analysis:** Hyde is clever because he is Jekyll: he manages to compose letters in Jekyll's hand because he is the very same person.
> **Discussion point**
> What truth is being revealed here?

Jekyll is Hyde separating himself from Hyde

Thenceforward **(from that point onwards)**, he sat all day over the fire in the private room, gnawing his nails; there he dined, sitting alone with his fears, the waiter visibly quailing **(shivering)** before his eye; and thence **(from there)**, when the night was fully come, he set forth in the corner of a closed cab, and was driven to and fro about the streets of the city. He, I say—I cannot say, I. That child of Hell had nothing human; nothing lived in him but fear and hatred. And when at last, thinking the driver had begun to grow suspicious, he discharged the cab and ventured on foot, attired **(dressed)** in his misfitting clothes, an object marked out for observation, into the midst of the nocturnal **(night-time)** passengers, these two base **(horrible/basic)** passions raged within him like a tempest **(storm)**. He walked fast, hunted by his fears, chattering to himself, skulking through the less frequented **(crowded)** thoroughfares **(streets)**, counting the minutes that still divided him from midnight. Once a woman spoke to him, offering, I think, a box of lights. He smote **(hit)** her in the face, and she fled.

When I came to myself at Lanyon's, the horror of my old friend perhaps affected me somewhat: I do not know; it was at least but a drop in the sea to the abhorrence **(horror)** with which I looked back upon these hours. A change had come over me. It was no longer the fear of the gallows **(being hung)**, it was the horror of being Hyde that racked me. I received Lanyon's condemnation partly in a dream; it was partly in a dream that I came home to my own house and got into bed. I slept after the prostration **(lying down)** of the day, with a stringent **(strict)** and profound **(very deep)** slumber **(sleep)** which not even the nightmares that wrung **(affected)** me could avail **(hope)** to break. I awoke in the morning shaken, weakened, but refreshed. I still hated and feared the thought of the brute that slept within me, and I had not of course forgotten the appalling dangers of the day before; but I was once more at home, in my own house and close to my drugs; and gratitude for my escape shone so strong in my soul that it almost rivalled the brightness of hope.

> **Simple explanation:** Hyde stays in the hotel, biting his nails, and then when it was night he set off for Lanyon's, hitting a woman who offered him some matches in the face. He turns into Jekyll before Lanyon and then is very pleased and relieved to be home and safe.
>
> **Analysis:** Once again, Jekyll feels he has "got away with it". Safely locked within the respectable facade of his house, he is able to feel civilised again. Thus we realise that Jekyll has come to depend upon Hyde to feel "relieved" again: his relief is dependent upon Hyde because without Hyde he would have nothing to feel "relieved" about.
>
> ### Discussion Point
> Why does Jekyll enter into this cycle of doing something bad in the name of Hyde and then feeling "relieved"?

I was stepping leisurely across the court after breakfast, drinking the chill of the air with pleasure, when I was seized again with those indescribable **(can't be described)** sensations **(feelings)** that heralded the change; and I had but the time to gain the shelter of my cabinet, before I was once again raging and freezing with the passions of Hyde. It took on this occasion a double dose to recall me to myself; and alas! six hours after, as I sat looking sadly in the fire, the pangs **(seizures)** returned, and the drug had to be re-administered **(taken again)**. In short, from that day forth it seemed only by a great effort as of gymnastics, and only under the immediate stimulation **(taking)** of the drug, that I was able to wear the countenance **(face)** of Jekyll. At all hours of the day and night, I would be taken with the premonitory **(foreseeing the future)** shudder; above all, if I slept, or even *subconscious is Hyde comes out when conscious is asleep*

dozed for a moment in my chair, it was always as Hyde that I awakened. Under the strain of this continually impending **(about to happen)** doom and by the sleeplessness to which I now condemned myself, ay, even beyond what I had thought possible to man, I became, in my own person, a creature eaten up and emptied by fever, languidly **(lazily)** weak both in body and mind, and solely **(only)** occupied by one thought: the horror of my other self. But when I slept, or when the virtue of the medicine wore off, I would leap almost without transition **(the process or a period of changing from one state or condition to another)** (for the pangs of transformation grew daily less marked) into the possession of a fancy **(idea/imagining)** brimming **(full of)** with images of terror, a soul boiling with causeless hatreds **(feeling hatred for no cause or reason)**, and a body that seemed not strong enough to contain the raging energies of life. The powers of Hyde seemed to have grown with the sickliness **(illness, cowardice)** of Jekyll. And certainly the hate that now divided them was equal on each side. With Jekyll, it was a thing of vital **(full of life)** instinct **(acting without thinking)**. He had now seen the full deformity **(ugliness)** of that creature that shared with him some of the phenomena **(situation)** of consciousness **(awareness)**, and was co-heir **(people legally entitled to equal property or rank of another on that person's death)** with him to death: and beyond these links of community, which in themselves made the most poignant **(sad)** part of his distress, he thought of Hyde, for all his energy of life, as of something not only hellish but inorganic **(not alive)**. This was the shocking thing; that the slime of the pit seemed to utter cries and voices; that the amorphous **(shapeless)** dust gesticulated **(made signs)** and sinned; that what was dead, and had no shape, should usurp **(steal)** the offices of life. And this again, that that insurgent **(rising in revolt/rebellion)** horror was knit to him closer than a wife, closer than an eye; lay caged in his flesh, where he heard it mutter and felt it struggle to be born; and at every hour of weakness, and in the confidence of slumber, prevailed **(prove more powerful or superior)** against him, and deposed **(remove from office suddenly and forcefully)** him out of life. The hatred of Hyde for Jekyll was of a different order. His terror of the gallows drove him continually to commit temporary suicide, and return to his subordinate **(less important)** station of a part instead of a person; but he loathed **(hated)** the necessity, he loathed the despondency **(depression)** into which Jekyll was now fallen, and he resented the dislike with which he was himself regarded. Hence the ape-like tricks that he would play me, scrawling in my own hand blasphemies **(swear words, unholy words)** on the pages of my books, burning the letters and destroying the portrait of my father; and indeed, had it not been for his fear of death, he would long ago have ruined himself in order to involve me in the ruin. But his love of me is wonderful; I go further: I, who sicken and freeze at the mere thought of him, when I recall the abjection **(humiliation/terrible fallen state)** and passion of this attachment, and when I know how he fears my power to cut him off by suicide, I find it in my heart to pity him.

> **Simple explanation:** Jekyll finds that he is constantly turning into Hyde and needs stronger and stronger drugs to stop Hyde taking over completely. Hyde writes swear words on Jekyll's religious books, and plays tricks on him. Jekyll feels pity towards Hyde because ultimately it will be Hyde who will be sorry to die, not Jekyll.
>
> **Analysis:** Hyde is "apelike" and irreverent, scrawling blasphemies on the religious books Jekyll reads to salve his conscience. What is most important to note here is how Hyde has a "love of life" and that Jekyll views this as "wonderful". Hyde is ultimately someone who is very positive about life, because there are so many opportunities for enjoyment. He is what the philosopher Nietzsche terms a "Yea-sayer": he says yes to life and all its possibilities. Jekyll is a "Nay-sayer": he is constantly saying "No" to things because they would not further his image of himself as a respectable and civilised man. Yet ultimately, Jekyll has the ultimate sanction: of killing himself. The ultimate "no" to all desires.
>
> ### Discussion Point
> Why does Hyde love life? Why does Jekyll contemplate killing himself?

It is useless, and the time awfully fails me, to prolong this description; no one has ever suffered such torments, let that suffice; and yet even to these, habit brought—no, not alleviation **(relief)**—but a certain callousness **(unfeelingness)** of soul, a certain acquiescence **(acceptance)** of despair; and my punishment might have gone on for years, but for the last calamity **(disaster)** which has now fallen, and which has finally severed me from my own face and nature. My provision of the salt **(chemical)**, which had never been renewed since the date of the first experiment, began to run low. I sent out for a fresh supply and mixed the draught **(drink)**; the ebullition **(bubbling**

liquid) followed, and the first change of colour, not the second; I drank it and it was without efficiency **(effect)**. You will learn from Poole how I have had London ransacked; it was in vain; and I am now persuaded that my first supply was impure, and that it was that unknown impurity which lent efficacy **(the ability to produce a desired or intended result)** to the draught.

About a week has passed, and I am now finishing this statement under the influence of the last of the old powders. This, then, is the last time, short of a miracle, that Henry Jekyll can think his own thoughts or see his own face (now how sadly altered!) in the glass. Nor must I delay too long to bring my writing to an end; for if my narrative has hitherto **(until now)** escaped destruction, it has been by a combination of great prudence and great good luck. Should the throes of change take me in the act of writing it, Hyde will tear it in pieces; but if some time shall have elapsed **(passed)** after I have laid it by, his wonderful selfishness and circumscription **(restrict (something) within limits)** to the moment will probably save it once again from the action of his ape-like spite **(hatred)**.

> **Simple explanation:** Jekyll is finding Hyde is taking over completely. Jekyll is running out of drugs and knows that he will die soon, either as Hyde, which may mean he will be hung, or as Jekyll because he will commit suicide.
> **Analysis:** Yet Hyde does not rip up the confession: why should he care after all?
> ### Discussion Point
> Why has Jekyll confessed do you think? What are his purposes in writing the confession?

And indeed the doom **(death/disaster)** that is closing on us both has already changed and crushed him. Half an hour from now, when I shall again and forever re-indue **(wear the clothes and attitudes of a person)** that hated personality, I know how I shall sit shuddering and weeping in my chair, or continue, with the most strained and fearstruck **(frightened)** ecstasy **(great intensity of feeling, great happiness)** of listening, to pace up and down this room (my last earthly refuge **(place of safety on earth)**) and give ear to every sound of menace. Will Hyde die upon the scaffold **(be hung)**? or will he find courage to release himself at the last moment? God knows; I am careless; this is my true hour of death, and what is to follow concerns another than myself. Here then, as I lay down the pen and proceed to seal up my confession, I bring the life of that unhappy Henry Jekyll to an end.

We, the reader, realise with a chill that Jekyll did win by killing himself.

Discussion Point

To what extent is this a chilling end to the novel?

Summary -- fill in the blanks (answers are at the back)

Jekyll talks about how he has since an early age two sides to his nature: the --- and the ---. When he became a scientist he became obsessed by how to separate these two elements of the human soul until one night he made a mixture which did precisely this: he became another ---, he became ----- ----. When he drank the potion again, he turned back into ----. He enjoyed changing into Hyde and doing whatever he wanted without being ----. He set up the laboratory for --- to live in, and ordered the servants to obey him. Things were tricky when Hyde was caught for trampling on the little girl and he had to pay compensation with a cheque written by Henry Jekyll. After this, Jekyll opened a bank account for ---- -. Two months before the murder of Carew, Jekyll found that he went to sleep as Jekyll but woke up as Hyde without taking the ----. After this, he decided not to take the potion but to be Jekyll all the time until one night he lost his ---- and took the potion; it had a very strong --- and he murdered Carew as a result. From then onwards, he decided ---- to become Hyde again. His dark side got the better of him and he did some bad things as ----. This caused him to - ---- into Hyde without taking the potion: one morning in Regent's Park, he found that he had changed into Hyde. He didn't know what to do. He decided to ask Lanyon to fetch the drugs from his laboratory, and then visited Lanyon where he took the ---- and changed back into Jekyll. From that moment onwards, he has had to take more and more drugs just to stay as ----. Hyde was ---- over him. He knows that either he will be hung as the ----- of Carew, or he will manage to --- himself.

Comprehension questions

What was Jekyll's upbringing like? Why were the seeds of him becoming "Jekyll and Hyde" sown then?

What experiments did Jekyll pursue and why did other scientists like Lanyon regard him as misguided for doing them?

What are Jekyll's emotions when he tramples on the girl talked about in the first chapter?

What were the circumstances that led up to the murder of Carew?

What does Jekyll decide to do after the murder of Carew?
What evidence is there that Jekyll is being taken over by Hyde?
What happens in Regent's Park that shocks Jekyll so much?
What does Jekyll feel towards Hyde and what does Hyde feel towards Jekyll?

Analytical questions

What evidence is there that Jekyll is an "unreliable narrator"?
Why do you think Stevenson wrote this last section of the novel when the reader already knows the answer to the mystery?
How does Stevenson build up a sense of drama and horror in this section?
How does Stevenson build up sympathy for Jekyll and, to a lesser extent, Hyde?

Evaluative questions

How successful is this last section of the novel?

Creative response tasks

Write Hyde's diary for the events described in this novel, describing his feelings when he tramples upon the girl, when he has to pay compensation, when he meets Utterson, when he murders Carew, when he goes on his nightly adventures, and when he returns in Regent's Park and visits Lanyon. Describe his feelings towards Jekyll.

You can watch YouTube videos I made about this section here:
http://www.youtube.com/watch?v=G842fM-0xuU
http://www.youtube.com/watch?v=Tm9zkeIq-fE

POSSIBLE ANSWERS in brief & bold

Comprehension questions

What was Jekyll's upbringing like? Why were the seeds of him becoming "Jekyll and Hyde" sown then? **He always had two sides to his nature: he had a "gaiety of disposition", which meant in those days that he wanted to be sexually promiscuous with the opposite sex, but he always wanted to be respectable and an important, high status member of society. The two things were only possible if he hid his reckless, wild side from the general public. Thus we can see that he had a "duality" of nature: two sides, a side that wanted to "appear good", and a side that wanted to commit what was regarded then as "sinful" or "bad" acts.**

What experiments did Jekyll pursue and why did other scientists like Lanyon regard him as misguided for doing them? **He pursued "transcendental" or "mystical" experiments which attempted to separate the different sides of the human soul. He was** regarded as being unscientific because what he was searching for was not viewed as a valid topic for scientific study.

What are Jekyll's emotions when he tramples on the girl talked about in the first chapter? **He doesn't appear to really care about the girl at all and views the matter as a problem only because he was nearly lynched for being violent to her.**

What were the circumstances that led up to the murder of Carew? **Jekyll had not taken the drug from some time, vowing to give it up altogether, but when he did "give in" and take it again its strength was greatly increased because he hadn't taken it in a long while. This meant that its effect was much stronger and this, in turn, led to him murdering Carew without any reason at all.**

What does Jekyll decide to do after the murder of Carew? **He decides to give up taking the drug altogether**

What evidence is there that Jekyll is being taken over by Hyde? **Sometimes he would go to sleep as Henry Jekyll but then wake up as Mr Hyde.**

What happens in Regent's Park that shocks Jekyll so much? **He turns into Hyde suddenly during the day. He had not taken the drug. Hyde is wanted for murder and therefore is terrified of being caught and hung for the crime.**

What does Jekyll feel towards Hyde and what does Hyde feel towards Jekyll? **Jekyll feels "paternal" towards Hyde: he wants to indulge Hyde like a kind father might indulge a spoilt son. Hyde has nothing but contempt for Jekyll and would get rid of him if he weren't killing himself as well.**

Analytical questions

What evidence is there that Jekyll is an "unreliable narrator"? **Jekyll is a narrator who does not fully describe things that might make him uncomfortable. For example, he only makes very short references to incidents that occupy a large part of the first part of the book: the trampling of the child, the murder of Carew and Lanyon's response to seeing Hyde turn into Jekyll are only briefly described. He appears to "skim" over these details because he doesn't want to think about the implications of what he is done. He comes across as a very selfish and self-obsessed man who cares much more about not being caught and his own enjoyment than other people: he never expresses guilt for what he has done, only regret that things have turned out badly for him.**

Why do you think Stevenson wrote this last section of the novel when the reader already knows the answer to the mystery? **Stevenson aimed to write much more than a horror story: he wanted to write a story which was a "psychological fable about the human condition". This section attempts to show the workings of**

Jekyll's mind and reveals that far from being the opposite of Hyde, Jekyll always had "Hyde" hidden inside him. Behind the veneer of respectability lurked a monster.

How does Stevenson build up a sense of drama and horror in this section? **The horror in this section is largely psychological. We feel horrified by the way in which Jekyll seems to love and care for Hyde, by the way in which he dismisses his crimes as unimportant and indeed at one point talks about how happy he felt when he was murdering Carew. Jekyll's self-pitying words are nauseating to read and make the reader angry that a man who had so much could enjoy becoming a psycho-path.**

How does Stevenson build up sympathy for Jekyll and, to a lesser extent, Hyde? **We feel sympathy for the way in which Jekyll becomes "corrupted" by the drug and the opportunities it offers to him. Even though he has confessed to enjoying murdering Carew, we can't help but feel a degree of sympathy for him when he talks about how degraded and humiliated he has become by his experiment. While we may hate Jekyll, we still see and, to a certain extent, feel his pain.**

Evaluative questions

How successful is this last section of the novel? **While the first half of the novel relied upon the classic tropes of the horror/mystery story to keep the reader interested, this last section maintains the reader's interest by getting us to think very carefully about Jekyll's state of mind and his perspective upon events we have already read about. Furthermore, this narrative "fills in the holes" of the narrative: we still don't quite know why Hyde had to demand Lanyon fetched the drugs from Jekyll's house. We realise now that Jekyll had turned into Hyde in Regent's Park and was desperate to change back to Jekyll but had no safe way of getting home. One of the chief pleasures in re-reading the novel is thinking again and again about Jekyll's predicament, which is possibly a predicament of many of us: how can we do what we want and yet be accepted in the eyes of society? Often our desires are in conflict with what society expects from us. This last part of the narrative explores this issue and reveals that we are all in a tragic situation like Jekyll: our inner-most desires will, in the end, kill us.**

Speaking and listening exercises to do on the novel

EXERCISE 1: Working in pairs, imagine you are a **psychiatrist** or **psychotherapist** or **counsellor** and you are **interviewing** various characters in the novel regarding their thoughts and feelings concerning the main events. You could interview:

Dr Jekyll: he could discuss his "duality of mind", his desire to appear respectable and yet indulge in "undignified pleasures", how the drug has got a grip on him, his fears about turning into Hyde, his love of Hyde etc., his reflections upon trampling upon the girl and murdering Carew.

Mr Hyde: he could discuss his love of pleasure, the sorts of things he likes doing, his hatred of Jekyll, his fear of being hung, his reflections upon trampling upon the girl, meeting Enfield, Utterson and Lanyon and murdering Carew

Mr Utterson: his shock regarding Jekyll and Hyde, how he discovered the truth about Jekyll, his worries for Jekyll throughout the novel.

Dr Lanyon: his shock at seeing Hyde turning into Jekyll, how all of his scientific ideas have been shattered now that he has seen this transformation.

Poole: his shock and concern at learning that his master was Hyde; his trauma regarding having to deal with Hyde for so long; his thoughts and feelings towards Jekyll.

EXERCISE 2: Put Jekyll and Hyde **on trial**. Set things up so that you have a prosecuting lawyer, who attacks Hyde and Jekyll for the murder of Carew and other crimes. Have a defence lawyer who tries to say that Jekyll was not in his right mind when he murdered Carew, he was Hyde. Call witnesses for prosecution and defence: these could be characters from the novel, but also could be police inspectors, psychotherapists, doctors etc.

EXERCISE 3: Hold a **chat show** a bit like Jeremy Kyle in which the main characters from the novel are invited to discuss what happened to them during the novel.

EXERCISE 4: Devise a series of **freeze-frames** for each chapter of the book which are pictures of the key moments in that chapter and include a narrator who explains what people in the freeze-frame are doing.

EXERCISE 5: Devise a **five minute drama** in groups of four in which you make use of a narrator and you show a very short version of the whole novel, boiling it down to its very basic actions, events and ideas. Use the chapter headings as your scenes, e.g. have a scene for 'Story of the Door' etc. You can also buy my script of the novel which includes a fully dramatized version of the play using the chapter headings.

Literary criticism of the novel

FIRST REVIEWS

The Times, 25th January 1885. Stevenson felt this positive review, published shortly after the book came out, helped make the book such a success:

> Nothing Mr. Stevenson has written as yet has so strongly impressed us with the versatility of his very original genius as this sparsely-printed little shilling volume...every connoisseur who reads the story once must certainly read it twice. He will read it the first time, passing from surprise to surprise, in a curiosity that keeps growing, because it is never satisfied...Never for a moment, in the most startling situations, has he lost his grasp of the ground-facts of a wonderful and supernatural problem.

Julia Wedgewood, *Contemporary Review*, April 1886 noted the lack of women in the story, an aspect which many critics have investigated since:

> Whereas most fiction deals with the relation between man and woman...the author of this strange tale takes an even narrower range, and sets himself to investigate the meaning of the word *self*. No woman's name occurs in the book, no romance is even suggested in it; it depends on the interest of an idea...

IS HYDE A RAPIST?

Gerald Manley Hopkins, *Letter to Robert Bridges*, October 28th 1886 noted that Hyde's crimes were probably too terrible to be written about in a novel:

> You are certainly wrong about Hyde being overdrawn: my Hyde is worse. The trampling scene is perhaps a convention: he was thinking of something unsuitable for fiction...Stevenson is master of a consummate style and each phase is finished as in poetry.

THE ORIGINALITY OF THE STORY

C. K Chesterton, *The Real Stab of the Story*, 1927

Chesterton believed that although Stevenson says the story is set in London, it felt it was "unmistakeably" taking place in Edinburgh, Stevenson's native city in Scotland. He felt that Utterson behaved like a Scottish lawyer, and that Jekyll's two-faced nature was "Caledonian" or Scottish, appearing to behave like a Scottish Puritan. Chesterton wrote:

> The real stab of the story is not in the discovery that the one man is two men; but in the discovery that the two men are one man...The point of the story is not that a man *can* cut himself off from his conscience, but that he cannot.

Chesterton was one of the first critics to notice the originality in this idea, and to explore the ways in which the novel is different from many other horror novels in that it is "psychological" in its structure and theme.

THE THREE PERSONALITIES

Vladimir Nabokov in *A Phenomenon of Style* made three major points about the book:

First, he felt that Jekyll was not a good man, but a "composite" character, a "mixture of good and bad"... Nabokov sees him as a hypocrite who hides his sins from other people. He is "vindictive, never forgiving Lanyon with whom he disagrees in scientific matters... Nabokov felt that Hyde was "mingled with him, within him. Into this mixture of good and bad in Dr. Jekyll, the bad can be separated as Hyde, who is a precipitate of pure evil..."

Second, Nabokov believed that Jekyll is not really changed into Hyde but "projects" his evil side which becomes Hyde.

Third, Nabokov believed that there were three personalities: Jekyll, Hyde and a "third, the Jekyll residue when Hyde takes over...Hyde still wants to change back to Jekyll. This is the significant point". For Nabokov this indicated that Jekyll still lives inside Hyde and is with Hyde when he is doing his evil.

Nabokov points out that Stevenson makes his story believable and realistic by having it observed by "matter-of-fact" persons, Utterson and Enfield, while Lanyon was used so that he could notice as a scientist all the details about the transformation. Nabokov noted like a number of other critics such as Elaine Showalter in her book *Sexual Anarchy: Gender and Culture at the Fin de Siecle* that the all-male atmosphere of the book, and the fact that Hyde is Jekyll's "benefactor" and "protégée" suggest that Jekyll was homosexual and liked to have homosexual adventures in London.

THE USE OF PRONOUNS

Peter Garrett in *Instabilities of Meaning, Morality and Narration*, from Cries and Voices: Reading *Jekyll and Hyde, Dr Jekyll and Mr Hyde after One Hundred Years* pp. 59-72

Garrett points out that the story constantly uses different pronouns when Jekyll and other characters talk about Hyde: sometimes Jekyll talks about Hyde in the first person, using "I", and, at other times, he calls him "he" or in some cases "it". Garrett points out that in his account, Jekyll often refuses to identify with Hyde by talking about Hyde's "infamy", but then at other times, Jekyll identifies with Hyde's feelings as in the passage when he describes murdering Carew: "With a transport of glee, I mauled the unresisting body, tasting delight from every blow." Sometimes, Garrett points out that there is an "unnamed narrator" telling Jekyll's account as in the sentence: "Between these two I now felt I had to choose", either the "I" of the narration has to choose between Jekyll and Hyde, and yet this is odd because it is Jekyll who is supposed to be narrating. Garrett asks who this "anonymous" narrator is. Garrett points out that Jekyll problem is the same as anyone who tells their story because they separate the "I" on the page from their actual self who is writing the story. Garrett goes on to show that after talking about Hyde in the first person at the very end of the narrative, Jekyll "reasserts his separation from Hyde" when he writes: "Will Hyde die on the scaffold?"

Garrett talks a great deal about the "instability" of who Jekyll is: he is not two people, but many, and we, the readers, and the other characters are constantly searching for an answer to this question. Ultimately, the quest for finding out who Jekyll is leads to Utterson and Poole breaking down the door in an act of violence which leads to Jekyll's suicide. Garrett notes that Jekyll's last words are spoken in the 'The Last Night': "Utterson for God's sake have mercy!" Again, we wonder who is speaking here. Is it Jekyll? Is it Hyde who is speaking with Jekyll's voice? Is it Jekyll speaking with Hyde's voice? Did Jekyll turn into Hyde when he killed himself, or did Hyde reply and then kill himself? There are no answers to these questions, and that's why the story remains a mystery after many readings.

HYDE AND EVOLUTION

Patrick Brantlinger, *An Unconscious Allegory about the Masses and Mass Literacy*

The critic Brantlinger examined in this essay the circumstances of the publication of the novel. She points out that Stevenson always had mixed feelings about the success of Dr. Jekyll, calling it a "Gothic gnome" and a "fine bogey tale". She shows that Stevenson's wife made him turn the story into a "moral allegory", i.e. a story that has a particular moral, or message in which Jekyll is effectively punished for his sins. Brantlinger shows that many critics have argued that the tale is an "allegory" about good and evil, but she argues that the novel be read as an allegory about "the emergence of a mass consumer society in the late-Victorian period." She argues that the murder of Sir Danvers Carew has some similarities with the real-life murders of the 1882 Phoenix Park murders in Dublin in which Irish nationalists murdered a respectable English gentleman. She argues that many readers of the time may have seen Hyde as being like an "Irish Fenian" or nationalist: most of these traits – his violence, his hairy arms, his short stature – were recognisably "working class" and possibly "Irish" for middle-class Victorian readers. He fits the stereotype of the criminal drawn up by the criminologist Cesar Lombroso in 1886, when he described criminals as having certain physical traits such as being ugly and deformed in their looks. She shows that one of Hyde's few "upper class" traits is his hand-writing and this is what makes him cause so much chaos and enables him to survive: he can write notes that enable him to get drugs, write cheques to pay off people who are unhappy with him, and write swear words all over Jekyll's sacred texts. Although Stevenson deliberately takes out all references to the contemporary society he was writing about such as the problem of the Irish/a criminal working class, for Brantlinger Hyde represents these worries and anxieties of upper-class Victorian society: he is a symbol of the destructiveness of the "lower orders".

THE "HYDING" OF CRIMES
Katherine Linehan, Sex, Secrecy and *Self-Alienation in Strange Case of Dr. Jekyll and Mr Hyde*

Lineham points out how Hyde is "closer than a wife" to Jekyll at the end of the book. She views Hyde as an "expression of underground sexual appetite on Jekyll's part" and discusses how critics have viewed Hyde's violence with some critics arguing that Hyde's shows "heterosexual sadism" while others like Nabokov and Showalter try to show that Hyde's acts suggest forbidden homosexual practices. Linehan points out that Stevenson openly rebelled against his Puritan upbringing which labelled sex as sinful. She refers to a letter of Stevenson's which vents his anger about Hyde being viewed as someone who is sinful because of his sexual appetite; as a result Stevenson thought that people failed to see that Hyde's cruelty comes not from his desire to have sex, but from Jekyll's desire to hide everything he did. Stevenson was angry because people mistake sexuality for evil, whereas it was actually hypocrisy that caused evil. Lineham develops a long and complex argument in her essay that essentially shows that it is the loss of Jekyll's "soul" which is the crime and that it happens because Jekyll is intoxicated with the way in which he can hide his actions by becoming Hyde. We see this in the 'Full Statement of the Case' because initially Hyde does not commit terrible crimes, but comes to become progressively worse because he realises that he can get away with it. Jekyll becomes obsessed by his disguise; this is what leads him astray and enables Hyde to grow in power and strength as the story progresses.

Writing essays on the novel, including exam responses

Here is a GSCE question on the novel, based on an extract. This is the extract, which is the opening of 'The Carew Murder Case':

Nearly a year later, in the month of October, 18—, London was startled by a crime of singular ferocity and rendered all the more notable by the high position of the victim. The details were few and startling. A maid servant living alone in a house not far from the river had gone upstairs to bed about eleven. Although a fog rolled over the city in the small hours, the early part of the night was cloudless, and the lane, which the maid's window overlooked, was brilliantly lit by the full moon. It seems she was romantically given, for she sat down upon her box, which stood immediately under the window, and fell into a dream of musing (she used to say, with streaming tears, when she narrated that experience), never had she felt more at peace with all men or thought more kindly of the world. And as she so sat she became aware of an aged beautiful gentleman with white hair, drawing near along the lane; and advancing to meet him, another and very small gentleman, to whom at first she paid less attention. When they had come within speech (which was just under the maid's eyes) the older man bowed and accosted the other with a very pretty manner of politeness. It did not seem as if the subject of his address were of great importance; indeed, from his pointing, it sometimes appeared as if he were only inquiring his way; but the moon shone on his face as he spoke, and the girl was pleased to watch it, it seemed to breathe such an innocent and old-world kindness of disposition, yet with something high too, as of a well-founded self-content. Presently her eye wandered to the other, and she was surprised to recognise in him a certain Mr. Hyde, who had once visited her master and for whom she had conceived a dislike. He had in his hand a heavy cane, with which he was trifling; but he answered never a word, and seemed to listen with an ill-contained impatience. And then all of a sudden he broke out in a great flame of anger, stamping with his foot, brandishing the cane, and carrying on (as the maid described it) like a madman. The old gentleman took a step back, with the air of one very much surprised and a trifle hurt; and at that Mr. Hyde broke out of all bounds and clubbed him to the earth. And next moment, with ape-like fury, he was trampling his victim under foot and hailing down a storm of blows, under which the bones were audibly shattered and the body jumped upon the roadway. At the horror of these sights and sounds, the maid fainted.

GCSE QUESTION

How does Stevenson's writing here make this moment in the novel so horrifying?

Remember to support your ideas with details from the extract.

What do you think of the following response and how do you think it could be improved? Re-write it, correcting any mistakes you spot, and adding detail where you think is necessary.

STUDENT RESPONSE

I fink this writing passage shows that Mr Hyde is a horrible bloke. I have a few reasons for showing this. First, you have to got to fink about wot happened before this scene happened, this is chapter 4 of the book, and so you realise that the writer has built up to this moment. We already don't like Mr Hyde because we have seen him trample on a young girl of eight and make Henry Jekyll really unhappy. He already seems to be a dodgy geezer. So that meanz you're on the edge of your seat before the scene begins; you know something dodgy is gonna happen the moment Hyde appearz.

That's important coz when the maid sees Mr Hyde carrying the "heavy cane" you fink, uh-oh wots gonna happen now, Mr Hyde is gonna do somefing real bad.

But wots horrifying is that the violence he commits is far worse than anything he has done before. Stevenson makes the scene horrifying by describing the scene in such detail. He uses a metaphor "great flame of anger" to suggest that Hyde is burning with anger; this makes you fink Hyde is like a great big bonfire full of hatred and anger. Then he uses a Similie to say that Hyde is like "a madman", this makes me fink Hyde is a syko who dosent care wot anyone finks of him. Wot makes it even worse is that the old geezer wot he tramples on and beats to death is very nice, he shows "a very pretty manner of politeness", in other words, he's very nice and polite to Hyde, and wot does Hyde do him but beats him to death? This is horrifying because it makes you realise that Hyde is a rite proper syko:

> The old gentleman took a step back, with the air of one very much surprised and a trifle hurt; and at that Mr. Hyde broke out of all bounds and clubbed him to the earth. And next moment, with ape-like fury, he was trampling his victim under foot and hailing down a storm of blows, under which the bones were audibly shattered and the body jumped upon the roadway.

This quote shows he is a rite proper syko. Don't you think? He is described as having "ape-like fury", this makes me fink that Hyde is like an animal who is less evolved than a human being. Then the description of the bones being "audibly shattered" make you hear the crunching of the bones of the poor old gentleman: this imagery makes you think of how painful the old man's death must be. You can see it clearly too because Stevenson uses visual imagery when he says there was a "storm of blows": this metaphor suggests that he hit the old man very quickly in the same way rain falls in a storm. Then, there's more horror when he is described as "jumping" on the old man. You know that the scene must have been terrifying coz the maid is described as "fainting". Overall, you see that Stevenson has made the scene horrifying by using a number of different techniques. 1. He has structured the story so that we're already worried about wot Hyde mite do 2. He has used some well good imagery to make us see the murder in very clear detail.

Oh and I almost 4got, the setting is described in a creepy way and this is somefing wot adds to the suspense coz it's a foggy, cloudless night wiv the full moon shinning. Spooky or wot? It's like there mite be wherewolves or somefing.

How you might improve this response:

First, this candidate needs to improve their spelling and grammar. Spelling mistakes such as "fink", "4got" and slang expressions such as "gonna" are not going to get you a top grade. Furthermore, the candidate is very repetitious: he repeats words like "described" far too much. He needs to find synonyms to describe this words.

Second, there are many good points in the essay that need to be further developed and re-phrased. The candidate makes a good point in the first paragraph by pointing out how Stevenson has "structured" the novel so that we're already in suspense BEFORE the chapter begins. He shows that he knows what has happened previously by referring to incidents that are quite frightening in the book. However, he could have discussed the structure of this particular passage as well; he could have talked about how the scene begins in a very peaceful fashion, with the street being quiet and the old man greeting Hyde in a polite fashion, and then ends with a terrible murder. Stevenson builds up a sense of horror by painting a vivid picture of a very nice old man being savagely murdered. He does this very "economically", that is he quickly sketches a picture of the old man being very pleasant: he is a "beautiful aged gentleman" who "bows" before Hyde. This accentuates the horror because it is a good and defenceless man who has been murdered.

Third, there are a number of good points about how the imagery of the passage adds to the horror. However, at one point, the candidate just copies out a large chunk of the passage and repeats a previous point, without analysing the passage in any depth. This is a common mistake of weaker answers, they tend to copy out passages and not really analyse them. To give the candidate credit, he does pick out some phrases which are relevant and analyse them: "great flame of anger", "audibly shattered", "ape-like fury", and "storm of blows" are all good phrases to analyse and by and large the candidate does tackle them in a reasonably analytical fashion, except that his expression can be too informal at times. Here we see him "integrating" the quotes into his answer, and talking about the effect of the quotations. He could have gone into more depth though, by discussing in more detail what the imagery makes the reader see, think and feel.

Fourth, the candidate could have looked in more depth at the characterisations, and shown how the writer builds up a sense of horror by slowly revealing the true depths of Hyde's evil. We also feel a deeper sense of unease because of Hyde's connection with Jekyll.

Fifth, the candidate could have examined Stevenson's use of punctuation to build up a sense of horror. There are a number of sentences you could analyse in depth but this one is good for examining to see the effect of the punctuation:

> And then all of a sudden he broke out in a great flame of anger, stamping with his foot, brandishing the cane, and carrying on (as the maid described it) like a madman.

Notice how Stevenson builds up a sense of horror by listing the various horrific events that happen and separating them off with commas: we have first of the "flame of anger" which describes Hyde's emotions, then the stamping of his foot which suggests the rage he feels and conveys the noises he is making, then we see him "brandishing his cane" and then finally, at the very end of the sentence the devastating simile that he is carrying on "like a madman". The commas enable the writer to build up a terrifying picture of Hyde's feelings, what he is physically doing and his psychotic demeanour.

Here is another question, which is a straight "essay" question rather than one that requires you to analyse a passage. Personally, I think it is a better question to respond to because it allows a good candidate to show more knowledge of the novel than the other question.

How far are you able to feel sympathy for Dr Jekyll? Remember to support your ideas with details from the novel.

To pen a good answer to this question, you will need to structure your answer carefully. First, you need to brainstorm all your thoughts in response to the question, using the **5Ws + H (What, where, when, who, why, how)** to help you:

When do we feel sympathy for Jekyll? **When** do we not feel sympathy for him?

What makes us feel sympathy towards him? What techniques does Stevenson use to make us feel sympathetic towards him?

Where in the novel are the moments in the novel that make us feel sympathetic towards him?

Who feels sympathy for him in the book and how does this affect our feelings towards him?

How does Stevenson makes us feel sympathy for him?

KEY POINTS

Stevenson **structures** the novel carefully so that there is a great deal of mystery about Dr Jekyll. While we may feel sympathy for him at certain points in the novel, this isn't the primary reason why we keep turning the pages: the central cause for our interest is the mystery. However, along the way, we feel sympathy, to a degree, that Jekyll has become "mixed up" with Mr Hyde: this is before we know the truth about who Hyde is. So, for example, there are key moments such as 'The Incident at the Window' when we see Jekyll looking so unhappy, when he shows he is full of "abject terror" that make us feel pity for him. But by the time of Jekyll's confession, which is the last section of the book, we have lost sympathy for him: he has conducted a dangerous experiment which has led to the abuse of many people and the murder of Carew. Even so, towards the end of the confession, we feel sympathy once again when he turns back into Mr Hyde in Regent's Park: Jekyll has determined to live a life without Hyde, but has failed and now is a hunted and humiliated man. Jekyll behaves like a drug addict, desperate for the drug to turn him back into Jekyll.

Stevenson's **characterisation** of Jekyll is complex: as the novel progresses he is revealed as a complicated man with contradictory desires and aspirations. This evinces a degree of sympathy because, in this sense, Jekyll is like all of us: we are all complicated and if we had discovered an "ebullition" like the one he finds, we may well have enjoyed being "Hyde" for a while. Thus we can see that Stevenson creates sympathy for Jekyll by describing his "duality of nature", by exploring how he always had "two sides" to him: the side that wanted to appear respectable and have people's admiration, and the side that wanted to act on his deepest desires. However, we are torn in our sympathies because it becomes clear that rather than Hyde being a "different person" created by the drug is actually a manifestation of Jekyll's innermost desires. This is clearly seen when Jekyll describes the murder of Carew:

> Instantly the spirit of hell awoke in me and raged. With a transport of glee, I mauled the unresisting body, tasting delight from every blow; and it was not till weariness had begun to succeed, that I was suddenly, in the top fit of my delirium, struck through the heart by a cold thrill of terror

The **pronoun** "I" is important here because Jekyll is actually Hyde when he murders Carew and has been describing what Hyde does in the third person at certain points, but here we see him using the first person. This indicates that it is actually Jekyll who is killing Carew and that Hyde is a "smoke-screen" for the dark side of Jekyll. Stevenson's writing here is full of energy and while we don't feel sympathy for Jekyll, we certainly are both fascinated and horrified to read the description of a murder: we see that Jekyll feels a "transport of glee", in other words he is ecstatically happy when he kills Carew, he feels "delight from every blow": this is a man who revels and enjoys violence, and only stops being violent when he is tired.

Stevenson uses a great deal of **emotive language** to evoke sympathy for Jekyll. This whole novel is an anatomy of the changing feelings of Jekyll: we see him exhibit a whole multiplicity of moods and "dispositions": he moves from feeling extreme joy or ecstasy, to feeling suicidally depressed.

Sequencing exercise

Learning objectives: to learn how Stevenson develops a sense of horror in his narrative through his use of description.

TASK 1: Read the quotes and then put the quotes in the order that they occur in the book, matching them with the correct chapter heading.

TASK 2: Order the quotes with the most horrifying first, and least horrifying last. Discuss and make notes upon WHY you have sequenced them in this way.

The extracts are taken from these chapters but not in this order:

Chapter 1 'Story of the Door'; Chapter 2, 'Search for Mr Hyde'; Chapter 4, 'The Carew Murder Case'; Chapter 7, 'Incident at the Window'; Chapter 8, 'The Last Night'; Chapter 9 'Dr Lanyon's Narrative'; Chapter 10, 'Dr Jekyll's Full Statement of the Case'.

QUOTE 1: Right in the midst there lay the body of a man sorely contorted and still twitching. They drew near on tiptoe, turned it on its back and beheld the face of Edward Hyde.
QUOTE 2: I knew myself, at the first breath of this new life, to be more wicked, tenfold more wicked, sold a slave to my original evil; and the thought, in that moment, braced and delighted me like wine.
QUOTE 3: But the hand which I now saw, clearly enough, in the yellow light of a mid-London morning, lying half shut on the bed-clothes, was lean, corded, knuckly, of a dusky pallor and thickly shaded with a swart growth of hair. It was the hand of Edward Hyde.
QUOTE 4: Instantly the spirit of hell awoke in me and raged. With a transport of glee, I mauled the unresisting body, tasting delight from every blow;
QUOTE 5: His face became suddenly black and the features seemed to melt and alter – and the next moment, I had sprung to my feet and leaped back against the wall, my arm raised to shield me from that prodigy, my mind submerged in terror.
QUOTE 6: The pleasures which I made haste to seek in my disguise were, as I have said, undignified; I would scarce use a harder term. But in the hands of Edward Hyde, they soon began to turn toward the monstrous.
QUOTE 7: Well, sir, the two ran into one another naturally enough at the corner; and then came the horrible part of the thing; for the man trampled calmly over the child's body and left her screaming on the ground.
QUOTE 8: My life is shaken to its roots; sleep has left me; the deadliest terror sits by me at all hours of the day and night
QUOTE 9: Mr Hyde was pale and dwarfish, he gave an impression of deformity without any nameable malformation, he had a displeasing smile...
QUOTE 10: And then all of a sudden he broke out in a great flame of anger, stamping with his foot, brandishing the cane, and carrying on (as the maid described it) like a madman.
QUOTE 11: 'That is just what I was about to venture to propose,' returned the doctor with a smile. But the words were hardly

uttered, before the smile was struck out of his face and succeeded by an expression of such abject terror and despair, as froze the very blood of the two gentlemen below.

Answers to sequencing exercise

Quote 1: from 'The Last Night'
Quote 2: from 'Dr Jekyll's Full Statement of the Case'
Quote 3: from 'Dr Jekyll's Full Statement of the Case'
Quote 4: from 'Dr Jekyll's Full Statement of the Case'
Quote 5: from 'Dr Lanyon's Narrative'
Quote 6: from 'Dr Jekyll's Full Statement of the Case'
Quote 7: from 'The Story of the Door'
Quote 8: from 'Dr Lanyon's Narrative'
Quote 9: from 'The Search for Mr Hyde'
Quote 10: from 'The Carew Murder Case'
Quote 11: from 'Incident at the Window'

Answers to fill-in-the-blanks summary exercises

1 Story of the Door – fill-in-the-gaps answers: Trouble; door; trample on; girl; £100; Henry Jekyll; respectable; genuine; blackmailed
2 Search for Mr Hyde – fill-in-the-gaps answers: Will; Edward Hyde; fallen out; face; address; key; obey
3 Dr Jekyll was Quite at Ease – fill-in-the-gaps answers: Dinner; trusted; blackmailed; Mr Hyde; disappears or dies.
4 The Carew Murder Case – fill-in-the-gaps answers: Death; breaks; Mr Utterson; clients; Henry Jekyll's; broken stick; cheque-book; bank; seen

5 Incident of the Letter – fill-in-the-gaps answers: deathly ill; Hyde; escaped; unworthy; letter; hand-writing; forge
6 Remarkable Incident of Dr Lanyon – fill-in-the-gaps answers: Found; good Lanyon and Utterson; anybody; die; dead; complain; punishment; after; refuses
7 Incident at the Window – fill-in-the-gaps answers: Open; Jekyll's; depressed; walk; terror; silence.
8 The Last Night -- fill-in-the-gaps answers: "foul play"; hallway; strange; "made away with"; ill; smaller; "have mercy!"; dressed; killed; Jekyll; Utterson's; Lanyon's; "confession"
9 Dr Lanyon's Narrative -- fill-in-the-gaps answers Drawer; drawer; midnight; watch; Satan; Jekyll; Hyde; murdered; "The deadliest terror"
10 Henry Jekyll's Full Statement of the Case -- fill-in-the-gaps answers: good and the bad; person; Edward Hyde; Jekyll; caught; Hyde; Hyde; potion; self-control; effect; Jekyll; change; drugs; Jekyll; taking; murderer; kill

Glossary

conventional morality – the ordinary rules of everyday life, the code of behaviour that 'normal' people abide by
dualistic -- dualism - the doctrine that reality consists of two basic opposing elements, often taken to be mind and matter (or mind and body), or good and evil
inarticulacy – being unable to express something in words
extraneous – irrelevant, not needed
hysteric – a person who reacts in a hysterical manner to life, making a great deal of fuss about nothing!
irreverent – not being respectful, disrespectful
malevolence – badness, nastiness, evil
motif – repeated idea
neurotic – a person who is obsessively and needlessly worried
perturbed – upset, disturbed
proto-existentialist – the forerunner of an existentialist, who were people believed that one should do what you want, follow your unconscious desires, rather than being constrained by conventional **morality** – a set of rules which enable you to live what society deems to be a good life.
repressed – holding back, keeping back your emotions
repression – see above
resonances -- associations

social position – your place in society
subconscious – another word for the 'unconscious'
the unconscious – the place in the human mind where one's repressed desires are kept
undiscriminating – not very picky, not being able to make good decisions about things and people

Select bibliography

Chesterton, C., 2001. *Robert Louis Stevenson*. New edition based on a much older book ed. London: House of Stratus.
Daiches, D., 1973. *Robert Louis Stevenson and His World*. London: Pictorial Biography.
Gray, W., 2004. *Robert Louis Stevenson -- A Literary Life*. Great Britain: Palgrave Macmillan.
Harman, C., 2006. *Robert Louis Stevenson -- A Biography*. Harper Perennial ed. London: Harper .
Linehan, E. b. K., 2003. *Strange Case of Dr. Jekyll and Mr Hyde -- A Norton Critical Edition*. New York: W.W. Norton.
Luckhurst, R., 2006. *Strange Case of Dr Jekyll and Mr Hyde and Other Tales*. Oxford World Classics ed. Oxford: Oxford University Press.
Mighall, E. b. R., 2003. *The Strange Case of Dr Jekyll and Mr Hyde and other tales of terror*. London: Penguin Classics.